GROWING OLD IN AMERICA

INFORMATION PLUS®
WYLIE, TEXAS 75098
© 1979, 1982, 1996, 1998
ALL RIGHTS RESERVED

EDITORS:
CORNELIA BLAIR, B.A., M.S.
MARK A. SIEGEL, Ph.D.
JACQUELYN QUIRAM, B.A.

CHAPTER I

OLDER AMERICANS — A DIVERSE AND GROWING POPULATION

AMERICA GROWS OLDER

Old age is the most unexpected of all the things that happen to a man.

—Leon Trotsky

America is aging and aging rapidly. The United States, indeed the world, is only beginning to experience the effects of an aging population. America began the twentieth century young — less than 1 in 25 residents was older than 65 in 1900. By 1995, 1 in 8 Americans was past the age of 65. The growth of America's older residents may be among the most important developments in the United States in the twenty-first century. Fewer children per family and longer life spans have transformed the aging from a small to a sizable portion of the U.S. population.

While the U.S. population under the age of 65 has tripled during the twentieth century, the number aged 65 and over is 11 times greater. And this is just the beginning of the "graying of America," for the large baby boom generation is expected to swell until, by mid-century, 1 in 5 Americans — approximately 80 million — will be 65 or older (Figure 1.1).

WHO IS OLD?

According to Webster, the word "old" means "having lived or been in existence for a long time." This definition works well for a car or a piece of

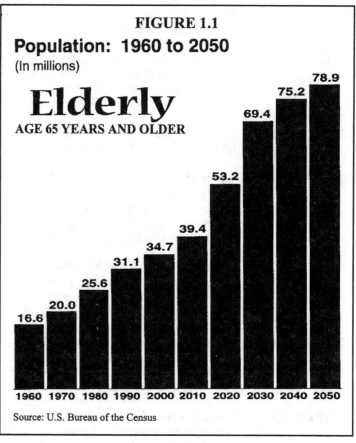

FIGURE 1.1

Population: 1960 to 2050
(In millions)

Elderly
AGE 65 YEARS AND OLDER

Year	Value
1960	16.6
1970	20.0
1980	25.6
1990	31.1
2000	34.7
2010	39.4
2020	53.2
2030	69.4
2040	75.2
2050	78.9

Source: U.S. Bureau of the Census

pottery, but when applied to people, it shows only a small part of a much larger picture — it indicates only the number of years a person has been alive.

Life expectancy (the anticipated average length of life) has changed throughout history. The average life expectancy of an ancient Greek was 18 years. Native Americans in the pre-Columbian Southwest could expect to live 33 years. The low life expectancy was based on a high infant mortality rate. Once a child survived through childhood, he or she had a better chance of making it into his or her fifties or sixties. In 1900, the life expectancy of the average American was 47 years. By 1998, the average American male born could expect to live more than 73 years, and a female, 79 years.

WHAT DOES OLD MEAN?

There are many ways to characterize an aging person, and everyone has an idea of what old means. Aside from the obvious measure of number of birthdays, people may be labeled old because of their appearance, their physical functioning, their mental capacity, or their lifestyle.

A Working Definition

In 1995, the American Association of Retired Persons (AARP), in its *Images of Aging in America*, conducted by FGI Research, tried to determine knowledge and attitudes regarding aging in American society. In both the 1981 and 1994 studies, when asked to define "old," most people defined the point of becoming old by a specific chronological number of years. In contrast, in the earlier 1974 sampling, respondents had tended to give non-chronological, or event-driven criteria for being old, such as retirement, menopause, or disability. (See Table 1.1.)

Old age does not happen overnight; aging is a process that begins before birth and ends with death. At what point does one become "old"? The problem of defining old age is reflected in the terminology used to describe those who are no longer "young" adults: for example, elder, older, aged, mature, or senior. Some researchers distinguish between various stages of the later

TABLE 1.1

AGE AT WHICH THE AVERAGE PERSON BECOMES OLD
(OPINION OF THE AMERICAN PEOPLE)

	Average Man			Average Woman		
	1974	1981	1994	1974	1981	1994
N =	4,254	3,427	1,200	4,254	3,427	1,200
	%	%	%	%	%	%
Under 40	1	1	2	1	2	2
40 to 49	4	4	5	5	5	7
50 to 59	11	13	14	11	14	16
60 to 69	23	36	35	18	35	31
70 to 79	13	24	24	12	20	22
80 or older	1	5	5	2	5	6
Never	2	1	1	2	2	2
It depends/event	40	14	9	43	13	8
Not sure	5	2	5	6	2	7
Mean	--	--	63	--	--	62
Median	63	66	65	62	65	65
Chronological (cited specific age)	58	83	85	49	86	84
Non-chronological (cited event/it depends)	42	17	15	51	14	17

NOTE: means and medians are based only on ages expressed in years, as opposed to events.

Source: Kathy Speas and Beth Obenshain, *Images of Aging in America*, AARP/FGI Integrated Marketing, Chapel Hill, NC, 1995

years: young-old, middle-old, and oldest-old. In the AARP study, most people thought old age began around 60 to 69, although a significant proportion thought it began around 70 to 79. (See Table 1.1.) For statistical and legislative purposes, however, some definition of "old age" is necessary.

The United States government has assigned a person's sixty-fifth birthday as the age when U.S. citizens become eligible for government benefits such as full Social Security and Medicare. The number 65 was not selected by any scientific process; it followed a precedent set by German Chancellor Otto von Bismark in 1899. In that year, Germany became the first western government to assume financial support of its older citizens by passing the Old Age and Survivors Pension Act. Chancellor von Bismark arbitrarily decided that eligibility for benefits would begin at age 65 (although he himself was an active and vigorous 74 years old at the time).

In this book, the terms "old," "older," and "elderly" are used interchangeably to describe people aged 65 and older. The term "oldest old" refers to people 85 and older.

THE "AGE WAVE"

Why is America getting older? One of the main reasons is that in the 20 years after World War II (1945-1965), as soldiers returned home eager to start families, as the world political climate stabilized and the U.S. economy prospered, there was an explosion of births. Children born during these years make up what is called the "baby-boom genera-tion." The baby boomers, who are now turning 50, will begin to turn 65 around 2010. The 65+ population will increase dra-matically between 2010 and 2030 as the baby-boomers complete their transition from "not-old" to "old."

Figure 1.2 shows the move-ment of the bulge in the numbers of Americans as these boomers age. While the baby boom generation initially re-duced the median age (half of all Americans are below and half are above) by the presence of so many young, as it grows older, it is moving the median age upward in what is being termed an "age wave." The

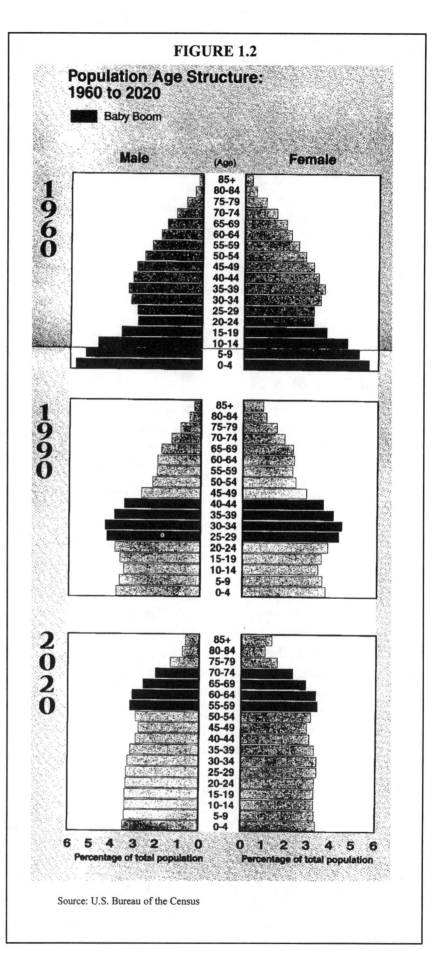

FIGURE 1.2

Population Age Structure: 1960 to 2020

◼ Baby Boom

Source: U.S. Bureau of the Census

TABLE 1.2

Resident Population—Estimates by Age, Sex, Race, and Hispanic Origin

(Numbers in thousands. Consistent with the 1990 Census, as enumerated.)

Date and age	Total			White			Black			American Indian, Eskimo, and Aleut			Asian and Pacific Islander		
	Total	Male	Female	Total	Male	Female	Total	Male	Female	Total	Male	Female	Total	Male	Female
November 1, 1997															
All ages	268,422	131,445	136,977	221,817	109,179	112,638	34,068	16,178	17,890	2,334	1,159	1,175	10,203	4,929	5,273
Under 5 years	18,982	9,713	9,269	15,060	7,724	7,336	2,857	1,448	1,409	200	101	99	865	440	425
Under 1 year	3,740	1,913	1,827	2,976	1,526	1,451	550	279	271	40	20	20	174	88	86
1 year	3,718	1,902	1,817	2,961	1,518	1,443	548	278	271	39	20	19	170	87	84
2 years	3,776	1,932	1,844	3,009	1,543	1,466	554	281	273	40	20	20	172	87	85
3 years	3,818	1,954	1,864	3,020	1,549	1,471	583	295	288	40	20	20	175	89	86
4 years	3,930	2,013	1,917	3,092	1,588	1,505	622	315	307	42	21	21	174	89	85
5 to 9 years	19,802	10,138	9,664	15,599	7,998	7,601	3,155	1,602	1,553	226	115	111	822	423	399
5 years	3,966	2,041	1,945	3,138	1,609	1,529	629	320	309	43	22	21	176	91	85
6 years	4,025	2,058	1,967	3,179	1,627	1,552	630	320	310	42	21	21	174	89	84
7 years	4,060	2,079	1,982	3,204	1,643	1,560	642	325	317	47	24	23	168	87	81
8 years	3,777	1,934	1,843	2,975	1,526	1,449	609	309	300	47	24	23	146	75	71
9 years	3,954	2,027	1,927	3,103	1,593	1,510	646	328	317	48	25	24	158	81	76
10 to 14 years	19,079	9,777	9,302	15,109	7,757	7,351	2,949	1,498	1,451	241	122	118	781	399	382
10 years	3,884	1,992	1,892	3,066	1,575	1,491	617	314	303	48	24	23	153	79	74
11 years	3,806	1,949	1,857	3,022	1,550	1,471	587	297	289	47	24	23	151	78	73
12 years	3,823	1,958	1,866	3,027	1,553	1,473	592	301	291	48	24	24	157	80	77
13 years	3,771	1,930	1,841	2,991	1,534	1,457	573	291	282	49	25	24	159	81	78
14 years	3,794	1,948	1,846	3,003	1,545	1,458	580	295	285	49	25	24	161	82	79
15 to 19 years	19,206	9,899	9,309	15,250	7,889	7,361	2,982	1,516	1,466	223	112	110	753	382	371
15 years	3,903	2,005	1,898	3,085	1,589	1,496	608	310	298	49	25	24	162	82	80
16 years	3,776	1,949	1,827	2,999	1,551	1,447	577	295	281	46	23	23	154	78	76
17 years	3,997	2,069	1,928	3,170	1,646	1,523	625	320	305	47	24	23	155	79	76
18 years	3,735	1,924	1,811	2,973	1,538	1,434	584	296	288	41	21	20	138	70	68
19 years	3,797	1,952	1,845	3,023	1,563	1,460	589	295	294	41	20	20	144	73	72
20 to 24 years	17,569	9,015	8,554	14,014	7,248	6,766	2,606	1,290	1,316	187	95	92	763	383	380
20 years	3,786	1,950	1,836	3,023	1,567	1,456	581	291	290	38	19	19	144	73	71
21 years	3,531	1,820	1,711	2,819	1,462	1,357	526	263	263	38	19	18	149	76	73
22 years	3,423	1,760	1,663	2,737	1,418	1,318	501	249	253	36	19	18	149	75	74
23 years	3,380	1,729	1,651	2,694	1,390	1,304	496	243	253	36	19	18	155	77	77
24 years	3,448	1,756	1,693	2,742	1,410	1,332	502	244	258	38	19	19	167	82	85
25 to 29 years	18,795	9,436	9,359	15,071	7,645	7,426	2,612	1,252	1,360	191	100	91	921	440	481
25 years	3,553	1,800	1,752	2,821	1,445	1,376	516	250	266	39	20	19	176	86	91
26 years	3,773	1,890	1,883	3,010	1,522	1,488	536	257	279	40	21	19	188	90	98
27 years	3,969	1,990	1,979	3,195	1,618	1,577	542	259	283	40	21	19	193	92	100
28 years	3,608	1,806	1,802	2,924	1,479	1,445	477	228	249	35	18	17	173	81	91
29 years	3,893	1,949	1,943	3,122	1,582	1,540	542	258	284	38	20	18	191	90	101
30 to 34 years	20,542	10,239	10,303	16,705	8,423	8,282	2,743	1,288	1,454	183	93	90	912	434	477
30 years	3,856	1,924	1,933	3,120	1,576	1,544	522	246	277	36	18	17	178	84	94
31 years	3,841	1,912	1,930	3,101	1,561	1,540	526	248	278	36	18	18	179	85	94
32 years	4,085	2,036	2,049	3,318	1,673	1,645	548	257	291	36	18	18	182	87	95
33 years	4,255	2,112	2,143	3,482	1,748	1,733	558	260	297	36	18	18	180	85	94
34 years	4,505	2,258	2,249	3,685	1,865	1,820	589	277	311	39	20	19	192	93	99
35 to 39 years	22,633	11,294	11,339	18,893	9,427	9,265	2,862	1,345	1,517	184	92	92	895	431	464
35 years	4,584	2,292	2,292	3,770	1,904	1,866	589	278	311	38	19	19	186	90	96
36 years	4,404	2,194	2,209	3,644	1,836	1,809	546	255	291	37	18	18	176	85	91
37 years	4,681	2,336	2,345	3,858	1,947	1,911	601	282	320	37	19	19	184	88	96
38 years	4,254	2,116	2,138	3,530	1,775	1,755	526	247	279	34	17	17	164	78	86
39 years	4,710	2,356	2,354	3,890	1,966	1,924	599	283	316	37	19	19	184	89	95
40 to 44 years	21,547	10,689	10,859	17,934	8,992	8,942	2,613	1,221	1,392	167	81	85	834	394	439
40 years	4,613	2,296	2,315	3,825	1,924	1,900	575	271	304	36	18	18	177	85	92
41 years	4,357	2,158	2,199	3,617	1,812	1,805	533	247	285	34	17	18	173	82	91
42 years	4,297	2,134	2,163	3,575	1,794	1,780	523	244	279	33	16	17	167	79	87
43 years	4,142	2,043	2,100	3,444	1,718	1,726	498	231	267	33	16	17	167	78	89
44 years	4,137	2,055	2,081	3,473	1,743	1,730	484	228	257	30	14	15	150	70	80
45 to 49 years	18,611	9,146	9,465	15,658	7,788	7,870	2,112	965	1,147	136	66	70	705	327	378
45 years	4,045	1,999	2,047	3,401	1,701	1,701	467	215	252	29	14	15	148	69	79
46 years	3,648	1,794	1,855	3,072	1,529	1,543	410	186	223	27	13	14	139	65	74
47 years	3,763	1,849	1,915	3,134	1,559	1,575	452	206	246	28	14	14	149	69	80
48 years	3,415	1,668	1,747	2,898	1,433	1,465	365	165	200	24	12	12	128	59	69
49 years	3,738	1,837	1,902	3,154	1,567	1,587	418	192	226	27	13	14	140	65	75
50 to 54 years	15,394	7,497	7,897	13,241	6,518	6,723	1,526	684	842	105	50	54	522	245	277
50 years	3,892	1,907	1,984	3,364	1,666	1,698	375	170	205	26	12	13	127	59	68
51 years	3,008	1,467	1,541	2,580	1,273	1,307	297	133	164	22	11	11	110	51	58
52 years	2,771	1,348	1,423	2,368	1,164	1,203	285	128	157	19	9	10	99	47	52
53 years	2,756	1,335	1,420	2,362	1,157	1,205	281	125	156	19	9	10	94	44	49
54 years	2,968	1,439	1,529	2,567	1,258	1,310	288	129	160	19	9	10	93	44	49
55 to 59 years	12,001	5,767	6,235	10,311	5,009	5,301	1,226	537	688	78	37	41	387	183	204
55 years	2,711	1,308	1,403	2,316	1,129	1,187	290	129	160	18	9	9	87	41	46
56 years	2,448	1,175	1,273	2,111	1,026	1,085	242	104	138	16	8	8	79	37	41
57 years	2,405	1,156	1,249	2,056	999	1,057	254	112	143	16	7	8	79	38	42
58 years	2,160	1,035	1,126	1,870	905	965	210	92	118	14	6	7	67	32	36
59 years	2,277	1,093	1,185	1,958	950	1,008	230	100	129	15	7	8	74	35	39
60 to 64 years	10,109	4,774	5,335	8,724	4,170	4,554	1,011	434	578	61	29	32	312	141	170
60 years	2,126	1,005	1,122	1,830	874	956	215	93	122	13	6	7	68	32	36
61 years	2,019	958	1,061	1,745	838	906	199	85	114	12	6	6	63	29	34
62 years	2,040	963	1,077	1,759	841	918	206	88	118	12	6	7	63	28	34
63 years	1,980	939	1,041	1,720	826	895	190	82	108	11	5	6	58	26	32
64 years	1,944	909	1,035	1,670	791	879	202	87	115	11	5	6	60	26	34
65 to 69 years	9,698	4,434	5,263	8,457	3,905	4,552	934	399	535	49	22	27	258	108	150
70 to 74 years	8,756	3,823	4,933	7,798	3,430	4,368	716	291	425	39	17	21	202	84	118
75 to 79 years	7,111	2,941	4,170	6,404	2,662	3,742	543	210	332	29	12	17	136	57	79
80 to 84 years	4,663	1,728	2,935	4,245	1,577	2,668	325	111	214	18	7	11	76	32	43
85 to 89 years	2,485	781	1,704	2,263	708	1,556	174	54	120	10	4	7	37	16	22
90 to 94 years	1,074	278	796	965	245	720	87	24	63	6	2	4	16	7	10
95 to 99 years	305	66	239	269	56	213	28	7	21	2	1	2	5	2	3
100 years and over	58	11	48	49	8	41	7	2	6	1	.	.	2	1	1
16 years and over	206,656	99,812	106,844	172,965	84,110	88,854	24,500	11,320	13,179	1,619	796	822	7,573	3,585	3,988
18 years and over	198,884	95,795	103,089	166,796	80,913	85,883	23,298	10,705	12,593	1,526	749	777	7,264	3,428	3,836
15 to 44 years	120,295	60,572	59,723	97,666	49,624	48,042	16,418	7,912	8,506	1,135	574	561	5,076	2,463	2,613
65 years and over	34,150	14,062	20,088	30,450	12,591	17,859	2,815	1,099	1,716	153	65	88	732	307	426
85 years and over	3,922	1,135	2,787	3,546	1,017	2,529	297	87	210	19	6	13	61	25	36
Median age	35.1	33.9	36.2	36.1	34.9	37.3	29.8	27.9	31.4	27.3	26.6	28.0	31.1	30.0	32.1
Mean age	36.1	34.8	37.4	37.0	35.7	38.4	31.7	30.2	33.1	30.1	29.3	30.9	32.2	31.2	33.2

(Continued on following page.)

TABLE 1.2 (Continued)

Resident Population--Estimates by Age, Sex, Race, and Hispanic Origin--Con.

(Numbers in thousands. Consistent with the 1990 Census, as enumerated.)

Date and age	Hispanic origin [1] Total	Male	Female	Not of Hispanic origin, by race White Total	Male	Female	Black Total	Male	Female	American Indian, Eskimo, and Aleut Total	Male	Female	Asian and Pacific Islander Total	Male	Female
November 1, 1997															
All ages	29,577	15,209	14,367	194,858	95,295	99,563	32,394	15,332	17,062	1,985	977	1,008	9,606	4,633	4,976
Under 5 years	3,336	1,711	1,625	12,012	6,161	5,852	2,667	1,350	1,317	165	83	82	801	407	393
Under 1 year	683	350	333	2,351	1,205	1,146	511	259	252	33	16	16	162	82	80
1 year	670	344	326	2,348	1,203	1,144	511	258	252	32	16	16	158	81	78
2 years	665	341	324	2,403	1,232	1,171	516	261	254	33	17	16	159	81	78
3 years	658	338	321	2,420	1,241	1,178	545	276	269	33	17	16	161	82	79
4 years	660	339	321	2,491	1,279	1,212	583	295	288	35	18	17	160	82	78
5 to 9 years	2,972	1,520	1,452	12,900	6,618	6,282	2,979	1,511	1,468	190	96	94	761	392	369
5 years	653	335	318	2,543	1,304	1,239	591	300	291	36	18	18	163	84	79
6 years	630	322	309	2,603	1,333	1,270	595	302	293	36	18	18	161	83	78
7 years	615	314	301	2,644	1,358	1,287	606	306	299	39	20	19	156	80	75
8 years	531	272	260	2,496	1,281	1,215	577	292	284	39	20	19	135	69	66
9 years	542	278	264	2,615	1,343	1,272	611	311	301	40	21	20	146	75	71
10 to 14 years	2,531	1,297	1,233	12,823	6,586	6,237	2,799	1,421	1,378	202	103	100	724	370	354
10 years	528	271	257	2,589	1,331	1,259	584	297	288	40	21	19	142	73	69
11 years	510	261	249	2,561	1,315	1,247	556	282	274	39	20	19	139	72	68
12 years	501	256	245	2,575	1,322	1,253	562	286	277	41	20	20	145	74	71
13 years	493	253	241	2,545	1,305	1,239	545	276	268	41	21	20	148	75	73
14 years	499	257	242	2,553	1,313	1,240	551	281	271	41	21	20	150	76	74
15 to 19 years	2,598	1,376	1,222	12,887	6,635	6,252	2,835	1,439	1,396	187	94	93	701	355	346
15 years	509	264	245	2,625	1,350	1,275	578	294	284	41	21	20	150	76	74
16 years	513	269	243	2,534	1,307	1,227	547	280	267	39	19	19	143	73	70
17 years	530	282	249	2,687	1,389	1,298	596	305	291	39	20	19	144	73	71
18 years	510	273	237	2,507	1,288	1,218	555	281	274	34	17	17	129	65	64
19 years	535	288	247	2,534	1,299	1,235	559	280	280	34	17	17	134	67	67
20 to 24 years	2,572	1,401	1,171	11,654	5,957	5,697	2,473	1,221	1,252	155	78	77	716	358	358
20 years	539	292	247	2,529	1,298	1,230	552	276	276	32	16	16	135	68	67
21 years	522	284	238	2,340	1,201	1,139	498	248	250	31	16	16	139	71	69
22 years	506	276	230	2,272	1,164	1,108	476	235	240	30	15	15	140	70	69
23 years	497	271	226	2,237	1,140	1,097	470	230	241	30	15	15	145	73	73
24 years	508	278	230	2,276	1,154	1,122	477	231	245	31	16	16	157	77	80
25 to 29 years	2,567	1,404	1,163	12,729	6,360	6,369	2,474	1,180	1,294	158	81	77	867	411	456
25 years	506	278	228	2,358	1,190	1,168	491	237	254	32	17	16	166	80	86
26 years	513	281	232	2,542	1,265	1,277	509	244	265	33	17	16	177	84	93
27 years	525	287	238	2,716	1,355	1,361	513	244	269	33	17	16	181	86	95
28 years	487	266	221	2,479	1,235	1,244	450	214	236	29	15	14	163	76	86
29 years	536	292	243	2,635	1,315	1,320	512	242	270	31	16	15	180	84	96
30 to 34 years	2,667	1,428	1,239	14,277	7,120	7,157	2,590	1,209	1,380	151	75	76	858	407	451
30 years	528	285	243	2,639	1,315	1,324	492	230	262	29	15	14	168	78	89
31 years	527	284	244	2,620	1,302	1,318	496	233	264	29	14	15	168	79	89
32 years	534	286	248	2,832	1,412	1,421	517	241	276	30	15	15	172	82	90
33 years	531	282	249	2,997	1,491	1,507	528	245	283	30	15	15	169	80	89
34 years	547	291	256	3,188	1,600	1,588	556	261	296	32	16	16	181	88	94
35 to 39 years	2,447	1,287	1,160	16,468	8,255	8,213	2,718	1,270	1,448	155	76	79	845	406	439
35 years	524	278	246	3,294	1,651	1,643	559	262	297	32	16	16	175	85	90
36 years	504	266	238	3,185	1,593	1,592	518	240	277	31	15	16	166	80	86
37 years	503	265	238	3,401	1,706	1,695	572	266	305	32	15	16	174	83	90
38 years	441	230	211	3,129	1,565	1,564	500	233	267	29	14	15	156	74	82
39 years	475	248	227	3,459	1,741	1,719	570	268	302	32	16	16	174	84	90
40 to 44 years	2,010	1,033	978	16,110	8,054	8,056	2,493	1,159	1,334	143	69	74	791	373	417
40 years	447	232	215	3,420	1,714	1,706	548	257	291	31	15	16	168	80	87
41 years	419	216	203	3,237	1,615	1,621	508	234	273	30	14	15	164	78	86
42 years	405	208	197	3,207	1,606	1,602	498	232	267	28	14	14	158	75	83
43 years	373	190	183	3,107	1,546	1,561	476	220	256	29	14	15	158	74	84
44 years	366	187	179	3,140	1,573	1,567	462	216	246	26	12	14	143	67	76
45 to 49 years	1,522	763	759	14,275	7,094	7,181	2,023	920	1,102	119	57	62	672	312	361
45 years	340	172	168	3,092	1,544	1,548	447	205	242	26	12	13	141	65	75
46 years	316	159	157	2,784	1,384	1,400	392	177	214	24	11	12	133	62	71
47 years	309	155	154	2,854	1,419	1,435	433	197	236	24	12	13	143	66	77
48 years	273	135	138	2,648	1,309	1,340	350	158	192	21	10	11	123	57	66
49 years	284	141	143	2,896	1,438	1,458	401	183	218	24	12	12	134	62	71
50 to 54 years	1,136	555	581	12,203	6,009	6,194	1,462	654	809	93	45	49	499	234	265
50 years	272	134	138	3,116	1,543	1,573	360	163	197	23	11	12	122	57	65
51 years	240	118	122	2,361	1,165	1,197	283	127	157	19	9	10	105	49	56
52 years	214	105	109	2,173	1,069	1,104	273	122	151	17	8	9	95	45	50
53 years	208	101	107	2,172	1,065	1,107	270	119	150	17	8	9	90	42	47
54 years	203	98	105	2,382	1,168	1,214	277	123	153	17	8	9	89	42	47
55 to 59 years	851	406	445	9,533	4,638	4,895	1,177	515	662	70	33	37	370	175	195
55 years	187	90	98	2,146	1,048	1,098	278	124	154	16	8	9	83	39	44
56 years	175	84	91	1,950	948	1,002	232	100	132	14	7	7	75	36	40
57 years	175	84	91	1,896	922	973	244	107	137	14	7	7	76	36	40
58 years	155	73	81	1,728	838	890	201	88	114	12	6	7	64	30	34
59 years	159	75	84	1,813	881	932	221	96	124	14	6	7	71	33	37
60 to 64 years	683	317	366	8,098	3,878	4,220	974	417	557	55	26	29	299	136	163
60 years	147	68	78	1,696	811	884	207	89	118	12	6	6	65	31	35
61 years	140	65	75	1,616	778	838	191	82	110	11	5	6	61	28	33
62 years	139	65	74	1,631	781	850	198	84	114	11	5	6	60	27	33
63 years	132	61	70	1,599	769	830	183	78	104	10	5	5	56	25	31
64 years	125	57	68	1,556	738	817	195	84	111	10	5	6	58	25	33
65 to 69 years	581	262	319	7,923	3,664	4,259	902	385	517	44	20	24	248	104	144
70 to 74 years	448	196	252	7,383	3,248	4,135	694	282	412	35	16	20	195	81	113
75 to 79 years	306	128	179	6,120	2,543	3,577	528	205	323	26	11	15	131	55	76
80 to 84 years	183	69	115	4,074	1,513	2,561	316	108	208	17	7	10	73	31	42
85 to 89 years	103	36	67	2,167	674	1,492	170	53	117	10	3	6	36	15	21
90 to 94 years	47	16	31	921	230	690	85	23	62	5	2	4	16	6	9
95 to 99 years	14	5	9	256	52	204	28	7	21	2	1	1	5	2	3
100 years and over	3	1	2	46	7	39	7	2	6	1			1		1
16 years and over	20,229	10,416	9,812	154,498	74,580	79,918	23,371	10,755	12,616	1,386	674	713	7,172	3,387	3,785
18 years and over	19,186	9,866	9,320	149,277	71,884	77,393	22,228	10,170	12,058	1,309	634	674	6,884	3,240	3,644
15 to 44 years	14,661	7,928	6,932	84,124	42,380	41,744	15,583	7,479	8,104	949	474	476	4,778	2,311	2,467
65 years and over	1,686	711	974	28,889	11,931	16,958	2,731	1,065	1,666	140	60	81	704	295	409
85 years and over	167	57	110	3,389	964	2,426	291	85	206	18	6	12	58	24	34
Median age	26.5	26.1	27.1	37.5	36.4	38.6	29.9	28.0	31.6	27.8	27.0	28.8	31.4	30.3	32.4
Mean age	28.7	27.9	29.4	38.2	36.8	39.6	31.9	30.4	33.3	30.7	29.8	31.5	32.5	31.5	33.4

[1] Persons of Hispanic origin may be of any race. The information on the total and Hispanic population shown in this report was collected in the 50 states and the District of Columbia, and therefore, does not include residents of Puerto Rico.

Source: U.S. Bureau of the Census

national median age was 16.7 years in 1820. It took 130 years for the median age to reach 30 years. In 1987, it exceeded 32 years and, in 1997, the median age of Americans reached 35.1 years. In 1997, in a U.S. population of 268.4 million people, 34 million (13 percent) were over the age of 65 (Table 1.2).

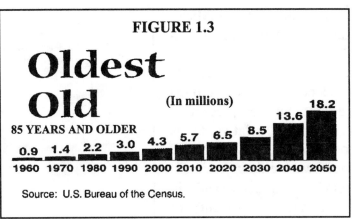

FIGURE 1.3

Oldest Old (In millions)

85 YEARS AND OLDER

1960	1970	1980	1990	2000	2010	2020	2030	2040	2050
0.9	1.4	2.2	3.0	4.3	5.7	6.5	8.5	13.6	18.2

Source: U.S. Bureau of the Census.

The Oldest Old

Even more dramatic than the growth of the 65+ population is the increase in the number of Americans over the age of 85, the "oldest old." In 1997, 3.9 million Americans (1.5 percent) were 85 years old or older, and the number of people over 85 will continue to grow through 2050 (Figure 1.3). By 2050, the 85+ age group will make up 5 percent of the total U.S. population and 22 percent of the 65+ age group. Among the oldest old, women outnumber men by a ratio of 5 to 2. Because women will continue to live longer into the middle of the next century, they will make up an even larger proportion of the older population and thereby a larger percentage of the total population in the future.

The 100 Club

Within the next 60 years, America will experience a "centenarian boom." The chances of living to age 100 have increased 40 times since 1900. The centenarian population more than doubled during the 1980s to reach 58,000 in 1997. The U.S. Census Bureau predicts that America will have 108,000 centenarians by 2000, 441,000 by 2025, and 1.3 million by 2050 — a phenomenal growth when compared to the 4,000 centenarians who were living in the United States in 1960. Not surprisingly, most centenarians live past the age of 100 by only a few years, the majority (90 percent) being less than 105 years of age.

RACIAL CHARACTERISTICS

The older population is becoming more ethnically and racially diverse, although at a slower pace than the overall population of the United States.

The non-White and Hispanic populations have a smaller proportion of elderly than the White population. In 1997, of the total population over 65, about 85 percent were non-Hispanic White; 8 percent, Black; 0.4 percent, American Indian; 2 percent, Asian and Pacific Islander; and 5 percent, of Hispanic origin (Table 1.2).

These differences in racial proportions are expected to continue into the next century, when the minority elderly are predicted to increase more rapidly than the White population, especially among Hispanics and Asian/Pacific Islanders.

ADDITIONAL REASONS FOR THE AGING OF AMERICA

In addition to the large number of births after World War II, there are additional reasons for the American population's aging. Foremost are medical advances that have greatly reduced infant mortality and death from childhood diseases; people have a greater chance of surviving the first years of life. (An extremely high infant and child mortality rate was the main reason that average life expectancy was so low in early civilizations.) At the other end of life, medical advances, life-sustaining technologies, and a greater awareness of and desire for a healthy lifestyle have helped lengthen the lives of Americans.

WHERE DO OLDER AMERICANS LIVE — AND WHERE ARE THEY GOING?

Nine states have more than 1 million elderly: California, New York, Florida, Pennsylvania,

Texas, Illinois, Ohio, Michigan, and New Jersey. Although California has the largest number of elderly residents, in 1995, Florida had the highest percentage (19 percent) relative to its total population. Alaska had the fewest elderly residents both in number and in percentage (5 percent) of population (Figure 1.4). Since 1980, most states have experienced a steady rise in the proportion of elderly persons.

The number of 65+ residents will increase in all regions of the United States into the next century, with the South gaining the greatest number and the Midwest the fewest. By 2025, Florida is expected to remain the "oldest" state with more than 26 percent of its population age 65 or older. Alaska will still rank as the "youngest" state with 10 percent elderly (Figure 1.5). (Some states "age" not only due to the in-migration of elderly but also to the out-migration of the young.) To further show the growth in the aging population, only five states had at least 15 percent of their population in the elderly segment in 1995. By 2025, that number is expected to grow to 48 states.

The U.S. Bureau of the Census ("Census Brief — State-By-State Population Changes to 2025," December 1996) predicted that, by 2025, 27 states will have at least 1 in 5 (20 percent) people elderly (Figure 1.6). Every state but Alaska and California will have 15 percent or more of their population over the age of 65 in 2025, up from five states in 1995. Twenty-one states will at least double their elderly population. Except for New Hampshire, these states are in the South or West. Nineteen-eighty marked the first time in American history that a greater number of elderly people lived in the

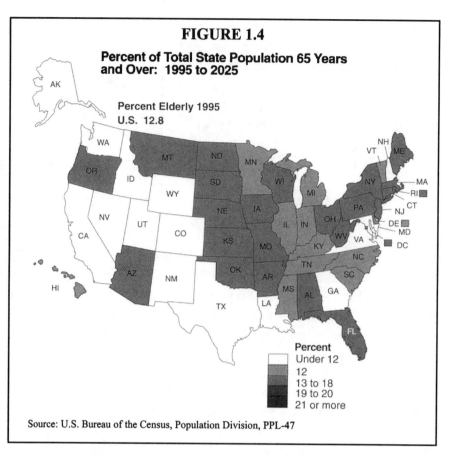

FIGURE 1.4

Percent of Total State Population 65 Years and Over: 1995 to 2025

Percent Elderly 1995
U.S. 12.8

Percent
Under 12
12
13 to 18
19 to 20
21 or more

Source: U.S. Bureau of the Census, Population Division, PPL-47

suburbs than in central cities. These were older suburbs known to have lower resident income levels, more rental housing, lower home values, and higher population densities.

Most older Americans still live in, or have returned to, their native states. Older Americans are less likely than the average American to move across state lines. They tend to remain where they spent their adult lives. In 1996, only 4.3 percent of people 65 to 84 and 5.4 percent of those over 85 made an interstate move (Figure 1.7). Although migration is less common among the elderly, when older citizens do move, they generally move to the Sunbelt states of the South and Western regions, especially Florida, Arizona, Texas, and Washington.

Long-distance retirees have become coveted prizes for state economic developers. Some retirement areas get such a rich monthly boost of money from pensions, investments, and Social Security checks that their civic leaders boast of a "mailbox economy." Nonetheless, older people who move to retire are a small percentage of the elderly. According to the AARP, 84 percent of adults 55 and older report they would prefer to stay in their current homes.

What retirees want most is easy access to important services — grocery stores, pharmacies, hospitals. Only 40 percent of older adults report that they want to live close to children or grand-children, although that de-sire increases with age. Retirement migrants are in-creasingly concerned about getting away from crime and congestion, one of the rea-sons that Florida's share of in-migrants has declined in recent years as the state has grown rapidly.

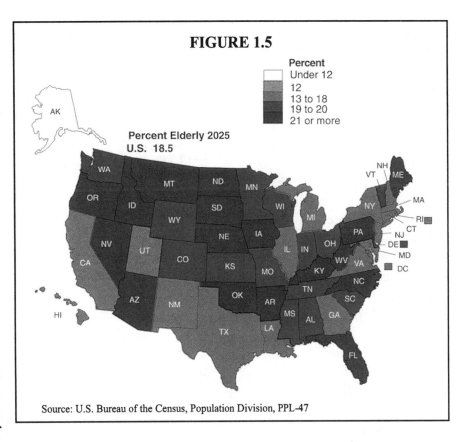

FIGURE 1.5

Percent
Under 12
12
13 to 18
19 to 20
21 or more

Percent Elderly 2025
U.S. 18.5

Source: U.S. Bureau of the Census, Population Division, PPL-47

MARRIED MEN, UNMARRIED WOMEN, AND LIVING ALONE

The ratio of women to men varies dramatically by age, with the disparity becoming most marked among the oldest. At age 65, there are 81 men for every 100 women; by age 100, only 27 men are living for each 100 women. (Figure 1.2 demonstrates the moving of the baby boom cohort through the population over time. The diagrams illustrate the increase of the population at the oldest ages and the especially noticeable increase in the female elderly.) Higher female life expectancy, combined with the fact that men are generally older than their spouses, contributes to the higher proportions or women living alone — widowed or unmarried.

Most younger elderly are married, but the number decreases with age, especially among women. In 1995, 64 percent of persons age 65 to 74 were married and living with their spouses; 24

percent (17.3 percent of men and 41.6 percent of women) were living alone. Among those 75 and older, 22.8 percent of men and 53.4 percent of women lived alone (Figure 1.8). Among those 85 and over, only 21 percent lived with their spouse, and 54 percent lived alone.

The possibility of widowhood increases with age and is greater among women than men. In 1995, 33 percent of women age 65 to 74, 59 percent of those 75 to 84, and 81 percent of women 85 years and over were widowed. Elderly men were much less likely to be widowers: 9 percent of men 65 to 74, 18 percent of those 75 to 84, and 41 percent of men 85 years and older were widowers. Researchers estimate that the average age of widowhood was 68.9 years for women and 72.3 years for men. On average, women spend 15.3 years as widows, while men live 8.4 years as widowers.

The large discrepancy between the percentage of elderly men and elderly women who are married results from women living longer than men, men tending to marry women younger than themselves

9

(and, therefore, being more likely to die before their spouses), and men who are widowed or divorced remarrying more often than do women in the same situation.

As life expectancy increases, the proportion of those widowed may decline. For the immediate future, however, the proportion who are divorced is expected to rise.

ATTITUDES ABOUT AGING

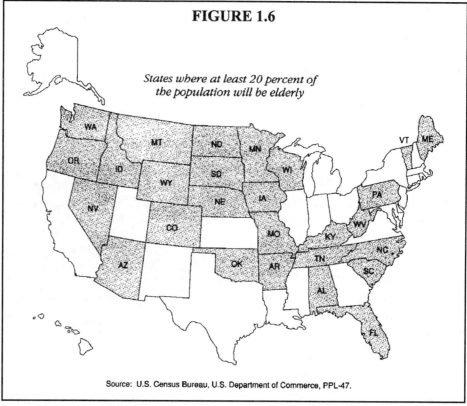

FIGURE 1.6

States where at least 20 percent of the population will be elderly

Source: U.S. Census Bureau, U.S. Department of Commerce, PPL-47.

In non-industrialized countries, old people are often held in great respect and esteem. Not only have they weathered years of what may have been harsh living conditions, but they have accumulated wisdom and knowledge that younger generations need to survive and carry on the traditions of their cultures. In many industrialized societies, such as the United States, a person's worth is measured largely by the type of work he or she does and the amount of wealth accumulated. When people retire from full-time employment, they may lose status because they are no longer working, earning money, or "contributing" to society. People's identity is often bound to their former jobs, and without them, they may feel worthless. Their lifetime of experience may not seem relevant in an ever-changing world where computers become outdated every year.

Until recently, partly in jest and partly reflecting real fears, many people did not acknowledge any birthday from 40 onward and became "39 and holding" — indefinitely. "Old" people were thought to have wrinkled faces, to walk with canes, to be generally irritable and demanding, to be forgetful, and to spend their waking hours playing bingo and shuffleboard — passing time until they died. While this stereotype was probably never an accurate representation of most older people, it is even less true today. As technology and better living conditions increase the number of years a human being can survive and as people actively strive to improve and preserve their health, "old age" becomes harder to portray.

One Definition Does Not Fit All

Individuals age very differently. In fact, the differences between individuals in the latter years of their lives are much greater than in their early years. Although they may have diverse personalities and intellects, most babies and young children behave and develop within fairly predictable patterns. Even our educational system, rightly or wrongly, presupposes a uniformity among children that allows them to be taught and to learn specific materials at specific ages.

On the other hand, one 65-year-old man may go to work every day as he has for the past 40 years, while another requires constant care. One 70-year-old woman may play 18 holes of golf four times a week, while another is crippled with arthritis. One 80-year-old couple may volunteer to be foster grandparents, another spends most of their days in front of the TV.

Challenging the Myth

During the past few years, a revolution has been taking place. Older people are no longer content to be regarded as "old." They want to be recognized as individuals rather than as stereotypes. Most of them are healthier and better educated, and many are wealthier, than at any time in history. They are demanding the respect and recognition they feel they have earned. Older activists are involved in causes ranging from job retraining to long-term care to saving historical buildings to changing the public's perception of old age.

many years. When the baby boomers were young, their needs dominated society. It was not until 1983 that the number of elderly equaled the number of teenagers for the first time. The complexion of the nation is changing and will change even more dramatically in the years to come.

FIGURE 1.7

Percent of Movers by Age: 1996

Age	Percent
1-4	25.1
5-9	18.5
10-14	14.6
15-19	15.3
20-24	33.7
25-29	33.2
30-34	21.9
35-44	14.1
45-54	9.9
55-64	6.6
65-84	4.3
85 and over	5.4

Source: U.S. Census Bureau, Department of Commerce, *Geographical Mobility: March 1995 to March 1996*, Series P20-497.

RESHAPING AMERICAN SOCIETY

The aging of America means much more than just having more old people around. Attitudes about older people are changing as the elderly become more numerous and vocal, and the focus of daily life is shifting from a youth culture to a mature one. This is unfamiliar territory. America has never been old before.

It is little wonder that the United States has been a youth-oriented society for so

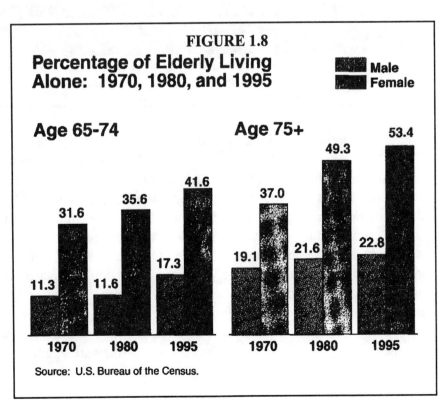

FIGURE 1.8
Percentage of Elderly Living Alone: 1970, 1980, and 1995

■ Male
■ Female

Age 65-74

	1970	1980	1995
Male	11.3	11.6	17.3
Female	31.6	35.6	41.6

Age 75+

	1970	1980	1995
Male	19.1	21.6	22.8
Female	37.0	49.3	53.4

Source: U.S. Bureau of the Census.

FIGURE 1.9
THE WORLD'S OLDEST COUNTRIES: 1996
(Percent of population age 60 and over)

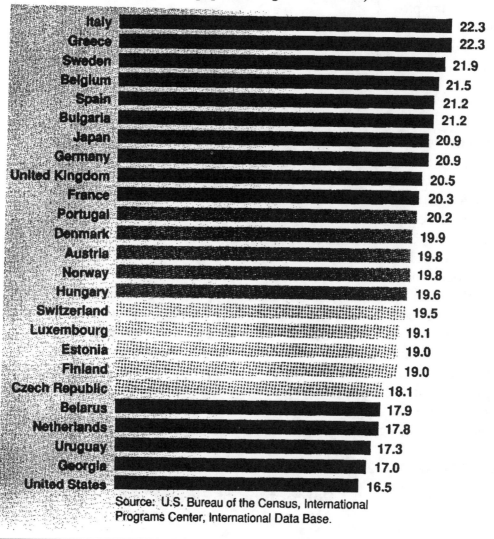

Italy	22.3
Greece	22.3
Sweden	21.9
Belgium	21.5
Spain	21.2
Bulgaria	21.2
Japan	20.9
Germany	20.9
United Kingdom	20.5
France	20.3
Portugal	20.2
Denmark	19.9
Austria	19.8
Norway	19.8
Hungary	19.6
Switzerland	19.5
Luxembourg	19.1
Estonia	19.0
Finland	19.0
Czech Republic	18.1
Belarus	17.9
Netherlands	17.8
Uruguay	17.3
Georgia	17.0
United States	16.5

Source: U.S. Bureau of the Census, International Programs Center, International Data Base.

Changing the Marketplace

Because spending power has traditionally been in the hands of young adults and their children, manufacturers and retailers have targeted these age groups almost exclusively. Now a whole new market is surfacing. Today's older adults worked in the prosperous post-war years, earned good wages, and were often conscientious about saving. Having completed child rearing responsibilities, many now have considerable discretionary money.

Many manufacturers have no idea how to tap this potential market. Older consumers, especially those between ages 50 and 75, are a very diverse group with wide-ranging interests and needs. Marketing programs sometimes fail because manufacturers promote items designed specifically for "old" people, only to find that older people reject products marketed on the basis of age. It is often harder to develop a product that universally appeals to the old because they are old than one that appeals to the young simply because they are young.

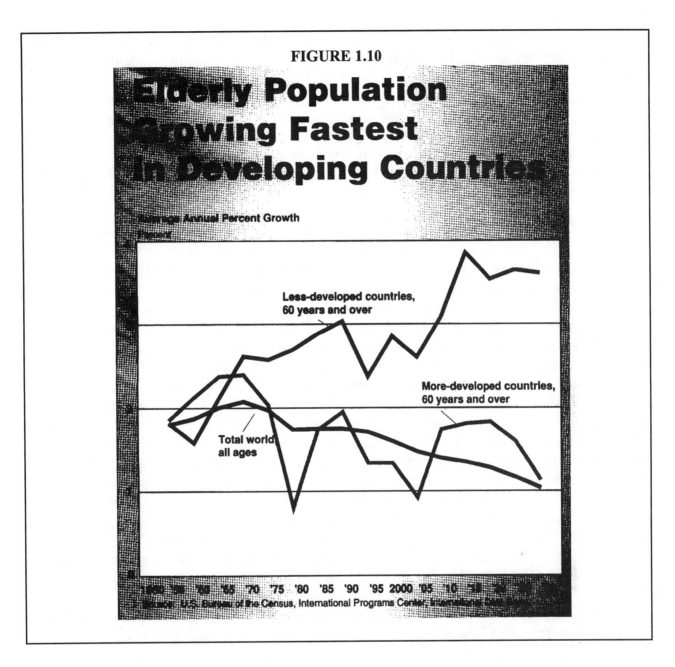

FIGURE 1.10

Elderly Population Growing Fastest in Developing Countries

Average Annual Percent Growth

Less-developed countries, 60 years and over

More-developed countries, 60 years and over

Total world all ages

'60 '65 '70 '75 '80 '85 '90 '95 2000 '05 '10

Source: U.S. Bureau of the Census, International Programs Center, International Data Base

The Need for New Marketing Approaches

Television commercials may look very different in the years ahead. The emphasis on youthfulness may find less acceptance in a generally aging community. Modeling and advertising agencies increasingly demand the over-50 model. Magazines aimed at the mature audience, such as *Modern Maturity*, published by the AARP, almost exclusively use advertisements with older models. However, the image of older people in advertising will almost certainly retain the healthy, vital qualities of younger models, while emphasizing the wisdom and experience gained with age.

The increasing number of elderly, the hours they spend watching television and otherwise attuned to the media (see Chapter XI), and the considerable discretionary income available to many of them are making the elderly a prime target for consumer marketing.

The Need for New and Different Housing

In the future, the privately-owned, one-family residence with a lawn may be only one of the housing options preferred by the elderly. Houses that accommodate the physical limitations of the elderly will become more necessary, as will apartment complexes for those no longer able or interested in maintaining a single-unit home for physical, financial, or security reasons. Entire developments devoted to elderly retirees have sprung up in several states. Chapter III explores more fully the housing options for the elderly.

Caring for the Elderly

While many older people are remaining active and independent longer than ever before, there are many others who are in poor health and live at the brink of poverty. With time, even the sturdiest body weakens and mental faculties may decline. Long or catastrophic illnesses can deplete a lifetime of savings. Almost all of the oldest old require some kind of assistance — financial, physical, or often both — just to survive the day. This assistance must come from somewhere, whether the family, private organizations, or the government. Caring for a much larger, older population in the future will require foresight and planning. For more information, see Chapters VIII and IX.

GLOBAL AGING

Population aging is not confined to the United States. The size of the world's population has been growing for centuries. What is new is the accelerated pace of aging. According to United Nations projections, 1 in 10 persons worldwide will be age 65 or older by 2025 — up from 1 in 15 today. As fertility levels decline throughout the world, all major areas will have a greater share of elderly population. The elderly in Asia and Latin America will nearly double to about 10 percent in 2025. The elderly in North America will increase from 12.5 percent in 1995 to 18.5 percent; Europe, from 13.8 to 20.2 percent; and Africa, from 3.2 to 4.2 percent. Figure 1.9 shows that, in 1996, the United States was one of the youngest countries in the developed world.

Less developed nations generally are aging much faster than their more developed counterparts. Nearly 80 percent of the increase in 1995 occurred in less developed countries (Figure 1.10). In 1996, more than 43 percent of those over 75 years lived in just four countries: the People's Republic of China, the United States, India, and Japan. In many countries, such as the United States, those 75 and older constituted the fastest-growing segment of the population. Growth of aging populations around the world reflects major social and economic achievements — declines in infant mortality, decreases in infectious diseases, and improvements in nutrition and education. This unprecedented growth challenges social planners, since the oldest old consume disproportionate amounts of health and long-term care services.

CHAPTER II

THE ECONOMIC STATUS OF OLDER AMERICANS

The economic status of older Americans is more varied than that of any other age group. The elderly were once popularly stereotyped as generally poor, ill, and in need of public and private economic support. Today that image has changed, and some observers now even suggest that because many older people are financially well off, they do not need as much assistance, especially from the government. Elderly-rights advocates, on the other hand, point out that many older Americans have high out-of-pocket medical expenses and are sharply affected by inflation and the overall economic climate. They have few opportunities to increase, or even maintain, their incomes.

Unfortunately for most elderly retirees who live off their investments, the recent trend in the U.S. economy toward lower interest rates has led to significant cuts in their monthly incomes, sometimes by several hundreds, and even many thousands of dollars. In addition, changes in governmental programs, such as Medicare and Social Security, may threaten the economic stability of many elderly and soon-to-be-elderly persons.

The elderly are well represented in every economic bracket — affluence, middle class, and poverty. The major questions are how many elderly are in each segment, how wealth and poverty are defined, and how severe poverty is among the poor.

NET WORTH

A person's net worth is the sum of all his or her financial resources, including assets (items of value) and income, minus all debts and liabilities. When estimating the net worth of Americans, the U.S. Bureau of the Census uses the household,* rather than the individual, as the basic unit of calculation.

Are the Elderly Worth More?

The median net worth of households headed by a person 65 years or older in 1993 (the latest data available), including home equity (the market value of the home less the amount remaining on the mortgage), was $86,324, the highest of any age group except those persons 55 to 64 years of age ($91,481) (Table 2.1 and Figure 2.1). These figures seem to support the argument that the elderly are generally more wealthy than the non-elderly. However, many elderly people have fixed incomes, about three-quarters of their equity is in their home, and what they own cannot always be easily converted into cash if needed. Older people often have higher per person living

---

* A household consists of all persons occupying one housing unit and includes related and nonrelated persons. Household income includes the income of every person in the household. The Bureau assumes that everyone living in one household shares the income and assets as well as the debts and liabilities.

TABLE 2.1
Median Measured Net Worth by Age of Householder 1993

[Excludes group quarters]

Monthly household income	Total	Less than 35 years	35 to 44 years	45 to 54 years	55 to 64 years	65 years and over			
						Total	65 to 69 years	70 to 74 years	75 years and over
1993									
All households (thousands)	96,468	24,361	22,790	16,258	12,291	20,768	6,132	5,504	9,131
Median measured net worth (dollars)..	37,587	5,786	29,202	57,755	91,481	86,324	92,500	95,748	77,654
Excluding home equity	9,505	3,297	8,219	14,499	25,108	20,642	23,650	23,054	18,125

Source: T.J. Eller and Wallace Fraser, *Asset Ownership of Households, 1993*, U.S. Bureau of the Census, Washington, DC, 1995

costs. In addition, among the elderly, net worth is much lower for Blacks, Hispanics, and unmarried persons, with unmarried householders' net worth being less than half that of married couples (Table 2.2).

As shown in Table 2.1, net worth in 1993 increased for each successive age group up to age 74. This increase is largely due to the fact that at some time during their lives most people work, and a working person generally earns more money and accumulates more assets as he or she gets older.

By age 65, most people are retired from the work force. They must then rely on fixed resources, such as interest income, Social Security, or pension benefits, or compensate by tapping other, perhaps non-replaceable resources, such as savings accounts or investments.

Assets

The elderly hold more assets than the non-elderly because of people's tendency to accumulate savings, home equity, and property in their lifetimes. Older Americans will usually have a greater percentage of their assets in bank accounts (23.2 percent) than the non-elderly (Table 2.3).

In all age groups, home equity accounts for most of the household's net worth. In 1993, it represented 43.6 percent of net worth of households headed by an elderly householder. Regardless of how valuable a home might be, it cannot be used for daily expenses. Generally, the only time a house provides any monetary value to the owner is when it is sold, and even then, new accommodations must be found and paid for. Many older people have lived in their homes for a long time and do not want to move. Money can often be borrowed against the value of a home, but elderly people may be reluctant to take on any new debt, especially if they are on a fixed income, and they may fear losing their home.

FIGURE 2.1
Median Measured Net Worth by
Age of Householder: 1993

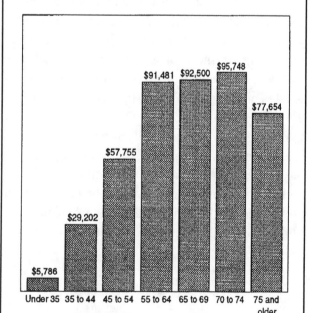

Source: T.J. Eller and Wallace Fraser, *Asset Ownership of Households, 1993*, U.S. Bureau of the Census, Washington, DC, 1995

TABLE 2.2

Median Measured Net Worth by Type of Household and Age of Householder: 1993 and 1991

[Excludes group quarters]

Type of household by age of householder	1993			1991		
		Median measured net worth (dollars)			Median measured net worth (in 1993 dollars)	
	Number of households (thousands)	Total	Excluding equity in own home	Number of households (thousands)	Total	Excluding equity in own home
Married-couple households	52,891	61,905	17,051	52,616	63,599	19,557
Less than 35 years	12,141	12,941	5,677	12,247	12,702	5,548
35 to 54 years	23,983	61,874	17,436	23,080	64,047	19,801
55 to 64 years	7,568	127,752	43,543	7,849	123,138	47,158
65 years and over........................	9,199	129,790	44,410	9,040	142,517	59,200
Male householders	15,397	13,500	5,157	15,297	12,698	5,963
Less than 35 years	5,285	4,300	2,890	5,746	5,027	3,668
35 to 54 years	6,157	18,426	6,156	5,409	18,391	7,420
55 to 64 years	1,437	44,670	10,905	1,514	32,330	5,988
65 years and over........................	2,518	60,741	12,927	2,627	69,157	17,489
Female householders.......................	28,180	13,294	3,363	27,179	15,518	3,762
Less than 35 years	6,935	1,342	790	7,038	1,383	953
35 to 54 years	8,908	8,405	2,652	7,959	11,294	3,308
55 to 64 years	3,286	44,762	6,475	3,211	41,635	6,229
65 years and over........................	9,050	57,679	9,560	8,972	62,746	13,015

TABLE 2.3

Distribution of Measured Net Worth by Age of Householder and Asset Type: 1993 and 1991

[Excludes group quarters]

Asset type	1993						1991					
	Total	Less than 35 years	35 to 44 years	45 to 54 years	55 to 64 years	65 years and over	Total	Less than 35 years	35 to 44 years	45 to 54 years	55 to 64 years	65 years and over
Total measured net worth	100.0	100.0	100.0	100.0	100.0	100.0	100.0	100.0	100.0	100.0	100.0	100.0
Interest-earning assets at financial institutions	11.4	10.9	7.9	7.7	9.6	16.7	14.3	12.3	9.6	9.5	12.2	21.1
Other interest-earning assets	4.0	2.1	2.5	2.6	4.1	6.1	5.0	1.9	3.0	3.7	5.1	7.3
Checking accounts	0.5	1.2	0.7	0.5	0.4	0.4	0.5	1.2	0.7	0.4	0.4	0.4
Stocks and mutual fund shares	8.3	8.9	6.4	8.1	8.8	9.1	7.1	4.7	5.9	5.4	6.7	9.4
Own home	44.4	43.8	47.7	45.3	42.4	43.6	42.1	42.1	45.3	41.0	41.2	41.6
Rental property	6.7	5.3	6.4	7.2	9.1	5.2	6.5	6.0	7.7	9.1	6.6	4.4
Other real estate..........	4.6	5.1	5.0	5.5	4.9	3.6	5.4	6.2	5.4	6.8	6.3	4.0
Vehicles	6.4	18.2	8.8	6.5	4.9	3.7	6.4	18.1	8.8	6.4	5.2	3.5
Business or profession.....	6.4	10.6	9.5	9.0	6.1	2.4	7.3	13.5	11.6	10.8	6.8	2.1
U.S. savings bonds........	0.8	1.0	1.2	0.7	0.7	0.8	0.6	0.7	0.5	0.5	0.7	0.6
IRA or Keogh accounts	6.7	3.9	6.3	7.4	8.8	5.7	5.2	3.2	5.7	5.8	7.1	3.8
Other financial investments[1]..................	3.0	3.6	2.9	2.6	3.0	3.2	3.0	3.5	1.7	4.1	4.3	2.4
Unsecured liabilities[2]	-3.4	-14.5	-5.3	-3.3	-2.8	-0.6	-3.4	-13.6	-5.8	-3.7	-2.6	-0.5

[1]Includes mortgages held from sale of real estate, amount due from sale of business, unit trusts, and other financial investments.
[2]Since net worth is the value of assets less liabilities, unsecured liabilities are subtracted from the distribution of net worth and are shown as negative.

Source of both tables: T.J. Eller and Wallace Fraser, *Asset Ownership of Households, 1993*,
U.S. Bureau of the Census, Washington, DC, 1995

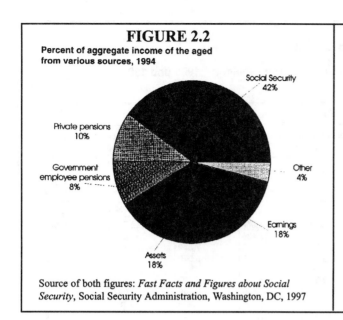

FIGURE 2.2

Percent of aggregate income of the aged from various sources, 1994

- Social Security 42%
- Private pensions 10%
- Government employee pensions 8%
- Other 4%
- Earnings 18%
- Assets 18%

Source of both figures: *Fast Facts and Figures about Social Security*, Social Security Administration, Washington, DC, 1997

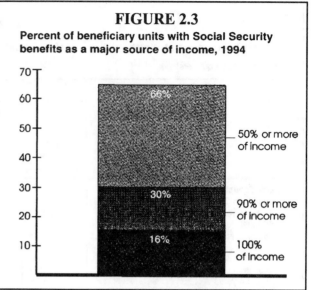

FIGURE 2.3

Percent of beneficiary units with Social Security benefits as a major source of income, 1994

- 66% — 50% or more of income
- 30% — 90% or more of income
- 16% — 100% of income

Although the elderly maintain the greatest percentages in bank accounts, these assets are not "fixed" in the strict sense because they do represent available cash. Many older people, however, are reluctant to "touch their savings," except in an extreme emergency. They know that one major or prolonged illness can use up a lifetime of savings. Many elderly reserve their savings for illness or long-term care, such as residence in a nursing home — costs which can wipe out all their financial reserves.

Changing Assets

Numbers such as net worth do not always accurately describe the condition of elderly people. Some older people in the United States are, indeed, very rich. When their wealth is averaged into income and asset statistics, it masks the fact that a large number of old people live below — often far below —the poverty level (see THE ELDERLY POOR, below).

SOURCES OF INCOME

Unlike younger people, who may get almost all their income from regular paychecks, the elderly rely on a variety of sources to meet the expenses of daily living. Usually unable to improve their incomes through work, they often are vulnerable to circumstances beyond their control, such as the death of a spouse, health problems, Social Security and Medicare variations, and inflation.

As a group, in 1994, the elderly derived 42 percent of their income from Social Security benefits, 18 percent from assets (returns on stock investments, interest from savings accounts, etc.), 18 percent from earnings, 18 percent from government and private employee pensions, and 4 percent from "other" sources. (See Figure 2.2.) Very few elderly people receive income from all these sources at any one time. In addition, many elderly receive favorable treatment in taxes and government in-kind transfers, such as Medicare, Medicaid, food stamps, and housing assistance.

Rising health care costs, rather than funding for retirement, account for most of the increasing public spending on the elderly. In the mid 1990s, programs benefitting the elderly accounted for more than 30 percent of the federal budget, double the 15 percent spent on the elderly in 1960. Over the same period, spending on health programs for the elderly increased five-fold, from 6 percent in 1960 to more than one-third today.

Social Security

The elderly depend on Social Security for their incomes more than on any other source. In

1994, the Social Security program paid benefits to 90 percent of those over 65. For 66 percent of the elderly, Social Security provided more than 50 percent of their income; for 30 percent, it was 90 percent of their income; and for 16 percent of the elderly, Social Security was their only source of income (Figure 2.3). As the number of elderly increases in the next decades, the number of Social Security participants will rise. For more information on Social Security, see below.

Assets and Earnings

The percentage of employed men age 65 and older has declined over the past few decades. In 1997, there were 3.8 million employed people over 65. For more information on employment among the elderly, see Chapter IV.

TABLE 2.4
Private Pension Coverage*
(% covered)

Hourly Wage Quartiles	No Pension	One Pension	Two or More Pensions
Whites and Others			
Lowest	48	43	10
Second	23	56	20
Third	14	63	23
Highest	5	66	28
Blacks			
Lowest	59	30	10
Second	25	57	18
Third	11	68	21
Highest	6	73	21
Hispanics			
Lowest	70	27	3
Second	36	48	16
Third	20	66	13
Highest	24	47	29

*Excluding self-employed.

Source: *University of Michigan Health and Retirement Study, 1993.* Funded by the National Institute of Aging

The trend toward earlier retirement has led to a decline in the role of earnings in supporting the aged. As earnings account for a smaller proportion of income, assets and pensions have become more important. Assets represent one-fifth of the income of the elderly. It must be emphasized that this is an average figure; while some elderly have large assets, one-third of the elderly have *no* income from assets.

Pension (Retirement) Funds

Many large companies, along with most local and state governments and the federal government, offer pension plans. (The first employer-provided retirement plan in the United States was started in 1875.) Employees are eligible for pension benefits when they retire or leave a company if they have worked for the company for a designated number of years and/or have reached a specified age. A pension benefit is usually money in the form of a monthly check beginning at retirement and ending at death. A few companies pay for 100 percent of pension benefits, but more commonly, companies provide a portion of the benefits, and employees contribute a percentage of their salaries to the pension fund during their working years.

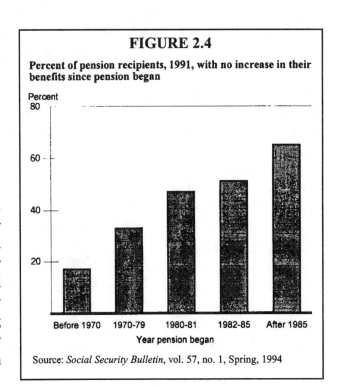

FIGURE 2.4

Percent of pension recipients, 1991, with no increase in their benefits since pension began

Source: *Social Security Bulletin*, vol. 57, no. 1, Spring, 1994

19

Employers are not required to provide pensions. In addition, pension plans do not have to include all workers; they may exclude certain jobs and/or individuals. Before 1976, pension plans could require an employee to work a lifetime for one company before being eligible for pension benefits. As required by the Employee Retirement Income Security Act of 1974 (ERISA — see below), as of 1976, an employee becomes eligible after 10 years of service. Most current plans require five years of work before an employee becomes vested (eligible for benefits).

The Social Security Administration reports that, in 1962, private pensions accounted for 3 percent of the income for the elderly. By 1994, pensions supplied 10 percent of older persons' income. (The spouse of a person who actually participated in a pension plan is also considered a recipient.)

Employees in larger firms were more likely to be covered than those in smaller firms. Highly paid workers were more likely to have coverage, as were workers in industries covered by union contracts. White-collar workers were somewhat more likely to receive pensions than blue-collar (66 percent versus 58 percent). Private pension coverage is greater among Whites than Blacks or Hispanics and is strongly related to a worker's wage level. (See Table 2.4.) Also, employer pensions are more prevalent in goods-producing industries than in service-producing industries. There are fewer government pension plans

than private plans, but average benefits are substantially larger.

Women over the age of 65 are much less likely to have worked outside the home than are younger women; therefore, they are less likely to have

---

TABLE 2.5

Legislation Related to Pensions

Employee Retirement Income Security Act of 1974 (ERISA)

Establishes individual rights under pension plans, investment rules for plan officials, funding requirements, and the Federal pension insurance program. Rules on individual rights went into effect in 1976. Other rules became effective in 1974 and 1975.

Multiemployer Pension Plan Amendments Act of 1980 (MPPAA)

Establishes financial obligations for companies that withdraw from multi-employer pension plans and provides Government insurance protection for financially troubled plans. Applies to companies that withdraw from multi-employer plans after September 25, 1980.

Tax Equity and Fiscal Responsibility Act of 1982 (TEFRA)

Includes provisions requiring "top-heavy" pension plans to provide at least minimum benefits for secretaries, nurses, paralegals, and others working in small offices. Applies to benefits earned by employees working under pension plans in 1984 and after.

Retirement Equity Act of 1984 (REA)

Increases pension protection for widowed and divorced spouses, lowers minimum ages for vesting and participation, and liberalizes break-in-service rules. Generally helps spouses of workers employed under pension plans as of August 23, 1984, or later; applies to divorce court orders issued in 1985 or later.

Single Employer Pension Plan Amendments Act of 1986 (SEPPAA)

Strengthens the Federal insurance program for single-employer pension plans that terminated in 1986 or after.

Tax Reform Act of 1986 (TRA)

Includes provisions to shorten pension vesting, increase coverage, and restrict integration of pensions with Social Security. Applies to workers on the job in 1989 and after.

Omnibus Budget Reconciliation Act of 1986 (OBRA)

Includes pension provisions requiring plans to give benefits to employees who work past age 65. Prevents plans from setting a maximum age limit that excludes older employees from pension plan membership. Applies to workers on the job in 1988 and after (6).

Older Worker Benefit Protection Act of 1990 (OWBPA)

Amends the 1967 Age Discrimination Employment Act to clarify protection guaranteed to older individuals in regard to employee benefit plans (14).

Source: Nancy E. Schwenk, "Trends in the Economic Status of Retired People," *Family Economics Review*, vol. 7, no. 2, 1995

access to pension and Social Security income in their own name. This is likely to change, however, because of the large increase in the number of women who have entered the labor force over the past two decades. In the future, it is expected that many women over 65 will have earned their own pension and Social Security benefits.

Unlike Social Security, most pension plans do not provide automatic cost-of-living adjustments, which can gradually erode retirees' incomes. Among pension recipients, those who have been receiving their pensions the longest were the least likely to report no increases in benefits (Figure 2.4). Those persons receiving pensions from the military, the government, or Railroad Retirement were more likely to receive increases than were those receiving pensions from the private sector. Fifty-six percent of those with private pensions reported no change in their benefit amounts, and 4 percent reported that their payments had been reduced.

The proportion of retirees receiving pension benefits is expected to rise over the next 20 to 30 years because of growth in coverage and vesting. By 2018, the percentage of elderly households receiving pension benefits is projected to reach 88 percent. This growth will reflect the increasing coverage of women by pension plans due to the continually increasing numbers of women in the labor force. However, some sources contend that downsizing efforts by many companies may result in reduced benefits.

Federal Pension Laws

A company that has a pension plan will often invest the money received into the plan in an investment fund (for example, stocks or bonds), much as a bank does with its depositors' money. If the investment choice is a good one, the company makes a profit on the money in the fund; a bad investment results in a loss. During the early 1970s, several major plans collapsed, leaving retirees without benefits even though they had contributed to a plan for many years.

These collapses led to the passage in 1974 of the Employment Retirement Income Security Act (ERISA) (PL 93-406). ERISA established participation and vesting (eligibility for benefits) guidelines and standards to ensure that funds are managed in the best interest of plan participants. It also created the Pension Benefit Guaranty Corporation, a federal agency, to take over benefit payments when underfunded plans are terminated. (See Table 2.5 for laws relating to pensions.)

Before 1983, some plans paid lower monthly benefits to women because, statistically, women lived longer than men and, on average, collected pension benefits for a longer period of time. In 1983, the Supreme Court, in *Arizona Governing Committee for Tax Deferred Annuity and Deferred Compensation Plan v. Natalie Norris* (463 US 1073), ruled that pension plans must make payments based on gender-neutral actuarial tables (statistical calculations for insurance purposes).

The Retirement Equity Act of 1984 (PL 98-397) requires pension plans to pay a survivor's benefit to the spouse of a deceased vested plan participant. Prior to 1984, some spouses received no benefits unless the employee was near retirement age at the time of death. Under the 1984 law, pension vesting begins at age 21 or after five years on the job, and employees who have a break in employment for reasons such as maternity leave will not lose any time already accumulated.

Problems with Pension Management

A variety of flaws bedevil the American pension system, some of which may deprive retired workers of part, or all, of their pensions. A 1995 audit by the federal Pension Benefit Guaranty Corporation, a Washington, DC-based advocacy group, found an 8 percent error rate in the administration of pension payments, and some sources believe it is higher.

A major trouble spot arises from corporate mergers and downsizings. Employees may lose out when dissimilar pension plans are consolidated. Problems also arise when widows and divorced spouses fail to get a rightful share of their spouses' pension. Ex-spouses are often entitled to pension benefits, but terms must be included in divorce decrees or filed with a plan administrator. Divorce lawyers or judges may fail to include pensions when dividing assets, or wives may unknowingly sign away their rights. Pension calculations are often very complicated, and errors are easily made in calculating amounts due.

IRAs and 401(k)s — The Shift toward Self-Reliance

Individual Retirement Accounts (IRAs) were first established in 1974 as a means of retirement savings for those not covered by pensions. Another thrift plan, which is employer-provided, is the 401(k). An employee may have both a pension and a 401(k).

During and immediately following the Great Depression, when so many people felt vulnerable to poverty, America developed a "one-for-all" or "we're all in this together" economic system. New government safety nets, such as Social Security, came into existence, and corporations took on

new responsibilities for the well-being of their workers. This communal system is giving way to a do-it-yourself approach that increasingly asks Americans to make their own way. (Other signs are the trends in Americans assuming more responsibility for their own health insurance premiums, once covered by corporations, and new, more demanding hurdles to staying on welfare.) Likewise, workers are increasingly financing their own retirements by means of savings plans such as 401(k)s and IRAs.

Family Support

While the contribution by the family, both in financial support and the value of the care and time they give to an elderly parent or relative, has not been statistically determined, numerous studies suggest that it is substantial. According to these studies, income from Social Security plays a minor role compared to the amount of support contributed by family members. When elderly persons outlive their family members, they are often faced with serious problems of financial security and personal care.

Although nobody knows the exact extent of financial support given to aging parents by their children, most sources believe that 10 to 12

TABLE 2.6

Median Income of Households by Selected Characteristics, Race, and Hispanic Origin of Householder: 1996, 1995, and 1994

[Households as of March of the following year. An asterisk (*) preceding percent change indicates statistically significant change at the 90-percent confidence level. For meaning of symbols, see text]

Characteristic	1996			1995			1994			Percent change in real median income (1995-1996)
	Number (1,000)	Median income		Number (1,000)	Median income		Number (1,000)	Median income		
		Value (dollars)	Standard error (dollars)		Value (dollars)	Standard error (dollars)		Value (dollars)	Standard error (dollars)	
ALL RACES										
All households...............	101 018	35 492	179	99 627	34 076	197	98 990	32 264	146	* 1.2
Age of Householder										
Under 65 years........................	79 610	40 941	188	78 141	39 148	217	77 625	37 247	173	* 1.6
15 to 24 years....................	5 160	21 438	417	5 282	20 979	462	5 444	19 340	403	-.7
25 to 34 years....................	19 314	35 888	355	19 225	34 701	378	19 453	33 151	359	.5
35 to 44 years....................	23 823	44 420	446	23 226	43 465	406	22 914	41 667	310	-.7
45 to 54 years....................	18 843	50 472	484	18 008	48 058	525	17 590	47 261	473	* 2.0
55 to 64 years....................	12 469	39 815	615	12 401	38 077	545	12 224	35 232	497	1.6
65 years and over........................	21 408	19 449	208	21 486	19 096	203	21 365	18 095	192	-1.1
65 to 74 years....................	11 679	23 411	339	11 908	23 031	384	11 803	21 422	270	-1.3
75 years and over..................	9 729	15 995	246	9 578	15 342	237	9 562	14 731	188	1.3

Source: *Money Income in the United States: 1996*, Bureau of the Census, Washington, DC, 1997

---

percent of the work force is caring for older parents in some capacity. Andrew Scharlach, professor at the University of California at Berkeley, predicts that, by 2020, 1 in 3 people will have to provide care for an elderly parent, much of that in the form of financial assistance. The Conference Board, a business research group, estimates as many as 40 percent will be affected shortly after the turn of the century. For more information on elder care, see Chapter VIII.

MEDIAN INCOME

Households

In 1996, the elderly had the lowest median incomes of all age groups. In 1996, the median income for a household headed by someone 65 years and older was $19,449, slightly up from $19,096 in 1995 (i.e., half of all persons aged 65 years or older made less than $19,449 and half

---

TABLE 2.7

Age of reference person: Average annual expenditures and characteristics, Consumer Expenditure Survey, 1995

Item	All consumer units	Under 25	25-34	35-44	45-54	55-64	65 and over	65-74	75 and over
Number of consumer units (in thousands)	103,123	7,093	19,540	23,440	18,633	12,624	21,792	11,933	9,860
Consumer unit characteristics:									
Income before taxes [1]	$36,918	$17,274	$35,655	$45,133	$52,044	$38,326	$22,148	$25,553	$18,006
Age of reference person	48.0	21.6	29.9	39.4	49.1	59.4	74.4	69.3	80.6
Average number in consumer unit:									
Persons	2.5	1.9	2.8	3.2	2.8	2.2	1.7	1.9	1.5
Children under 18	.7	.4	1.1	1.3	.6	.2	.1	.1	(2)
Persons 65 and over	.3	(2)	(2)	(2)	(2)	.1	1.4	1.4	1.4
Earners	1.3	1.2	1.5	1.7	1.9	1.4	.4	.6	.2
Vehicles	1.9	1.2	1.7	2.1	2.5	2.2	1.4	1.8	1.0
Percent homeowner	64	12	44	63	76	81	79	82	76
Average annual expenditures	$32,264	$18,425	$31,493	$38,397	$42,179	$32,626	$22,24	$25,277	$18,572
Food	4,505	2,690	4,469	5,368	5,468	4,541	3,388	3,895	2,767
Food at home	2,803	1,407	2,758	3,345	3,223	2,833	2,367	2,610	2,069
Cereals and bakery products	441	227	422	539	501	425	385	419	344
Meats, poultry, fish, and eggs	752	331	724	900	899	807	610	699	500
Dairy products	297	155	301	352	338	293	248	274	217
Fruits and vegetables	457	213	433	509	513	496	437	459	409
Other food at home	856	482	878	1,044	973	812	687	759	599
Food away from home	1,702	1,283	1,711	2,023	2,245	1,708	1,021	1,285	698
Alcoholic beverages	277	277	299	314	348	253	171	206	129
Housing	10,458	5,908	10,532	12,625	12,886	10,294	7,585	7,918	7,185
Shelter	5,928	3,622	6,157	7,551	7,556	5,359	3,666	4,011	3,247
Owned dwellings	3,749	484	3,096	5,060	5,572	3,799	2,398	2,815	1,894
Rented dwellings	1,788	2,984	2,876	2,106	1,335	988	933	782	1,116
Other lodging	391	154	185	385	649	572	335	415	237
Utilities, fuels, and public services	2,191	1,160	1,987	2,386	2,627	2,443	1,981	2,151	1,775
Household operations	509	200	701	604	446	375	465	342	614
Housekeeping supplies	430	135	360	490	501	514	423	481	351
Household furnishings and equipment	1,401	792	1,327	1,595	1,755	1,604	1,051	933	1,197
Apparel and services	1,704	1,207	1,907	2,079	2,088	1,835	875	1,115	583
Transportation	6,014	4,022	6,198	7,472	8,027	5,732	3,374	4,481	2,035
Vehicle purchases (net outlay)	2,638	1,901	2,857	3,626	3,529	2,112	1,164	1,710	503
Gasoline and motor oil	1,006	701	1,013	1,181	1,324	1,062	604	749	428
Other vehicle expenses	2,015	1,236	2,029	2,289	2,723	2,144	1,284	1,597	905
Public transportation	355	184	299	376	451	414	323	424	199
Health care	1,732	466	1,096	1,607	1,851	1,911	2,648	2,618	2,683
Entertainment	1,612	1,083	1,685	1,951	2,137	1,578	926	1,153	651
Personal care products and services	403	243	387	450	517	407	326	380	260
Reading	162	71	134	173	199	187	161	179	138
Education	471	667	335	437	1,029	364	155	237	54
Tobacco products and smoking supplies	269	246	269	310	347	314	139	183	85
Miscellaneous	766	347	688	815	1,018	949	602	628	572
Cash contributions	925	114	456	908	1,463	1,043	1,099	1,164	1,021
Personal insurance and pensions	2,964	1,083	3,038	3,889	4,802	3,217	799	1,122	408
Life and other personal insurance	373	69	251	438	562	556	244	304	172
Pensions and Social Security	2,591	1,013	2,786	3,451	4,240	2,660	555	818	236

[1] Components of income and taxes are derived from "complete income reporters" only;
[2] Value less than 0.05.

Source: *Consumer Expenditures in 1995*, Bureau of Labor Statistics, Washington, DC, 1997

made more than that amount), just half the income of those 55 to 64 years of age ($39,815). Income continues to decline with age after age 65, with those over 75 receiving $15,995. (See Table 2.6.) Of course, the main reason income declines is that most people over 65 have retired and are, therefore, not receiving income from a job.

Black and Hispanic elderly have lower incomes than their White counterparts. The 1996 median income for families headed by Whites 65 and older was $29,470; for Blacks, $21,328; and for Hispanics, $21,068.

Personal

As with every other age group, women 65 years and older had a lower median personal income ($9,626) in 1996 than older men ($16,684). The lower incomes of older women are largely associated with their greater likelihood of lifelong economic dependence on men. The earnings gap between American men and women accelerates as people grow older. The already lower women's income increases until age 45, the peak of a woman's earnings, while men's income peaks a decade later. This results in substantial differences in male and female income among the elderly and also results in differences in pensions and Social Security payments, which are based on earnings.

Many factors contribute to this wage gap, among them differences in education, experience, and union affiliation. Many sources believe that the primary reason is job segregation. Older women are confined more narrowly in traditionally "women's occupations," which are generally lower paying. Unflattering stereotypes of older women as weak, incapable, and inflexible also encourage discrimination against women from mid-life on.

The Older Women's League reported that, in 1995, among retired workers receiving Social Security benefits based on their own work records, women's average monthly benefits were $538 compared to an average of $858 for men. In addition, just 13 percent of women over 65 had private pensions, compared to 33 percent of older men. The mean private pension for women was $3,940 a year, compared to $7,468 for men.

EXPENSES

The elderly spend their money differently from younger people. Table 2.7 shows expenditures for consumers in 1995. Older households spend less than younger households because they have less money to spend, fewer people to support, and different needs and values. The annual expenditure for those older than 65 was $22,240, lower than all other age groups except

---

TABLE 2.8
Persons and Families in Poverty by Selected Characteristics: 1995 and 1996

[Numbers in thousands]

Characteristic	1996 Below poverty		1995 Below poverty		Difference 1996 less 1995	
	Number	Percent	Number	Percent	Number of poor	Poverty rate
PERSONS						
Total	36,529	13.7	36,425	13.8	105	- 0.1
Age						
Under 18 years	14,463	20.5	14,665	20.8	-202	-0.3
18 to 24 years	4,466	17.9	4,553	18.3	-87	-0.4
25 to 34 years	5,093	12.7	5,196	12.7	-103	-
35 to 44 years	4,343	9.9	4,064	9.4	* 279	0.5
45 to 54 years	2,516	7.6	2,470	7.8	* 46	-0.2
55 to 59 years	1,086	9.4	1,163	10.3	-76	-0.9
60 to 64 years	1,134	11.5	996	10.2	* 137	* 1.3
65 years and over....................	3,428	10.8	3,318	10.5	110	0.3

Source: *Poverty in the United States: 1996*, Bureau of the Census, Washington, DC, 1997

---

those under the age of 25. Those over 75 spent only $18,572, the least of all the elderly. The greatest amounts were spent on housing (including utilities), food, transportation, and health care. Not surprisingly, the elderly spent more money on health care than any other age group, both in actual dollars and in percentage of expenditures. They spent less on entertainment, tobacco and smoking products, alcoholic beverages, apparel, food eaten away from home, and vehicle-related items than other groups.

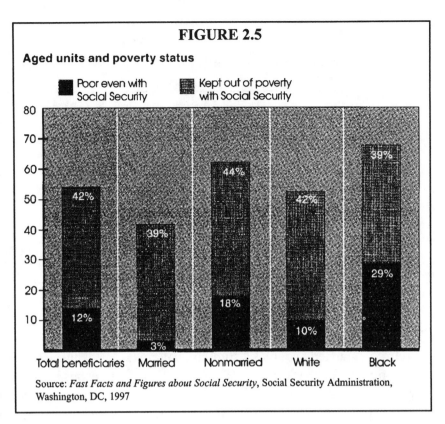

FIGURE 2.5

Aged units and poverty status

Source: *Fast Facts and Figures about Social Security*, Social Security Administration, Washington, DC, 1997

One measure of the economic differences among the elderly is shown in those who have discretionary income, that is money left over after the person has paid everything needed to maintain their standard of living. Many sources believe that those over the age of 65 have a smaller percentage of discretionary income than all groups except persons under 24, although most experts estimate that at least one-quarter of the elderly have some discretionary income.

Smaller Households Are More Expensive to Run

Almost all elderly households are made up of fewer persons than younger households. Generally, while larger households, in general, cost more to operate, they are less expensive on a per capita basis. For example, the Bureau of the Census reports that the basic cost of living for two people is less than twice as much as the cost for one person living alone; the living cost of four people is significantly less than four times that of someone living alone.

Larger, younger households often have multiple incomes. Repairing a leaky roof or buying a new refrigerator costs the same for both households, but the larger the household, the less the cost *per person* as a percentage of total income. Buying small quantities of food for one or two persons may be almost as expensive as buying in bulk for three or four. Because the elderly often have limited mobility, they may be forced to buy food and other necessities at small neighborhood stores that generally charge more than supermarkets.

Expenditures of Retired and Nonretired Elderly

R. M. Rubin and Z. M. Nieswiadomy, in "Expenditure Patterns of Retired and Nonretired Persons" (*Monthly Labor Review*, Vol. 117, No. 4, 1994, U.S. Department of Labor), reported a survey of retirees and nonretirees age 50 or older about their income and expenses. They found that income of retired married couples was 58 percent that of employed couples. Retired women had 53 percent of the income of employed single women, and retired men had 48 percent of the income of employed single men. Retired single women received only half as much pension income as retired single men and less than one-third as much

TABLE 2.9

Poverty Thresholds in 1996 by Size of Family and Number of Related Children Under 18 Years
(Dollars)

Size of family unit	Weighted average thresholds	Related children under 18 years								
		None	One	Two	Three	Four	Five	Six	Seven	Eight or more
One person (unrelated individual) ..	7,995									
Under 65 years	8,163	8,163								
65 years and over	7,525	7,525								
Two persons	10,233									
Householder under 65 years	10,564	10,507	10,815							
Householder 65 years and over .	9,491	9,484	10,774							
Three persons	12,516	12,273	12,629	12,641						
Four persons	16,036	16,183	16,448	15,911	15,967					
Five persons	18,952	19,516	19,800	19,194	18,725	18,438				
Six persons	21,389	22,447	22,536	22,072	21,627	20,965	20,573			
Seven persons	24,268	25,828	25,990	25,434	25,046	24,324	23,482	22,558		
Eight persons	27,091	28,887	29,142	28,617	28,158	27,506	26,678	25,816	25,597	
Nine persons or more	31,971	34,749	34,917	34,453	34,063	33,423	32,542	31,746	31,548	30,333

Source: *Poverty in the United States: 1996*, Bureau of the Census, Washington, DC, 1997

as retired married couples. Similar patterns existed for financial assets.

Nonretired married couples spent 45 percent more than retired couples, while nonretired single men spent 65 percent more than retired men, and nonretired women spent 50 percent more than retired women. All retired groups spent a significantly larger share of their total expenditures on food at home, utilities, and health care than did nonretired groups but less on food away from home and entertainment. Working couples and single women allocated more to work-related apparel and services, transportation, alcoholic beverages, and insurance.

THE ELDERLY POOR

Poverty standards are based on the "Economy Food Plan," developed by the U.S. Department of Agriculture (USDA) in the 1960s. The plan calculates the cost of a minimally adequate household food budget for different types of households. Since USDA surveys showed that the average family spends one-third of its income on food, it was decided that a household with an income three times the amount needed for food was living fairly comfortably. The poverty level, then, is calculated by multiplying the cost of a minimally adequate food budget by three.

The overall economic position of those 65 and over has improved significantly in recent decades. In 1966, more than 1 in every 4 elderly Americans lived in poverty. During the 1960s and early 1970s, the average income of the elderly increased. This was largely due to increases in Social Security and pension benefits. As a result, by 1989, the poverty rate of those 65 and older had dropped to 11.4 percent and, in 1996, to 10.8 percent (Table 2.8). The poverty rate of the nation's population in 1996 as a whole was 13.7 percent. However, the elderly (7.6 percent) were more likely than nonelderly (4.4 percent) to have incomes just above the poverty level, to be "near poor."

Social Security has played a significant role in reducing poverty among the aged. In 1994, more than two-fifths of the aged were kept out of poverty by their Social Security benefits. Overall, 12 percent of the aged were poor; without Social Security, the overall poverty rate would have been 54 percent. (See Figure 2.5.)

The elderly are underrepresented in the poverty population. In 1996, persons 65 and older were approximately 12 percent of the total population but made up only 9 percent of the poor, although experts note the high numbers of elderly concentrated just above the poverty threshold.

Consequently, many of the nation's "near-poor" persons were elderly.

The Old-Poor versus the Young-Poor Debate

In 1996, the poverty rate among the elderly was below that of the general population and well below that of those younger than 18 (20.5 percent), which was almost twice the elderly poverty rate. Many people use these statistics to support the argument that the elderly do not need as much support, especially from the government, as they currently receive. Some people assert that the elderly get benefits at the expense of the young. Other sources vigorously challenge this claim, noting that many elderly people have incomes that barely cover their needs (if it covers them at all) and that the oldest old are among the poorest poor. In addition, many elderly are near-poor.

A Different Standard for the Old

The Economy Food Plan used in determining poverty levels assumes that a healthy elderly person has lower nutritional requirements than a younger person and, therefore, an elderly person needs less money for food. This assumption has resulted in different poverty standards for the old and for the young. For example, in 1996, the Census Bureau's statistical poverty level for a single adult under 65 years of age was $8,163; for a single adult 65 or older it was $7,525. A 64-year-old woman, then, with a yearly income of $7,600 is poor, but on her sixty-fifth birthday, she becomes "not poor." (See Table 2.9.)

This method of defining poverty does not recognize the specialized problems of the elderly. For example, no household costs other than food are counted, even though the elderly spend a much greater percentage of their incomes on health care than younger people. In addition, the Economy Food Plan considers only the nutritional needs of a healthy person; many of the elderly are in poor health and may need special diets or nutritional supplements.

When comparing the percentage of old and very young people who live in poverty, it is important to note that the same poverty standard is not applied to both groups. If it were, the percentage of elderly poor would increase relative to the younger poor. In addition, most young people are poor for a limited period of time; as they become old enough to enter the work force they often have the opportunity to increase their income. Poor older people, on the other hand, have almost no option but to remain poor, and they may be poor for the rest of their lives.

Differences among the Poor Old

There are significant differences in poverty levels among the elderly. As a group, women over 65 (14 percent) were more than twice as likely to live below the poverty level as men (6 percent). Poverty rates for elderly Blacks (25 percent) and Hispanics (24 percent) were much higher than for elderly Whites (9 percent). Typically, poverty rates are high among the oldest old, women living alone, and minorities.

THE AFFLUENT ELDERLY

Certainly, more older Americans live comfortably today than at any other time in history. People now in their 60s and 70s were children of

TABLE 2.10

Trust fund operations:

Fiscal year	Income	Outgo	Fund at end of year
1996 (actual)			
OASI	$356.8	$305.2	$499.5
DI	59.2	44.3	50.1
1997 (estimated)*			
OASI	$383.3	$319.3	$564.4
DI	59.6	48.2	61.5

(In billions)

*Office of the Chief Actuary, SSA.

Source: *Fast Facts and Figures about Social Security*, Social Security Administration, Washington, DC, 1997

the Great Depression that began in 1929 and lasted through the 1930s. Many of them learned to economize and save. In their 20s and 30s, the men returned from World War II to inexpensive housing and G.I. bills that provided a free or inexpensive college education. During their 40s and 50s, their peak earning years, they participated in an unprecedented economic expansion. Today, many of them have raised their children, paid off their mortgages, invested wisely, and are in relatively good health. In addition, Social Security payments are larger than ever.

The Center for Social Research in Aging at the University of Miami (Coral Gables, Florida) defines the "comfortably retired" as those who live in households with incomes more than double the poverty level. It estimated, in 1994, that 59 percent of retired 55- to 64-year-olds were comfortably retired, as were 51 percent of retired 65- to 74-year-olds, and 37.5 percent of those 75 years and older. The center estimated that Hawaii had the highest percentage of comfortably retired persons in all three age groups, while Mississippi and South Dakota had the lowest percentage of comfortably retired elderly.

THE SOCIAL SECURITY PROGRAM

Congress passed the Social Security Act in 1935 to provide economic assistance to retirees, the blind, and mothers and their dependent children. It has since been amended innumerable times and is currently composed of many sections including Medicare (see Chapter VIII) and Supplemental Security Income (see below). The section authorizing the Old-Age, Survivors, and Disability Insurance (OASDI) program provides monthly benefits to retired and disabled workers and their dependents, and to survivors of insured workers.

The Social Security program is funded with a mandatory tax that is withheld from workers' earnings and is matched by the employer. When a covered worker retires (or is disabled), he or she draws benefits based on the amount he or she has contributed to the fund. The longer the time of employment and the higher the earnings, the larger the benefit. Today, worker and employer each contribute 7.65 percent of the worker's salary to the fund. In 1996, the fund took in $356.8 billion and paid out $305.2 billion (Table 2.10).

Although Social Security was not initially presented as a full pension with which a recipient could maintain his or her pre-retirement standard of living, many elderly people depend almost solely on it. Before Social Security was created, the poverty rate for those 65 and over was over 47 percent. The Social Security Administration has concluded that the program enables 38 million Americans to live above the poverty level and that it is the country's most effective anti-poverty program.

Ever since 1940, when Americans first received Social Security benefits, average monthly retirement benefits have steadily increased, but in the early 1970s, they soared. In 1972, the average benefit was indexed to keep up with inflation as reflected by the Consumer Price Index (CPI). This meant that recipients receive periodic "raises" or COLAs (cost of living adjustments) that were based upon the economic situation at that particular time. The 1970s were characterized by growing inflation, and within a few years, the whole system was facing serious

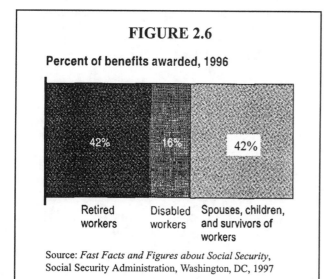

FIGURE 2.6

Percent of benefits awarded, 1996

42% — Retired workers

16% — Disabled workers

42% — Spouses, children, and survivors of workers

Source: *Fast Facts and Figures about Social Security*, Social Security Administration, Washington, DC, 1997

TABLE 2.11

Average monthly benefits by sex, December 1996

Type of beneficiary	Men	Women
Total	$819	$611
Retired workers	838	644
Spouses	226	385
Disabled workers	788	577
Spouses	125	173
Survivors:		
Nondisabled widows and widowers	521	708
Disabled widows and widowers	318	474
Mothers and fathers	416	520

Source:
Fast Facts and Figures about Social Security, Social
Security Administration, Washington, DC, 1997

eficiaries were retired workers and 16 percent were disabled workers. The remaining 42 percent were survivors and/or dependents of workers (Figure 2.6).

Of all adults receiving monthly Social Security benefits in 1996, 42 percent were men and 58 percent were women. Slightly less than one-fourth of the women received survivor benefits. In 1996, the average Social Security check was $819 for men and $611 for women. Retired workers received the highest amount, and spouses of disabled workers, the least. (See Table 2.11.)

Dual Entitlement

The number of women who are receiving benefits as dependents (based on their husband's earnings) has been declining. At the same time, the number of women with dual entitlement (based on both their own earnings and their husbands) has risen from 5 percent in 1960 to 26 percent in 1996. (See Figure 2.7.) This does not

long-range financial troubles which many observers linked to the 1972 amendments.

Some legislators felt that indexing vastly overcompensated for inflation, causing relative benefit levels to rise higher than at any time in the history of the program. In many cases, if the formula had remained in effect, benefit levels for some future retirees would be higher than their earnings before retirement. In an attempt to prevent future Social Security benefits from rising to what many considered excessive levels, Congress passed the Social Security Amendments of 1977 (PL 95-216) to restructure the benefit plan and design more realistic formulas for benefits.

Benefits and Beneficiaries

In 1996, Social Security made payments to 43.7 million persons. More than 3.7 million persons began receiving Social Security benefits in 1996. Forty-two percent of all ben-

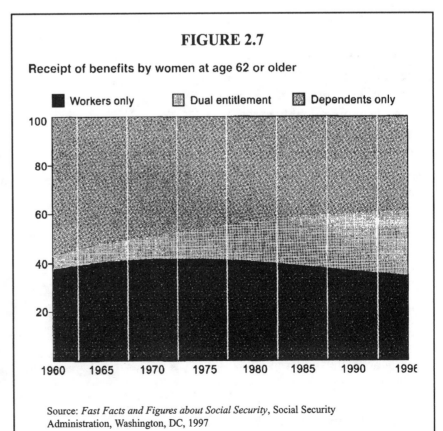

FIGURE 2.7

Receipt of benefits by women at age 62 or older

■ Workers only   ▨ Dual entitlement   ▨ Dependents only

Source: *Fast Facts and Figures about Social Security*, Social Security
Administration, Washington, DC, 1997

mean they get two Social Security payments, but that they are eligible for either and normally will get the larger of the two possibilities.

The Earnings Test

The Social Security program includes a retirement, or earnings, test. Under current law, the test allows beneficiaries age 62 to 69 to earn income to a specified annual limit without losing their Social Security benefits. When earnings exceed this limit, benefits are reduced $1 for every $3 earned over the limit for those 65 to 69 and $1 for every $2 for those age 62 to 64. The dollar amount depends on the worker's age — $8,640 annually for people 62 to 64 and $13,500 for those 65 to 69. The Social Security Administration has found that workers tend to keep earnings at or below the annual earnings limit. The earnings test may, therefore, depress the income of older workers.

Supplemental Security Income (SSI)

Supplemental Security Income (SSI) is a joint federal/ state welfare program designed to supply monthly cash payments to needy aged, blind, or disabled Americans. Instituted in 1974, it replaced many local public assistance programs. SSI benefits are financed from general revenues, not from the Social Security Trust fund, and are issued in addition to Social Security benefits. Individual payments vary from state to state, depending on whether the federal or state government administers the program.

About 6.6 million persons, 22 percent of them elderly,

received SSI payments in 1996 (Figure 2.8). The average payment to an aged individual was $254 and for an aged couple, $679. About 60 percent of all SSI payments went to women.

The percentage of SSI recipients under 65 years of age increased between 1974 and 1996, while the percentage of recipients over 65 decreased (Figure 2.9). Critics of the program believe that the SSI program could do more to help the elderly. For one thing, it provides only enough income to bring an individual to 70 percent, and a couple to 90 percent, of the poverty level. Its strict assets test excludes many elderly people from receiving benefits, and many low-income people are unaware of the program.

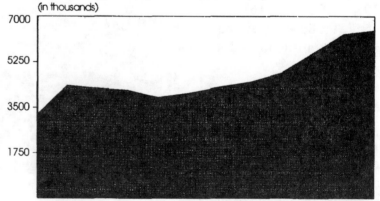

FIGURE 2.8

Persons receiving federally administered SSI payments

Year	Total number (in thousands)
1974	3,216
1976	4,326
1978	4,217
1980	4,142
1982	3,858
1984	4,029
1986	4,269
1988	4,464
1990	4,817
1992	5,566
1994	6,296
1996	6,614

Persons receiving federally administered SSI payments
(in thousands)

Source: *Fast Facts and Figures about Social Security*, Social Security Administration, Washington, DC, 1997

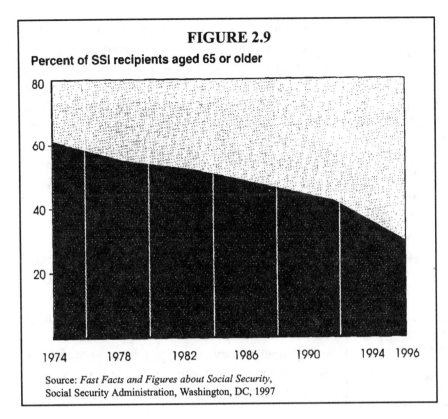

FIGURE 2.9

Percent of SSI recipients aged 65 or older

1974   1978   1982   1986   1990   1994 1996

Source: *Fast Facts and Figures about Social Security*,
Social Security Administration, Washington, DC, 1997

THE FUTURE OF THE SOCIAL SECURITY PROGRAM

Most experts believe that the Social Security program faces a shaky future and that its solvency is threatened in the next decades. In 1982, the OASDI trust fund almost went bankrupt. Then-President Ronald Reagan and Congress instituted higher Social Security taxes, along with a one-time delay in the cost of living adjustment and increased the amount of salary subject to taxation.

Social Security is a "pay-as-you-go" program, with con-

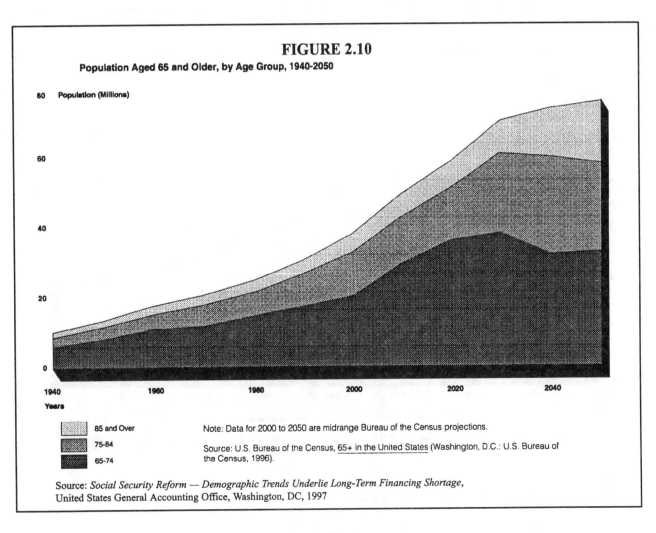

FIGURE 2.10

Population Aged 65 and Older, by Age Group, 1940-2050

80   Population (Millions)

60

40

20

0

1940   1960   1980   2000   2020   2040

Years

85 and Over

75-84

65-74

Note: Data for 2000 to 2050 are midrange Bureau of the Census projections.

Source: U.S. Bureau of the Census, 65+ in the United States (Washington, D.C.: U.S. Bureau of the Census, 1996).

Source: *Social Security Reform — Demographic Trends Underlie Long-Term Financing Shortage*,
United States General Accounting Office, Washington, DC, 1997

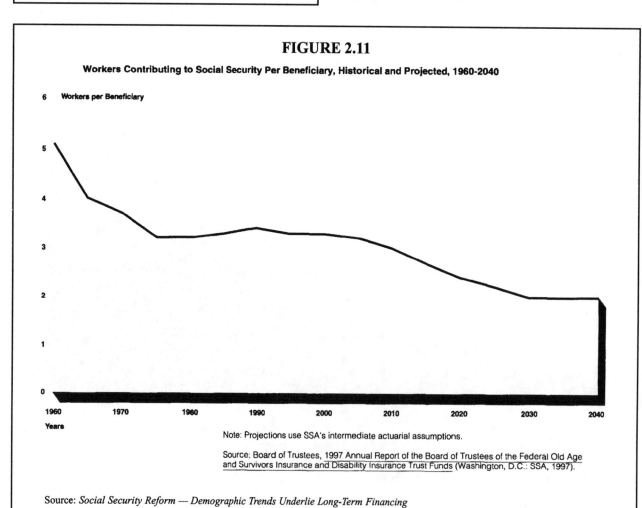

TABLE 2.12
Perceptions about Social Security

Probability Scale (Chances in 10)	Probability that Social Security Will Become MORE Generous (%)	Probability that Social Security Will Become LESS Generous (%)
0	31	9
1,2,3	38	15
4,5,6	23	31
7,8,9	5	31
10	3	14
Average	26	58

a Most HRS respondents expect that the Social Security system will become less generous in the future — that is, they expect either a cut in benefits or an increase in the degree to which Social Security benefits are subject to tax.

Source: *University of Michigan Health and Retirement Study, 1993.* Funded by the National Institute of Aging

tributions of present workers paying the retirement benefits of those currently retired. The program is solvent at this time, the result of a larger number of employees contributing funds to the system and fewer retirees than expected. The earliest wave of "baby boomers," those individuals who were born between 1946 and 1964, are still in the work force and reaching their peak earning years.

At the same time, people who are now retiring were born during the low birth rate cycle of the Great Depression, so there are now fewer retirees depleting funds than there are workers contributing to it. The federal government has been using some of the current surplus in the Social Security fund to make the federal deficit appear smaller. By using this money to pay current non-Social Security expenses, there will be less money for Americans when they retire.

FIGURE 2.11

Workers Contributing to Social Security Per Beneficiary, Historical and Projected, 1960-2040

Note: Projections use SSA's intermediate actuarial assumptions.

Source: Board of Trustees, 1997 Annual Report of the Board of Trustees of the Federal Old Age and Survivors Insurance and Disability Insurance Trust Funds (Washington, D.C.: SSA, 1997).

Source: *Social Security Reform — Demographic Trends Underlie Long-Term Financing Shortage,* United States General Accounting Office, Washington, DC, 1997

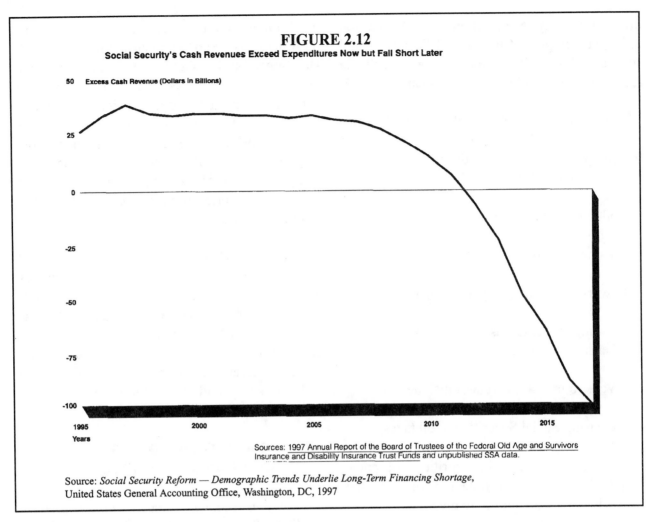

FIGURE 2.12

Social Security's Cash Revenues Exceed Expenditures Now but Fall Short Later

Excess Cash Revenue (Dollars in Billions)

Sources: 1997 Annual Report of the Board of Trustees of the Federal Old Age and Survivors Insurance and Disability Insurance Trust Funds and unpublished SSA data.

Source: *Social Security Reform — Demographic Trends Underlie Long-Term Financing Shortage*, United States General Accounting Office, Washington, DC, 1997

At the present time, a retiree who has paid approximately $25,000 into the system will have that amount returned in about three years. However, that will not be the case for a retired worker of the future. He or she will have paid considerably more money into the system and get back much less. Furthermore, since there will be a much larger percentage of retirees as the baby boomers reach 65, starting in 2011, the younger generation of workers will face greater financial responsibility for the support and care of an increasing population of older Americans. Figure 2.10 shows the expected growth in the Social Security age population through the year 2050.

The retirement age is already scheduled to rise from 65 to 67, to be phased in between 2000 and 2027. In 1993, Social Security Commissioner Shirley Sears Chater warned that the retirement age may have to be increased further and that benefits may need to be reduced. Table 2.12 shows that Americans generally believe that Social Security will become less generous in the future.

At the same time that the elderly population is growing, life expectancy is growing, resulting in even more elderly who will become eligible for Social Security. Additionally, the falling fertility rate caused by fewer children born to couples means there will be fewer workers contributing to Social Security for each aged, disabled, dependent, or surviving beneficiary (Figure 2.11).

Currently, because there are more contributing to the system and fewer elderly to use the funds, contributions to the system exceed expenses paid out to the aging by roughly $30 billion each year. That excess goes into a trust fund, which helps reduce the federal budget deficit. The U.S. General Accounting Office predicts, however, that trust fund will be depleted in approximately 15 years (Figure 2.12). So, while most sources predict that Social Security could still pay full benefits to recipients until 2029, the federal budget will be impacted as early as 2012.

Restoring Social Security's long-term financial balance will require a combination of increased revenues and reduced expenditures. Some ways to reduce expenditures include:

• Reducing initial benefits to retirees

• Raising the retirement age

• Lowering cost-of-living adjustments

• Limiting benefits based on the beneficiaries' other income and assets

Ways to increase revenues include:

• Increasing Social Security payroll taxes

• Investing trust funds in securities with potentially higher yields than the government bonds in which they are currently invested

• Increasing income taxes on Social Security benefits.

A Contract between the Generations?

A "pay-as-you-go" pension system means that current workers finance the retirement of their elders. Some sources have predicted that with fewer workers to pay for more retirees, young people will have to sacrifice a good part of their own well-being to keep their elders living in the style they expect. They contend that, in most national systems in both Europe and the United States, this "contract between generations" is headed for trouble.

Rethinking the Future of Social Security

The debate over Social Security is not just about how to prevent the retirement system itself from going broke, but also about a number of much bigger questions. Among these questions, do Americans spend too much and save too little? How much burden should the old impose on the working generations? Is it better to continue the "all-for-one-and-one-for-all" notion embodied in Social Security and other benefit programs, or should Americans be asked to assume more responsibility for their own needs? These are complicated issues, with those on one side the long-time supporters of Social Security, believing a commitment was made to the aging.

On the other side are those who argue that Social Security, in its current form, undermines the economy by discouraging Americans from saving more for the future. As Lester C. Thurow, professor at MIT, contends, in *The Future of Capitalism* (William Morrow and Co., 1996), "Today's elderly are bringing down the social welfare state and threatening the nation's economic future."

FACING THE FUTURE — FUNDING RETIREMENT

Retirement income security in the United States has traditionally been based on the so-called three-legged stool: Social Security, private pensions, and personal savings. Since World War II, that formula has served the elderly well — the poverty rate among elderly fell from 35 percent in 1959 to 11 percent in 1995.... But the future is uncertain.... The prospect of a huge generation edging unprepared toward retirement raises worrisome questions about the living standards of the baby boomers in retirement, the concomitant pressure on government policies, and the stability of the nation's retirement system. — William G. Gale, The Brookings Review, Summer 1997

The largest federal study of Americans approaching retirement, performed by the National Institute on Aging, the University of Michigan, and the Alliance for Aging Research from 1990 to 1993, reported that many of the

12,600 respondents age 51 to 61 or married to someone in that age range face an uncertain financial future. Although these "fifty-some-things" are better off than their counterparts decades ago, they are less prepared to face retirement. Among the findings:

- Two of every 10 households had no assets;

- Two of every 5 interviewees had no expectation of receiving pension income of any type other than Social Security;

- One in 7 lacked health insurance, public or private;

- Almost half of those surveyed believed there was a likelihood they could lose their job in the next year and that they may be unable to find a new job in a few months.

In 1995, *Gallup Poll Monthly* surveyed Americans about their retirement plans. When asked when they expected to retire, 29 percent responded age 65; 23 percent, age 60 to 64; 15 percent, under 55; 12 percent, over 65. Five percent expected never to retire. (See Table 2.13.) When asked if they felt sure of receiving income for retirement, 83 percent said yes from savings and investments; 66 percent, pensions;

and 35 percent from Social Security (Table 2.14). Seventy-four percent said having enough money for retirement was very important, and 21 percent responded somewhat important. Sixty-two percent were very concerned (30 percent) or somewhat concerned (32 percent) that their savings would run out.

TABLE 2.13
At what age do you expect to retire?

Dec 15-18

Under 55	15%
55-59	12
60-64	23
65	29
Over 65	12
Expect never to retire	5
No opinion	4
	100%

Mean: 60.

TABLE 2.14

For each of the following, please tell me whether or not you feel fairly sure you can count on it as a source of income during your retirement years: Social Security; pension from your place of employment; income from savings and investments.

(% responding "yes")

Dec 15-18

Savings and investments	83%
Pension from job	66
Social Security	35

TABLE 2.15

Next, how much money did you save last year for retirement – including such savings plans as IRAs and 401Ks?

Last Year's Savings – Trend

	Nov 6-8	Dec 15-18
None	44%	49%
Less than $1,000	8	7
$1,000 up	29	31
No opinion	19	13
	100%	100%

Mean: including "none" **$1468**; excluding "none" **$3368.**

Source of above tables: Gallup Polls, Princeton, NJ, !995

When asked if they or their spouse had personally set aside money in investment plans, 68 percent said they had invested in bank savings or certificates; 40 percent, IRAs or 401(k)s; 26 percent, individual stocks or bonds; 18 percent, stock mutual funds; and 9 percent each in bond mutual funds or other (work retirement plan, life insurance, or savings plan). However, when asked how much money they saved the previous year for retirement, including IRAs and 401(k)s, 49 percent said none; 31 percent, less than $1,000; 7 percent, more than $1,000; and 13 percent, no opinion (Table 2.15).

Will Baby-Boomers Be Ready for Retirement?

America is a consumer society that prefers to spend rather that save. Despite the fact that the baby boomer generation is the richest in history and many of its members have profited from the recent stock market surge, the average American saves only about 3.5 percent of his or her earnings, far less than people in other developed nations. This low savings rate could leave older Americans in trouble, especially if problems do develop with the Social Security system.

As a society, Americans understand little about the dynamics of retirement. Only one or two generations have had lengthy retirements. Many critical issues affecting retirees — health care technology and cost, Social Security, investment markets — are rapidly changing, making predictions even more difficult.

THE AGING CONSUMER

Today's elderly (and their caregivers) have proven to be a lucrative market for many products. In addition to the products traditionally offered to the aging, such as health and life insurance and burial plots, marketers have discovered the elderly are interested in a new range of products and services. Today's healthier, more affluent aging population desires products that make dressing and routine chores simpler, products that promote health, travel, and recreation. Direct marketers find that elderly consumers readily shop mail-order catalogs. Many older shoppers now expect more attractive and comfortable clothing and footwear.

Mature consumers respond to marketing that reflects autonomy and self-sufficiency, social and spiritual connectedness, altruism, personal growth, and revitalization. Older customers are often suspicious of claims about a product's attributes, are less influenced by peers, less materialistic, and more subjective in their purchasing.

"The Eisenhower Generation"

Americans born during the Great Depression (beginning in 1929) and World War II (1941 - 1945) are now in their most affluent years. They spend freely on grandchildren, new cars, homes, and travel but have also been saving for retirement. Marketers have found in the "Ikes" (named for President Dwight Eisenhower) an aging, but definitely not elderly, target.

Approximately 15 percent of the U.S. population is wedged between seniors and baby boomers. They are at the top of their careers and earning power and, hence, their spending power. Most of today's corporate leaders come from their ranks. Most "Ikes" have the work ethic of their elders and believe in thrift and self-sufficiency. With their housing investments appreciating and pension plans still essentially sound, the "Eisenhowers" may be the last American generation with reasonably bright prospects for retirement. They are at a stage in life where they may begin experiencing many life changes, such as grandparenthood, loss of a spouse, career down-shifting or retirement, and traveling. Many have discretionary income and the time to enjoy it, and these events have affected their buying behavior.

CHAPTER III

LIVING ARRANGEMENTS OF THE ELDERLY

ELDERLY HOUSEHOLDS

The Bureau of the Census reports that of the 109 million households in the United States in 1996, one in five (21.7 percent) was headed by a person 65 years or older (Table 3.1). In several states — Rhode Island, Pennsylvania, Iowa, North and South Dakota, Florida, West Virginia, and Arkansas — approximately one-fourth of households are headed by someone 65 and older.

Most elderly prefer to live independently as long as possible. Today, most elderly Americans are adequately housed, but there is a range of conditions, from the affluent "younger-old" homeowner, to the very elderly and often very poor nursing home resident, to the homeless.

THE "MODIFIED EXTENDED" FAMILY

The "modified extended" family is the dominant form of family organization found in industrialized societies today. It is also the arrangement that most older people say they prefer. In this setting, older and younger generations live in separate households but are in touch with each other on a fairly regular and frequent basis.

LIVING WITH A SPOUSE

The number of elderly people living with their spouses varies greatly between men and women. In 1995, 74.5 percent of all noninstitutionalized men aged 65 or over lived with their spouse, compared to only 40.6 percent of women. The difference is even more dramatic in the 75 to 84 age group: 72.8 percent of men lived with their spouse, compared to only 30.4 percent of women. By the age of 85, 46.8 percent of men lived with their spouse, while only 9.7 percent of women did. (See Table 3.2.) This occurs because women tend to live longer than men, and widowers are far more likely to remarry than widows.

LIVING WITH OTHER RELATIVES

In 1995, approximately 12 percent of people over age 65 lived with a relative other than a spouse. Again, the difference between men and women was significant. Sixteen percent of women lived with a relative other than their spouse, but only 7 percent of men did. This would follow, naturally, since so many more men lived with their spouse.

GRANDPARENTS AS PARENTS

With drug addiction, alcoholism, divorce, AIDS, family violence, and crime shattering thousands of young American families each year, large numbers of seniors find themselves raising their grandchildren. Over the past 25 years, the number of children living in households headed by grandparents has increased by 79 percent. In 1995, 6 percent (4 million) of all children under 18 years of age lived with their grandparents. Some also had one or both of their parents with them in the home of the grandparent, although 37 percent did not. (See Table 3.3.).

TABLE 3.1

Estimates of housing units and households and percent of households by age of householder: July 1, 1996

U.S., region, division and state	Total housing units	Total house-holds	Percent of householders by age Ages 15-24	Ages 25-34	Ages 35-44	Ages 45-54	Ages 55-64	Ages 65+	Persons per household
United States	109,568	98,751	5.3	18.7	23.3	18.6	12.5	21.7	2.62
Northeast	21,515	19,298	3.7	17.8	23.1	18.9	12.8	23.7	2.64
Midwest	25,997	23,390	5.4	18.4	23.3	18.2	12.5	22.2	2.59
South	39,283	34,949	5.7	18.7	22.8	18.4	12.8	21.6	2.58
West	22,773	21,113	5.8	19.6	24.5	18.9	11.7	19.4	2.70
New England	5,786	5,078	4.0	19.0	23.6	18.8	11.9	22.8	2.61
Connecticut	1,365	1,231	3.5	18.1	23.5	19.2	12.4	23.3	2.65
Maine	630	483	5.1	17.4	23.9	18.9	12.2	22.5	2.54
Massachusetts	2,544	2,322	3.8	19.7	23.1	18.8	11.8	23.1	2.61
New Hampshire	531	439	4.4	20.3	26.1	18.8	10.9	19.4	2.62
Rhode Island	427	378	4.2	18.6	22.7	17.6	11.4	25.5	2.56
Vermont	289	227	5.2	18.5	24.9	19.9	11.7	19.8	2.57
Middle Atlantic	15,728	14,219	3.6	17.4	22.9	19.0	13.2	24.0	2.65
New Jersey	3,184	2,889	2.9	17.0	23.9	19.7	13.2	23.3	2.75
New York	7,381	6,737	3.7	18.2	23.0	19.2	13.3	22.6	2.65
Pennsylvania	5,163	4,594	3.9	16.4	22.2	18.1	13.0	26.4	2.58
East North Central	18,035	16,339	5.2	18.5	23.4	18.5	12.6	21.8	2.61
Illinois	4,723	4,352	4.7	18.9	23.5	18.5	12.6	21.6	2.65
Indiana	2,442	2,209	5.6	18.7	23.1	18.5	12.8	21.4	2.57
Michigan	4,067	3,576	5.1	18.4	23.8	18.9	12.4	21.4	2.66
Ohio	4,586	4,260	5.3	18.1	23.0	18.4	12.9	22.5	2.54
Wisconsin	2,217	1,943	5.4	18.4	23.7	18.0	12.2	22.2	2.61
West North Central	7,962	7,051	6.0	18.3	23.0	17.5	12.3	22.9	2.54
Iowa	1,197	1,103	6.0	17.2	21.8	17.3	12.8	24.9	2.51
Kansas	1,109	982	6.6	18.3	23.0	17.4	11.8	22.9	2.54
Minnesota	1,980	1,763	5.6	19.3	24.6	18.0	11.7	20.8	2.58
Missouri	2,371	2,052	5.5	18.2	22.5	17.8	12.9	23.3	2.51
Nebraska	698	631	6.8	17.9	22.7	17.3	12.1	23.2	2.54
North Dakota	291	247	7.2	17.7	22.4	16.3	12.1	24.2	2.51
South Dakota	316	273	7.1	17.0	22.6	16.4	12.2	24.8	2.56
South Atlantic	20,751	18,146	5.2	18.7	22.6	18.4	12.6	22.6	2.56
Delaware	318	276	4.7	20.4	23.5	18.1	12.4	20.9	2.62
District of Columbia	268	231	4.3	21.7	21.5	18.1	12.6	21.7	2.24
Florida	6,769	5,648	4.9	16.3	20.5	16.6	12.6	29.0	2.45
Georgia	3,011	2,723	6.0	21.1	24.4	19.3	12.0	17.1	2.65
Maryland	2,044	1,871	3.9	19.8	25.2	19.9	12.2	19.0	2.70
North Carolina	3,197	2,796	5.6	19.6	22.4	18.4	12.9	21.1	2.53
South Carolina	1,604	1,376	5.4	18.7	22.6	19.0	13.2	21.0	2.64
Virginia	2,747	2,511	5.2	20.4	24.0	19.5	12.3	18.7	2.61
West Virginia	793	714	5.3	14.5	20.7	18.9	14.4	26.1	2.50
East South Central	6,760	6,122	5.7	18.1	22.2	18.5	13.5	21.9	2.56
Alabama	1,814	1,624	5.9	17.9	21.8	18.2	13.6	22.6	2.56
Kentucky	1,635	1,478	5.7	17.9	22.3	18.6	13.6	21.8	2.55
Mississippi	1,081	979	5.9	18.0	22.0	17.9	13.5	22.7	2.66
Tennessee	2,229	2,041	5.6	18.5	22.5	19.0	13.4	21.1	2.52
West South Central	11,772	10,681	6.7	19.2	23.5	18.4	12.6	19.6	2.65
Arkansas	1,075	951	6.2	17.0	20.5	17.8	13.7	24.8	2.51
Louisiana	1,777	1,572	6.1	18.0	23.2	18.7	13.4	20.6	2.67
Oklahoma	1,452	1,265	7.0	17.2	21.5	17.9	13.5	23.0	2.50
Texas	7,468	6,894	6.9	20.2	24.3	18.5	12.1	18.0	2.69
Mountain	6,649	6,022	6.9	18.7	24.0	18.9	12.4	19.2	2.61
Arizona	1,889	1,687	6.7	19.1	22.6	17.7	12.1	21.7	2.59
Colorado	1,628	1,502	6.4	18.8	26.0	20.4	12.1	16.3	2.47
Idaho	477	430	8.0	17.0	23.3	18.8	12.7	20.1	2.68
Montana	373	341	6.7	14.6	23.5	19.7	13.5	21.9	2.50
Nevada	684	619	5.8	19.7	23.4	19.2	13.3	18.5	2.53
New Mexico	705	619	6.3	17.5	24.3	19.1	13.0	19.7	2.64
Utah	682	639	9.3	21.6	23.3	17.2	11.1	17.5	3.06
Wyoming	209	184	7.9	15.4	24.8	19.7	12.9	19.3	2.55
Pacific	16,124	15,092	5.4	20.0	24.7	19.0	11.4	19.5	2.73
Alaska	241	214	7.9	18.9	30.1	22.7	11.4	9.1	2.76
California	11,811	11,101	5.2	20.8	24.8	18.6	11.3	19.4	2.79
Hawaii	433	389	4.2	15.7	24.7	20.5	12.6	22.4	2.97
Oregon	1,342	1,249	6.1	16.7	23.6	19.8	12.0	21.8	2.51
Washington	2,296	2,139	6.2	19.0	24.9	19.5	11.3	19.0	2.53

Source: U.S. Census Bureau, Department of Commerce, *Estimates of Housing Units and Households of States: 1990 and 1996*, Series PPL-73.

In cities with substantial drug and crime problems, the numbers of children being raised by grandparents are much greater. In Washington, DC, for example, more than 27,000 children — one-fourth of all children in the District — lived with their grandparents. In some schools in Oakland, California, 50 percent of the children are living with their grandparents.

According to the Association of Retired Persons Women's Initiative 1995 survey (*The Real Golden Girls: The Prevalence and Policy*

Treatment of Midlife and Older People Living in Nontraditional Households, the average age of grandparent caregivers was 59; the median age was 57. More than 75 percent were between 45 and 64; 23 percent, 65 or older, and 7 percent, 75 or older. Sixty percent were grandmothers, and 40 percent were grandfathers. Three-fourths of the grandparents were married; 13 percent, widowed; and 7 percent, divorced. Sixty-eight percent of grandparents raising their grandchildren were White; 29 percent were Black.

LIVING ALONE

Most elderly people who live alone have outlived their spouses, and in some cases, their children and siblings. As a result, the percentage of persons living alone increases with age. Forty-two percent of women between 65 and 74, and 53 percent of women 75 and over lived alone in 1995. In contrast, only 17 percent of 65- to 74-year-old men and 23 percent of men over 75 lived alone (Figure 3.1). These figures reflect the fact that women generally live longer than men, are more likely to be widowed, and are less likely to remarry.

Differing Views on Living Alone

Are those elderly who live alone enjoying the freedom and lack of responsibility for others, or are they a sad, lonely group isolated from the rest of the community? Certainly one can find positive and negative examples for every situation and condition. For those in good health, socially active, and financially comfortable, living alone does not have to be a problem. However, this is not the case with the majority of those who live alone. On the average, they have lower incomes than older couples, particularly if they are female, are members of a minority group, or are over the age of 85. In addition, a very high proportion of elderly who live alone suffer from chronic health problems and report their health to be only fair or poor.

The combination of poor health, poverty, and solitude is not a formula for happy living.

Substantial numbers of elderly persons living alone experience loneliness and fear. Fewer of them consider themselves happy than do those who live with others, and they are generally less satisfied with life. They frequently say that if they needed help, they would have no one to call on for a period of days, perhaps even weeks.

A Transitional Stage

Living alone is often a transitional stage between living with a spouse or other relative and, as health deteriorates, living in a nursing home or institution. Most older people prefer to remain independent as long as possible. While some have the physical and financial resources to live alone comfortably, others, especially very elderly women, are often extremely poor and isolated from the community.

LIVING IN A NURSING HOME

One of the main reasons for entering a nursing home or similar long-term care facility is to receive medical care. However, some experts suggest that between 10 and 60 percent of persons in nursing homes could live in the community if appropriate supportive (primarily nonmedical) services were available. Groups representing the elderly also believe that 30 to 50 percent of those in nursing homes could and would live elsewhere, if such facilities were available.

Only about 5 percent of the older population is living in nursing homes at any one time. The average nursing home resident is very old, female, and unmarried. Most nursing home residents are there because they are sick or disabled and cannot obtain adequate care in the community. However, health policy experts agree that many people live in nursing homes not because they need medical attention, but because that is the most available — and most likely to be financed — option. (See Chapter IX for a further discussion of nursing homes.)

TABLE 3.2

Marital Status of Persons 15 Years and Over, by Age, Sex, Race, Hispanic Origin, Metropolitan Residence, and Region: March 1995

[Numbers in thousands. For meaning of symbols, see text]

Subject	Total, 15 years and over	15 to 17 years	18 and 19 years	20 to 24 years	25 to 29 years	30 to 34 years	35 to 39 years	40 to 44 years	45 to 54 years	55 to 64 years	65 to 74 years	75 to 84 years	85 years and over	Total, 18 years and over	Total, 65 years and over
UNITED STATES															
All Races															
Both sexes	202 732	11 136	7 016	18 142	19 400	21 988	22 241	20 094	30 693	20 755	18 214	10 188	2 865	191 596	31 267
Never married	54 979	11 038	6 644	13 371	8 373	5 186	3 649	2 271	2 174	961	750	415	146	43 941	1 311
Married, spouse present	109 888	49	318	3 963	9 166	13 603	14 588	13 874	22 239	14 973	11 704	4 821	590	109 839	17 114
Married, spouse absent	6 846	24	40	443	747	1 042	1 076	905	1 225	667	416	182	78	6 822	676
Separated	4 864	21	20	277	533	762	867	706	894	492	220	62	9	4 843	291
Other	1 982	3	20	168	214	280	208	199	331	175	196	120	69	1 979	385
Widowed	13 366	4	2	17	23	80	156	205	808	1 680	4 045	4 361	1 985	13 362	10 392
Divorced	17 653	21	13	347	1 091	2 076	2 773	2 838	4 246	2 474	1 299	409	65	17 632	1 773
Percent	100.0	100.0	100.0	100.0	100.0	100.0	100.0	100.0	100.0	100.0	100.0	100.0	100.0	100.0	100.0
Never married	27.1	99.1	94.7	73.7	43.2	23.6	16.4	11.3	7.1	4.6	4.1	4.1	5.1	22.9	4.2
Married, spouse present	54.2	.4	4.5	21.8	47.2	61.9	65.6	69.0	72.5	72.1	64.3	47.3	20.6	57.3	54.7
Married, spouse absent	3.4	.2	.6	2.4	3.9	4.7	4.8	4.5	4.0	3.2	2.3	1.8	2.7	3.6	2.2
Separated	2.4	.2	.3	1.5	2.7	3.5	3.9	3.5	2.9	2.4	1.2	.6	.3	2.5	.9
Other	1.0	–	.3	.9	1.1	1.3	.9	1.0	1.1	.8	1.1	1.2	2.4	1.0	1.2
Widowed	6.6	–	–	.1	.1	.4	.7	1.0	2.6	8.1	22.2	42.8	69.3	7.0	33.2
Divorced	8.7	.2	.2	1.9	5.6	9.4	12.5	14.1	13.8	11.9	7.1	4.0	2.3	9.2	5.7
Male	97 704	5 696	3 522	9 023	9 689	10 900	11 041	9 931	15 022	9 878	8 097	4 066	840	92 008	13 003
Never married	30 286	5 658	3 441	7 285	4 944	3 075	2 241	1 390	1 214	494	342	160	41	24 628	543
Married, spouse present	54 944	10	67	1 505	4 043	6 463	7 114	6 866	11 361	7 821	6 340	2 960	393	54 934	9 693
Married, spouse absent	2 806	10	13	133	294	424	447	394	487	276	209	82	39	2 796	329
Separated	1 796	10	6	66	191	264	330	292	328	182	97	27	3	1 786	127
Other	1 011	–	8	67	103	160	116	102	158	95	112	55	36	1 011	202
Widowed	2 284	2	–	–	6	11	35	46	153	275	693	720	342	2 282	1 755
Divorced	7 383	17	–	100	401	927	1 204	1 234	1 807	1 011	513	144	24	7 367	682
Percent	100.0	100.0	100.0	100.0	100.0	100.0	100.0	100.0	100.0	100.0	100.0	100.0	100.0	100.0	100.0
Never married	31.0	99.3	97.7	80.7	51.0	28.2	20.3	14.0	8.1	5.0	4.2	3.9	4.9	26.8	4.2
Married, spouse present	56.2	.2	1.9	16.7	41.7	59.3	64.4	69.1	75.6	79.2	78.3	72.8	46.8	59.7	74.5
Married, spouse absent	2.9	.2	.4	1.5	3.0	3.9	4.0	4.0	3.2	2.8	2.6	2.0	4.6	3.0	2.5
Separated	1.8	.2	.2	.7	2.0	2.4	3.0	2.9	2.2	1.8	1.2	.7	.4	1.9	1.0
Other	1.0	–	.2	.7	1.1	1.5	1.1	1.0	1.1	1.0	1.4	1.3	4.2	1.1	1.6
Widowed	2.3	–	–	–	.1	.1	.3	.5	1.0	2.8	8.6	17.7	40.7	2.5	13.5
Divorced	7.6	.3	–	1.1	4.1	8.5	10.9	12.4	12.0	10.2	6.3	3.5	2.9	8.0	5.2
Female	105 028	5 440	3 494	9 119	9 712	11 088	11 200	10 163	15 672	10 878	10 117	6 122	2 025	99 588	18 264
Never married	24 693	5 380	3 202	6 087	3 429	2 111	1 408	881	959	467	408	255	105	19 312	768
Married, spouse present	54 944	39	251	2 458	5 123	7 140	7 474	7 008	10 878	7 152	5 364	1 861	196	54 905	7 421
Married, spouse absent	4 040	14	26	311	453	618	629	511	739	391	207	100	39	4 026	347
Separated	3 068	11	14	211	342	498	537	414	566	311	123	35	6	3 057	164
Other	971	3	12	99	111	120	92	97	173	80	84	65	33	968	182
Widowed	11 082	2	2	17	17	69	120	159	655	1 405	3 352	3 641	1 643	11 080	8 637
Divorced	10 270	4	13	247	689	1 150	1 569	1 604	2 441	1 463	786	264	41	10 266	1 091
Percent	100.0	100.0	100.0	100.0	100.0	100.0	100.0	100.0	100.0	100.0	100.0	100.0	100.0	100.0	100.0
Never married	23.5	98.9	91.7	66.7	35.3	19.0	12.6	8.7	6.1	4.3	4.0	4.2	5.2	19.4	4.2
Married, spouse present	52.3	.7	7.2	27.0	52.8	64.4	66.7	69.0	69.4	65.7	53.0	30.4	9.7	55.1	40.6
Married, spouse absent	3.8	.3	.8	3.4	4.7	5.6	5.6	5.0	4.7	3.6	2.0	1.6	1.9	4.0	1.9
Separated	2.9	.2	.4	2.3	3.5	4.5	4.8	4.1	3.6	2.9	1.2	.6	.3	3.1	.9
Other	.9	.1	.3	1.1	1.1	1.1	.8	1.0	1.1	.7	.8	1.1	1.7	1.0	1.0
Widowed	10.6	–	–	.2	.2	.6	1.1	1.6	4.2	12.9	33.1	59.5	81.1	11.1	47.3
Divorced	9.8	.1	.4	2.7	7.1	10.4	14.0	15.8	15.6	13.4	7.8	4.3	2.0	10.3	6.0
White															
Both sexes	170 051	8 776	5 604	14 557	15 651	18 088	18 387	16 812	26 154	18 035	16 201	9 212	2 573	161 274	27 985
Never married	41 918	8 707	5 266	10 401	6 222	3 713	2 574	1 609	1 594	725	631	348	127	33 210	1 106
Married, spouse present	97 389	40	296	3 496	7 920	11 849	12 717	12 193	19 636	13 485	10 743	4 473	540	97 349	15 757
Married, spouse absent	4 658	16	31	339	552	711	683	600	791	431	277	158	70	4 642	505
Separated	3 226	13	20	213	399	508	560	443	574	302	137	48	9	3 214	194
Other	1 432	3	11	125	153	203	122	157	217	129	140	110	61	1 429	311
Widowed	11 320	2	–	14	23	54	121	138	597	1 280	3 446	3 668	1 776	11 318	9 090
Divorced	14 766	11	11	308	935	1 761	2 292	2 272	3 536	2 113	1 104	364	60	14 755	1 527
Percent	100.0	100.0	100.0	100.0	100.0	100.0	100.0	100.0	100.0	100.0	100.0	100.0	100.0	100.0	100.0
Never married	24.7	99.2	94.0	71.5	39.8	20.5	14.0	9.6	6.1	4.0	3.9	3.8	4.9	20.6	4.0
Married, spouse present	57.3	.5	5.3	24.0	50.6	65.5	69.2	72.5	75.1	74.8	66.3	48.6	21.0	60.4	56.3
Married, spouse absent	2.7	.2	.6	2.3	3.5	3.9	3.7	3.6	3.0	2.4	1.7	1.7	2.7	2.9	1.8
Separated	1.9	.1	.4	1.5	2.6	2.8	3.0	2.6	2.2	1.7	.8	.5	.4	2.0	.7
Other	.8	–	.2	.9	1.0	1.1	.7	.9	.8	.7	.9	1.2	2.4	.9	1.1
Widowed	6.7	–	–	.1	.1	.3	.7	.8	2.3	7.1	21.3	42.0	69.0	7.0	32.5
Divorced	8.7	.1	.2	2.1	6.0	9.7	12.5	13.5	13.5	11.7	6.8	3.9	2.3	9.1	5.5
Male	82 566	4 512	2 840	7 329	7 881	9 071	9 232	8 398	12 908	8 712	7 248	3 873	762	78 055	11 683
Never married	23 667	4 487	2 768	5 798	3 827	2 301	1 683	1 047	921	374	300	128	32	19 180	460
Married, spouse present	48 683	7	60	1 344	3 467	5 646	6 208	6 042	9 982	7 035	5 805	2 726	361	48 676	8 891
Married, spouse absent	1 975	9	12	97	228	297	281	267	326	216	138	74	31	1 966	244
Separated	1 212	9	6	51	150	164	203	183	222	135	64	22	3	1 204	90
Other	762	–	6	46	77	132	78	84	104	81	74	52	28	762	154
Widowed	1 921	2	–	–	6	10	30	44	128	214	564	618	314	1 919	1 495
Divorced	6 321	7	–	90	354	817	1 030	1 007	1 551	872	441	127	24	6 314	593
Percent	100.0	100.0	100.0	100.0	100.0	100.0	100.0	100.0	100.0	100.0	100.0	100.0	100.0	100.0	100.0
Never married	28.7	99.5	97.5	79.1	48.6	25.4	18.2	12.5	7.1	4.3	4.1	3.5	4.1	24.6	3.9
Married, spouse present	59.0	.2	2.1	18.3	44.0	62.2	67.2	71.9	77.3	80.8	80.1	74.2	47.3	62.4	76.1
Married, spouse absent	2.4	.2	.4	1.3	2.9	3.3	3.0	3.2	2.5	2.5	1.9	2.0	4.1	2.5	2.1
Separated	1.5	.2	.2	.7	1.9	1.8	2.2	2.2	1.7	1.6	.9	.6	.4	1.5	.8
Other	.9	–	.2	.6	1.0	1.5	.8	1.0	.8	.9	1.0	1.4	3.6	1.0	1.3
Widowed	2.3	–	–	–	.1	.1	.3	.4	1.0	2.5	7.8	16.8	41.2	2.5	12.8
Divorced	7.7	.2	–	1.2	4.5	9.0	11.2	12.0	12.0	10.0	6.1	3.5	3.2	8.1	5.1

Source: *Marital Status and Living Arrangements: 1995*, Bureau of the Census, Washington, DC, 1997

TABLE 3.3

Grandchildren Living in the Home of Their Grandparents: 1970 to 1995

(Numbers in thousands)

Year	Total children under 18	Grandchildren				
			With parent(s) present			Without parent(s) present
		Total	Both parents present	Mother only present	Father only present	
1995	70,254	3,965	427	1,876	195	1,466
1994	69,508	3,735	436	1,764	175	1,359
1993	66,893	3,368	475	1,647	229	1,017
1992	65,965	3,253	502	1,740	144	867
1991	65,093	3,320	559	1,674	151	937
1990	64,137	3,155	467	1,563	191	935
1980 Census	63,369	2,306	310	922	86	988
1970 Census	69,276	2,214	363	817	78	957

Source of CPS data: U.S. Bureau of the Census, Current Population Reports, Series P20-484, "Marital Status and Living Arrangements: March 1994," table 4 and earlier reports.

Source of Decennial Census data: 1980 Census of Population, PC80-2-4B, "Living Arrangements of Children and Adults," table 1. 1970 Census of Population, PC(2)-4B, "Persons by Family Characteristics," table 1.

Respite Care

A concept known as "respite care" offers hope for the disabled elderly and their families. Respite care involves short-term stays in nursing homes or hospitals. Reasons for choosing temporary care in an institution include vacation needs for adult caregivers, brief medical or therapeutic needs of an elderly person, and relief for both parties from the caregiver/receiver relationship. Despite the growing need, the number of institutions (10 percent of hospitals and 30 percent of nursing homes) offering such short-term stays is relatively small. The cost of respite care is often not reimbursable under private or federal insurance programs or Medicare.

LIVING HOMELESS

Very little research has been conducted on the homeless elderly. However, with approximately 12 percent of the population of the United States over 65, only 3 percent of homeless people who have sought care have been elderly. The relatively low proportion of elderly homeless suggested by this figure may be explained by their access to benefits (Social Security, Medicare, housing), by high death rates once they enter street life, or by their avoidance of high visibility shelters and programs which they fear may be dangerous. (For further information, see *Homeless in America — How Could It Happen Here?*, Information Plus, Wylie, Texas, 1997.)

NONTRADITIONAL LIVING ARRANGEMENTS

For those who have the option of selecting where and how they live, several alternatives to single-family housing have emerged in recent years. There is no perfect alternative; each type of arrangement has its own particular problems and benefits.

Family Is Relative to Seniors

In 1995, the American Association for Retired Persons (AARP), using the U.S. Census Bureau's Current Population Survey (CPS), surveyed of about 150,000 persons in nearly 60,000 households throughout the country. The CPS categorized households as single, traditional, or nontraditional. Nontraditional households were subdivided into four types including

- Grandparent Caregivers — households consisting solely of grandparents and their grandchildren (see above);

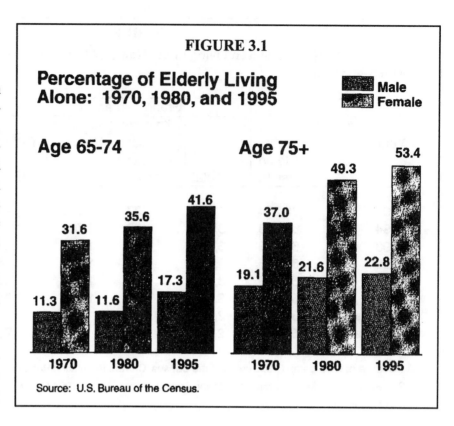

FIGURE 3.1

Percentage of Elderly Living Alone: 1970, 1980, and 1995

Male
Female

Age 65-74

1970: 11.3, 31.6
1980: 11.6, 35.6
1995: 17.3, 41.6

Age 75+

1970: 19.1, 37.0
1980: 21.6, 49.3
1995: 22.8, 53.4

Source: U.S. Bureau of the Census.

- Extended Families — households consisting solely of persons related to the householder by blood, marriage, or adoption but in which at least one of the relatives was not the spouse, parent, or child of the householder. Examples include cousins or siblings living together, a married couple caring for one spouse's great aunt, or two brothers and their families sharing a home. This was the most common nontraditional living arrangement among midlife and older persons.

- Partner/Roommate Households in which at least one person was a "partner/roommate" of the householder (Table 3.4);

- Miscellaneous Nontraditional Households — those not included in other categories, including an older man with a live-in employee to provide personal and household services, an older woman who rented an accessory apartment to a college student in exchange for household help, and a midlife woman who lived with her daughter and the daughter's unmarried partner. This category comprised 19 percent of nontraditional households in the midlife and older age group.

Eleven percent of persons over 65 and 16 percent of those over 85 lived in nontraditional households. Nontraditional households containing only midlife and older persons were rare (about 1 percent of U.S. households). Among those midlife and older who lived in nontraditional households, 35 percent were older than 65 (Figure 3.2). Midlife and older persons in nontraditional households were markedly poorer than those living in traditional households. Table 3.5 shows the demographic characteristics of persons living in nontraditional households.

Models of Nontraditional Living Arrangements

"Assisted Living"

The assisted living industry continues to be among the fastest-growing, most relatively problem-free senior living options as well as one of the hottest commodities — among all industries — on Wall Street. — Housing the Elderly Report, November 1997

42

Assisted living housing gets its name from the help provided to residents in the form of housekeeping, meal services, minor medical care, and personal care, such as help getting out of bed, bathing, or dressing. Assisted living sprang up to fill the gap in long-term care — elderly who are frail but not ill, who need some assistance but who are not in need of around-the-clock medical care. At $1,000 to $4,000 per month, assisted living can be as much as 30 percent cheaper than nursing home care.

Assisted living facilities can be large or small, institutional or home-like, expensive or affordable. In response to consumer demand, the private sector is increasingly developing facilities that are more bed-and-breakfast in appearance than nursing homes. On average, the residents-to-staff ratio in an assisted living home is 3 to 1, compared to 17 to 1 in an active living center, 4 to 1 in a congregate facility (nursing home), and 30 to 1 in an independent living setting.

Because of its immense growth, some people have expressed worry about assisted living as an industry. Among the concerns are the potential for serious waste, fraud, and abuse, problems that at times have plagued the nursing home industry and made them among the most regulated of health care components.

In 1996, the Assisted Living Federation of America, an industry association, in *Overview of Assisted Living*, studied 286 primarily for-profit assisted living residences in 35 states and Canada, to determine who the facilities served and what their residents felt were important. The study found that 75 percent of residents were female averaging 84 years of age, 22 percent were males averaging 82 years, and 3 percent were married couples.

The study categorized the ailments most affecting those in assisted living facilities. Forty-eight percent suffered some form of mental impairment, 38 percent used a wheelchair or walker, and 30. 2 percent were incontinent. Thirty-one percent had been hospitalized before moving into the residence. Among the services the residents felt they most needed help with were medication dispensing (70 percent), bathing (64 percent), medication reminders (50 percent), dressing (46 percent), toileting (32 percent), transferring from bed to chairs or wheelchairs (15.2 percent), and eating (10 percent).

TABLE 3.4

Estimate of Midlife and Older (45+) Partners and Roommates

(N=1,609,589 persons)

	Percentages
Partners	**55%**
Same-sex	7
Women	52
Men	48
Opposite-sex	93
Roommate	**44%**
Same-sex	49
Women	56
Men	44
Opposite-sex	51
Both	**1%**

Source: Unpublished data, 1992 Current Population Survey

Source: *The Real Golden Girls*, by Deborah Chalfie, a publication of the Women's Initiative, American Association of Retired Persons, Washington, DC, ©1995. Reprinted with permission only.

Life-Care Communities

Life-care communities provide their residents with housing, personal care, a variety of social and recreational activities, and, ultimately, nursing care. Typically, residents enter into a lifetime contractual arrangement with the facility for which they pay an entrance fee and a set monthly fee in return for services and benefits. Most facilities are operated by private, non-profit, and/or religious organizations.

According to government studies, entrance fees in these communities can vary substantially, from $20,000 to $200,000, and monthly fees range from $500 to $2,000 depending on the size of the facility and the quality and number of services. Services usually do not include acute health care needs such as doctor visits and hospitalization and, with few exceptions, are not covered by government or private insurance.

While life-care communities ensure their residents against rising health care costs and assure daily care, they have come under criticism in several areas. Sometimes fee calculations are not based on sound actuarial data, so that a facility may find itself without adequate financial resources, or residents may be paying more than necessary for care received. Residents sometimes find that if they decide to leave the community, none of their fees will be refunded. A few states have taken steps to regulate life-care communities, but there is little standardization in regulations between states.

Shared Housing

Some elderly persons share living quarters (and expenses) to reduce costs and responsibilities and also for companionship. Many elderly live in

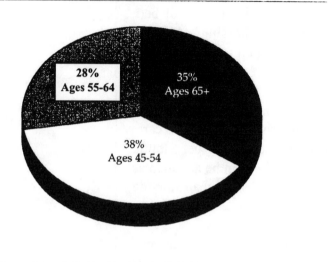

FIGURE 3.2
Age Distribution of Midlife and Older Persons (45+) in Nontraditional Households
(N=9,525,162 persons)

28% Ages 55-64

35% Ages 65+

38% Ages 45-54

Source: Deborah Chalfie, *The Real Golden Girls,* © 1995, American Association of Retired Persons. Reprinted with permission.

the same homes in which they raised their families. These houses may be too large for the needs of one or two persons. Shared housing can be very cost-effective for those who wish to remain in their own homes and for those who cannot afford a home of their own or the cost of a retirement community. About three-fourths of older home-sharing participants are women.

In its most common form, a single homeowner seeks a roommate to share living space and expenses. Shared housing can also include households with three or more roommates and family-like cooperatives in which large groups of people live together. Gregory Bergman, in "Shared Housing — Not Only for the Rent" (*Aging Today*, Jan/Feb 1994), reported that, nationwide, in 1994, there were 350 home-sharing programs in operation, which provide match-up services to home-seekers or providers.

Unfortunately, the elderly poor who desire to share housing may lose some of their already meager incomes. Under government regulations, supplemental Social Security eligibility and benefits are computed on the basis of the income of the entire household rather than the individual residents. Savings in living expenses may be more than offset by a reduction in benefits and money for food and medicine. Another barrier to shared housing is zoning restrictions. Some communities restrict people who are not related from sharing living quarters.

Intergenerational home-sharing may also fit the needs of younger and older people. While offering the usual benefits of cost-cutting and companionship, home-sharers may exchange services, for example, help with household maintenance in exchange for babysitting.

ECHO Units or "Granny Flats"

Elder Cottage Housing Opportunity (ECHO) units or "granny flats" are small, free-standing, removable housing units that are located on the same lot as a single-family house. Another term used in local zoning is "accessory apartments or units." Generally, they are constructed by a family for an elderly parent or grandparent so that they can be nearby while each party maintains a degree of independence. Zoning laws and concerns about property values and traffic patterns are major obstacles to granny flats, although as the elderly survive longer and nursing home costs increase, this concept may continue to gain support.

TABLE 3.5

Demographic Characteristics of Midlife and Older (45+) Persons Living in Nontraditional Households
(N=9,525,162 persons)

Characteristic	Percentage
Sex	
Women	54%
Men	46
Age	
45-64	66
45-54	38
55-64	28
65+	35
Mean Age	59
Marital Status	
Married	37
Separated	4
Divorced	21
Widowed	22
Never married	16
Race/Ethnicity	
White	76
Black	18
Asian/Pacific Islander	5
American Indian	1
Hispanic*	11
Education	
Less than high school	41
High school diploma	32
Some college	13
College degree+	14
Poverty Status	
Below poverty level	15
Near-poor (100-149% of poverty level)	11
At or above 150% of poverty level	74
Median household income	$37,420

* People of Hispanic origin can be of any race, therefore percentages do not total 100%.

Source: Deborah Chalfie, *The Real Golden Girls*, © 1995, American Association of Retired Persons. Reprinted with permission.

TABLE 3.6

Who Lives In Assisted Living?

Finances:
- Average annual income/assets: $28,000/$192,300
- Those with incomes less than $20,000: 34%
- Those receiving state Medicaid, SSI, etc.: 26%

Referral Sources:
- Family: 24%
- Hospitals: 15%
- Physicians: 11%
- Nursing Homes: 8%
- Current Residents: 7%
- Agencies/Churches: 7%
- Other: 27%

Source: *Housing the Elderly*, CD Publications, Silver Springs, MD, 1997

Retirement Communities

A number of developers have experimented with constructing entire cities just for the elderly. Examples are the Sun City communities in Florida, Arizona, and Texas. The Florida and Arizona locations opened in the 1960s; the Texas site in 1996. Homes in these properties are available only to those families in which at least one member is 55 or older, and no one under age 19 is allowed to stay permanently. Sun City offers clubs, golf courses, social organizations, fitness clubs, and recreational complexes. At the Texas location, 45 percent of the land will remain open space and natural areas. Medical facilities are located near the community.

Sun City is not for the poor. Forty percent of its residents have a net worth of $300,000, and 35 percent are worth $400,000 or more. About 60 percent have had at least some college education, compared with 20 percent of all adults aged 65 and older.

While cities devoted to the needs and interests of the elderly may seem ideal, they face a unique challenge: everyone is getting older. By the year 2000, the demand for social and health services for the thousands of people with a median age of 80 may prove overwhelming.

Cohousing and Intentional Communities

Cohousing, which originated in Denmark, is gaining interest in the United States. What distinguishes the arrangements in this category is planning — a group of individuals design and plan a community. Being in better health and living longer, many seniors wish to maintain their own private residences while also benefitting from certain features helpful to their age. They may find apartments less strenuous to maintain than single-family homes with lawns. They may also enjoy the camaraderie of others their age and some common areas, such as dining facilities.

For such seniors, many communities — or the seniors themselves — are building apartments, townhouses, and condominiums restricted to those over a specified age. Although acute medical needs are not provided, many such residences are physically equipped for older residences and, because of their specific clientele, accommodate some needs of the elderly, such as common transportation to senior centers, social activities tailored for various stages of aging, and checking on residents when asked. Most of these developments are private enterprises.

"Board and Care" Facilities

The Subcommittee on Health and Long-term Care of the Select Committee on Aging of the House of Representatives defines a board and care facility as one that "provides shelter, food, and protection to frail and disabled individuals." Typically, residents have their own bedroom and bathroom, or share them with one other person, but all other rooms are shared space. While the concept is praiseworthy, in actuality, the board and care business is riddled with fraud and abuses. Totally unregulated in many states, these facilities have frequently become dumping grounds for the old, the ill, the mentally retarded, and the disabled.

TABLE 3.7

Homeownership Rates by Age of Householder: Third Quarter 1997 and 1996

Age of householder	Third Quarter 1997	Third Quarter 1996	Standard error on 1997 rate	Standard error on difference
United States........................	66.0	65.6	0.2	0.2
Less than 25 years......................	18.3	18.2	0.6	0.9
25 to 29 years...........................	34.5	34.5	0.6	0.8
30 to 34 years...........................	53.4	52.8	0.6	0.8
35 to 39 years...........................	62.9	63.0	0.5	0.7
40 to 44 years...........................	70.1	69.7	0.5	0.7
45 to 49 years...........................	74.8	74.8	0.5	0.7
50 to 54 years...........................	78.2	77.4	0.5	0.8
55 to 59 years...........................	79.9	79.7	0.6	0.8
60 to 64 years...........................	80.2	79.8	0.6	0.9
65 to 69 years...........................	81.4	82.1	0.6	0.8
70 to 74 years...........................	82.3	80.7	0.6	0.9
75 years and over......................	76.1	75.3	0.5	0.7
Less than 35 years....................	38.9	39.0	0.4	0.5
35 to 44 years...........................	66.5	66.3	0.4	0.5
45 to 54 years...........................	76.3	75.9	0.4	0.5
55 to 64 years...........................	80.1	79.7	0.4	0.6
65 years and over......................	79.2	78.6	0.3	0.5

Source: U.S. Bureau of the Census and the U.S. Department of Housing and Urban Development

Medical experts believe that Supplemental Security Income (SSI) is the only form of income for three-fourths of these residents. It is not uncommon for a resident to turn over his or her entire SSI check to the facility's manager and receive less than minimal care in return.

In an attempt to stem abuses, the federal government passed the Keys Amendment in 1978. Under this amendment, residents in board and care facilities that do not provide adequate care are subject to reduced SSI income. The facility's owners would then suffer economically as a result of their tenants' reduced income. In fact, in most cases, the only ones who have suffered (even more than before) are the residents. Board and care facilities do provide an alternative living arrangement for the elderly, but it is one that, given the choice, probably very few would choose.

Demand Is Strong

A new study by the National Investment Conference for the Senior Living and Long-Term Care Industries, *National Survey of Adults Age 60+* (Annapolis, Maryland, 1997), found a strong demand for senior dwellings but too little attention on some groups, namely low-income elderly. The survey reported that 6 percent of adults over 60 lived in senior housing; 3.6 percent more have decided to move to senior housing sometime in the future, one-third of them within six months; and nearly 6 percent are considering a move to senior-specific housing. The study concluded that there is sufficient demand to build two additional senior housing units for every three currently in existence.

The demand is concentrated among those with lower incomes — lower-income seniors are less likely to have the resources to pay for the services that would enable them to remain in their homes as they age. As a result, they are more likely to want to move to senior housing. Table 3.6 shows characteristics of those who live in senior housing.

However, the growth in demand for assisted living exceeded the desire for active adult living housing. The survey found that the number of adults currently in or planning to move to active adult communities equaled the combined total seeking congregate, continuing care, and assisted living. Anthony Mullens, chairman of the Conference, reported, "Senior housing already has the highest occupancy rate of any housing — and is not yet at its market equilibrium."

A growing number of programs are becoming available to help lower-income seniors pay for such housing options. Through the Medicaid long-term care voucher program, seniors in 30 states can already use Medicaid funds to help pay for assisted living. In addition, other government programs, such as tax credits, state housing programs, and rural housing assistance are increasingly being used to help seniors afford housing.

Problems Faced by Nontraditional Households

In general, relationships and living arrangements not based on blood, marriage, or adoption are not formally recognized in public policy, leading to less favorable treatment than that accorded traditional family units. Persons in nontraditional relationships usually are not legally recognized as having rights. For example, without a blood or marital relationship, a person does not generally qualify for survivor, pension, or insurance benefits. A person cannot have the benefits of being a spouse or parent without legal standing as such. In medical matters, persons in nontraditional relationships may not be granted rights given to *family*, such as visitation or making medical decisions for the other person.

THE HIGH COST OF LIVING ARRANGEMENTS

Owning a Home — the American Dream?

In 1997, according to the Bureau of the Census, 79 percent of elderly householders owned the home in which they lived (Table 3.7). Home ownership peaks (82.3 percent) between the ages of 70 to 74. This was in sharp contrast to the situation with younger Americans for whom the home-ownership rate has declined since 1982. More than 1 in 5 householders are elderly.

Elderly householders are less likely than those under 65 to have mortgage indebtedness. Eighty percent of elderly homeowners have no mortgage payment. Even where there is no mortgage remaining on the home, however, the homeowner must still pay taxes, insurance, garbage collection, utility bills, and often high repair costs for what is most likely an older home.

Although elderly persons spend only half as much for housing as do younger owners, they spend an approximately equal percentage — one-fifth — of their income for housing. Their median monthly housing cost in 1995 was $282. (Seventy percent of young homeowners had a mortgage, which boosted their median housing cost to $480.) Among the 2.5 million elderly householders with a mortgage, the median housing cost was $445.

The Bureau of the Census reported that, in 1991, the elderly (69 percent) were more likely than other groups to be able to afford a medium-priced home in their area. Elderly married couples were the most able (75 percent), compared to older single males (51 percent) and single females over 65 (38 percent) (Table 3.8).

Nonetheless, failing health and physical disability, often accompanied by reduced or fixed income, can make home ownership a burden. The result is that the proportion of elderly who own

TABLE 3.8

Affordability Status of Families and Unrelated Individuals for a Median-Priced Home, by Age of Householder, Current Tenure, and Type of Financing: United States, 1991

(In thousands. Data may not add to total due to rounding)

Age of householder	Families – Total	Cannot afford median-priced home in area – Number	Per-cent	Married-couple – Total	Cannot afford median-priced home in area – Number	Per-cent	Male householder, no wife present – Total	Cannot afford median-priced home in area – Number	Per-cent	Female householder, no husband present – Total	Cannot afford median-priced home in area – Number	Per-cent	Unrelated individuals – Total	Cannot afford median-priced home in area – Number	Per-cent
USING CONVENTIONAL, FIXED-RATE, 30-YEAR FINANCING															
Total	69,543	35,668	51.3	53,249	22,449	42.2	2,810	1,904	67.8	13,484	11,314	83.9	36,010	27,433	76.2
Under 25 years	3,693	3,563	96.5	1,739	1,629	93.7	176	173	97.8	1,777	1,761	99.1	4,124	4,030	97.7
25 to 34 years	15,666	11,839	75.6	11,128	7,519	67.6	581	484	83.3	3,957	3,836	96.9	8,957	8,079	90.2
35 to 44 years	17,748	9,085	51.2	13,594	5,686	41.8	802	591	73.8	3,353	2,808	83.8	5,509	4,335	78.7
45 to 54 years	12,067	4,809	39.9	9,679	3,192	33.0	490	283	57.7	1,898	1,334	70.3	3,594	2,447	68.1
55 to 64 years	9,403	3,011	32.0	7,891	2,088	26.5	352	174	49.5	1,160	748	64.5	3,595	2,402	66.8
65 years or older	10,967	3,360	30.6	9,219	2,335	25.3	410	199	48.6	1,338	826	61.7	10,232	6,140	60.0
Median (years)	43.7	37.7	(X)	45.2	38.7	(X)	43.1	40.0	(X)	38.0	35.2	(X)	43.9	38.7	(X)
Current owners	49,881	17,742	35.6	41,875	12,591	30.1	1,804	967	53.6	6,202	4,185	67.5	16,311	9,291	57.0
Under 25 years	1,080	989	91.6	581	503	86.6	37	37	100.0	462	450	97.3	738	694	94.1
25 to 34 years	8,224	4,844	58.9	6,741	3,552	52.7	316	223	70.6	1,168	1,069	91.6	2,520	1,983	78.7
35 to 44 years	12,995	4,757	36.6	10,991	3,409	31.0	517	331	64.2	1,488	1,017	68.4	2,447	1,544	63.1
45 to 54 years	9,902	2,914	29.4	8,339	2,078	24.9	354	163	45.9	1,209	673	55.6	1,907	963	50.5
55 to 64 years	8,093	1,909	23.6	7,045	1,416	20.1	255	97	38.1	793	396	49.9	2,072	1,056	51.0
65 years or older	9,587	2,329	24.3	8,179	1,633	20.0	325	116	35.6	1,083	580	53.6	6,629	3,051	46.0
Median (years)	47.7	41.4	(X)	48.1	41.6	(X)	45.9	41.8	(X)	44.9	40.6	(X)	57.6	49.4	(X)
Current renters	19,662	17,926	91.2	11,373	9,859	86.7	1,007	937	93.1	7,282	7,130	97.9	19,699	18,142	92.1
Under 25 years	2,613	2,574	98.5	1,158	1,126	97.2	140	136	97.2	1,315	1,312	99.7	3,386	3,336	98.5
25 to 34 years	7,442	6,995	94.0	4,387	3,967	90.4	265	261	98.4	2,789	2,767	99.2	6,438	6,096	94.7
35 to 44 years	4,753	4,328	91.1	2,603	2,277	87.5	285	260	91.2	1,865	1,791	96.0	3,062	2,791	91.1
45 to 54 years	2,165	1,896	87.6	1,340	1,114	83.2	135	120	88.6	690	662	96.0	1,687	1,484	88.0
55 to 64 years	1,310	1,102	84.1	846	673	79.5	96	77	79.8	367	353	96.1	1,523	1,346	88.4
65 years or older	1,380	1,031	74.7	1,039	701	67.5	85	84	98.2	256	246	96.1	3,603	3,089	85.7
Median (years)	34.7	34.1	(X)	35.5	34.6	(X)	38.5	37.8	(X)	33.3	33.1	(X)	35.1	34.4	(X)
USING FHA, FIXED-RATE, 30-YEAR FINANCING															
Total	69,543	34,362	49.4	53,249	21,256	39.9	2,810	1,874	66.7	13,484	11,232	83.3	36,010	27,173	75.5
Under 25 years	3,693	3,507	95.0	1,739	1,573	90.5	176	173	97.8	1,777	1,761	99.1	4,124	4,019	97.5
25 to 34 years	15,666	11,386	72.7	11,128	7,092	63.7	581	484	83.3	3,957	3,810	96.3	8,957	7,966	88.9
35 to 44 years	17,748	8,651	48.7	13,594	5,293	38.9	802	581	72.4	3,353	2,777	82.8	5,509	4,302	78.1
45 to 54 years	12,067	4,612	38.2	9,679	3,013	31.1	490	277	56.7	1,898	1,322	69.6	3,594	2,428	67.6
55 to 64 years	9,403	2,931	31.2	7,891	2,022	25.6	352	164	46.7	1,160	744	64.2	3,595	2,383	66.3
65 years or older	10,967	3,275	29.9	9,219	2,262	24.5	410	196	47.7	1,338	817	61.0	10,232	6,075	59.4
Median (years)	43.7	37.6	(X)	45.2	38.7	(X)	43.1	39.8	(X)	38.0	35.2	(X)	43.9	38.7	(X)
Current owners	49,881	16,724	33.5	41,875	11,667	27.9	1,804	937	52.0	6,202	4,119	66.4	16,311	9,141	56.0
Under 25 years	1,080	946	87.7	581	460	79.2	37	37	100.0	462	450	97.3	738	694	94.1
25 to 34 years	8,224	4,526	55.0	6,741	3,255	48.3	316	223	70.6	1,168	1,048	89.7	2,520	1,938	76.9
35 to 44 years	12,995	4,402	33.9	10,991	3,089	28.1	517	321	62.1	1,488	993	66.7	2,447	1,521	62.2
45 to 54 years	9,902	2,753	27.8	8,339	1,929	23.1	354	158	44.5	1,209	666	55.1	1,907	950	49.8
55 to 64 years	8,093	1,852	22.9	7,045	1,373	19.5	255	87	34.2	793	392	49.4	2,072	1,044	50.4
65 years or older	9,587	2,246	23.4	8,179	1,562	19.1	325	112	34.4	1,083	571	52.8	6,629	2,994	45.2
Median (years)	47.7	41.6	(X)	48.1	41.9	(X)	45.9	41.5	(X)	44.9	40.7	(X)	57.6	49.4	(X)
Current renters	19,662	17,639	89.7	11,373	9,589	84.3	1,007	937	93.1	7,282	7,113	97.7	19,699	18,032	91.5
Under 25 years	2,613	2,561	98.0	1,158	1,113	96.1	140	136	97.2	1,315	1,312	99.7	3,386	3,325	98.2
25 to 34 years	7,442	6,861	92.2	4,387	3,837	87.5	265	261	98.4	2,789	2,763	99.0	6,438	6,028	93.6
35 to 44 years	4,753	4,249	89.4	2,603	2,205	84.7	285	260	91.2	1,865	1,785	95.7	3,062	2,781	90.8
45 to 54 years	2,165	1,859	85.9	1,340	1,084	80.9	135	120	88.6	690	656	95.1	1,687	1,478	87.6
55 to 64 years	1,310	1,079	82.4	846	650	76.8	96	77	79.8	367	353	96.1	1,523	1,339	87.9
65 years or older	1,380	1,029	74.6	1,039	700	67.4	85	84	98.2	256	246	96.1	3,603	3,082	85.5
Median (years)	34.7	34.1	(X)	35.5	34.6	(X)	38.5	37.8	(X)	33.3	33.1	(X)	35.1	34.4	(X)

X Not applicable.

Source: Howard A. Savage and Peter J. Fronczek, *Who Can Afford to Buy a House in 1991?*, U.S. Bureau of the Census, Washington, DC, 1993

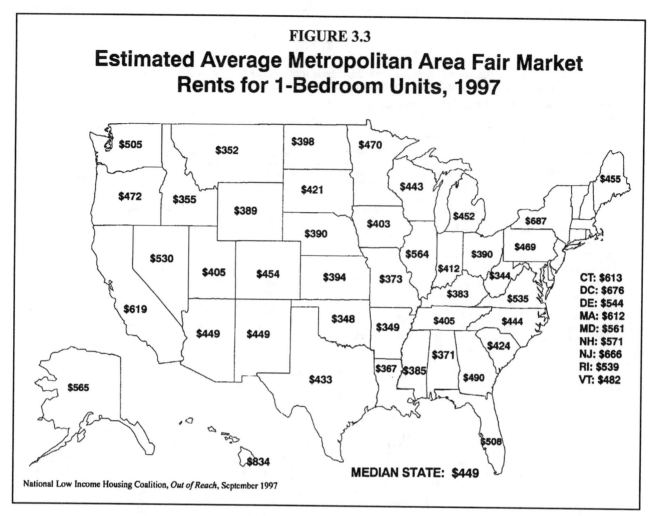

FIGURE 3.3

Estimated Average Metropolitan Area Fair Market Rents for 1-Bedroom Units, 1997

$505
$352
$398
$470
$455
$472
$355
$421
$443
$452
$687
$389
$403
$469
$390
$564
$390
$530
$412
$344
$405
$454
$394
$373
$383
$535
$619
$383
$348
$349
$405
$444
$449
$449
$371
$424
$565
$367 $385
$490
$433
$508
$834

CT: $613
DC: $676
DE: $544
MA: $612
MD: $561
NH: $571
NJ: $666
RI: $539
VT: $482

MEDIAN STATE: $449

National Low Income Housing Coalition, *Out of Reach*, September 1997

their own homes begins to decline at age 65. Most elderly owners have lived in their homes more than 17 years. About half of elderly owners paid less than $20,000 for their homes due to the age and size of the buildings. About 21 percent of the elderly had four or fewer rooms, while only 11 percent of younger owners' homes were that small.

Reverse Mortgages

Older homeowners sometimes need spendable cash. An arrangement known as a reverse mortgage allows a homeowner to "cash in" some of her home equity each month for cash, yet still retain ownership of the home. The money is paid out to a homeowner in monthly installments determined by the amount of home equity borrowed against, the interest rate, and the length of the loan. In most cases, no repayment is due until the homeowner dies, sells the house, or permanently moves.

Sale/Leaseback or Life Tenancy

In a sale/leaseback or life tenancy arrangement a homeowner sells the home to an investor, who then leases it back to the homeowner. The former homeowner retains the right to live in the house for life as a renter. The investor pays the former owner in monthly installments and also is responsible for property taxes, insurance, maintenance, and repairs.

Renting Is Even More Expensive

The National Low-Income Housing Coalition, in its study *Out of Reach* (1997), reported that the nationwide median fair market rent for a one-bedroom unit was $449 and for a two-bedroom, $558 (Figures 3.3 and 3.4).

About one-third of elderly households live in rented facilities. Renters pay a higher percentage

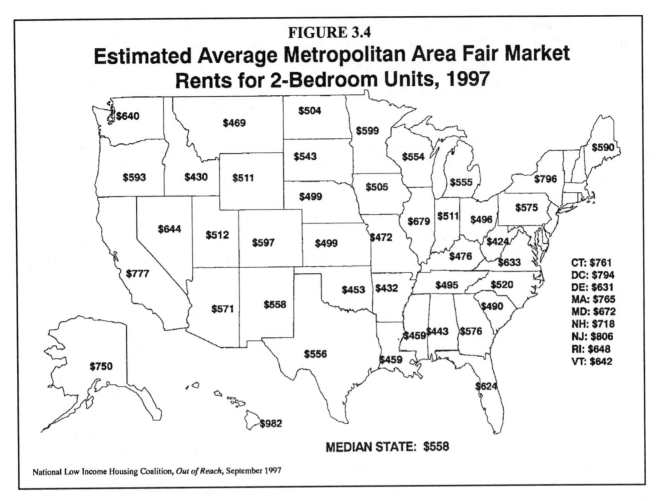

FIGURE 3.4
Estimated Average Metropolitan Area Fair Market Rents for 2-Bedroom Units, 1997

$640
$469
$504
$599
$590
$543
$554
$593 $430 $511 $505 $555 $796
$499 $575
$644 $512 $597 $499 $472 $679 $511 $496
$476 $424
$777 $633
$453 $432 $495 $520
$571 $558 $490
$459 $443 $576
$750 $556 $459
$624
$982

CT: $761
DC: $794
DE: $631
MA: $765
MD: $672
NH: $718
NJ: $806
RI: $648
VT: $642

MEDIAN STATE: $558

National Low Income Housing Coalition, *Out of Reach*, September 1997

of their incomes for housing than do homeowners. Renters are often faced with several additional drawbacks: mortgage payments generally remain the same over a period of years (often until the entire mortgage is paid off), but rents may increase each year while the renter remains on a fixed income. Also, homeowners have the equity in their homes to fall back on in times of financial crisis; the renter makes out a monthly check, but none of the money is ever returned as a tangible asset. Finally, mortgage payments are tax-deductible, while rent payments are not.

According to the Bureau of the Census (*Housing of the Elderly*, 1995), elderly renters spend an average of 36 percent of their income on housing, compared to 28 percent for younger renters. Four in 10 elderly renters receive some form of housing assistance, either from the government, such as rent control or public or subsidized housing, or some from landlords who

voluntarily lower rents to older renters. About one in 10 renters over 65 years of age paid no cash rent.

For many older renters, meals are part of their rental package. The Bureau of the Census reported that 1 in 10 elderly renters lived in homes where meals were provided as part of their rental agreement. The proportion with a rent-meals arrangement rose with age, reaching 23 percent for renters 85 and older. Most of these elderly renters paid $750 or more per month for this combination of housing and meals.

A Housing Problem for Older Women

Whether they are owners or renters, as people age, they can expect to spend more and more of their income on housing. While men may find it hard to find suitable housing, women are disproportionately affected because their retirement incomes are generally much smaller than

51

men's and because they live an average of seven years longer than men. As women age, they are increasingly more likely to live alone because of divorce or death of their spouse.

The Older Women's League, in its 1993 *Mother's Day Report*, "Room for Improvement," reported that housing is a critical problem for mid-life and older women. Among the problems they cited were

• Forty-five percent of older single women have an income of $10,000 a year or less;

• Nearly one-third of older women renters spend more than half their limited income on housing. On average, women renters spend a third of their income on housing compared to one-fourth for men;

• Almost 30 percent of homeless women are over the age of 50.

The result is that a majority of older women live in older suburbs that are falling into decay — homes built in the post-World War II boom that now need major repairs. And although most women in the suburbs are owners rather than renters, their homes are valued at less than those owned by single men or couples because single women's incomes often keep them from being able to make repairs. Older women also run a risk of becoming homeless through divorce, abusive marital situations, or loss of employment.

ADDITIONAL HOUSING PROBLEMS OF THE ELDERLY

Older Houses

Many older people live in older houses. The Bureau of the Census reported that, in 1991, 24 percent of the elderly, compared to 18 percent of the nonelderly, lived in houses built more than 40 years ago, over one-third of them before World War II. In four eastern states —Vermont, Pennsylvania, Maine, Massachusetts — and the District of Columbia, as many as 40 percent or more of elderly residents lived in older homes. Conversely, in four states — Alaska, Nevada, Arizona, and Florida — less than 10 percent lived in homes built before 1940.

It is quite common for elderly owners, especially those over 85, to have lived in their homes for at least 30 years. The Bureau of the Census reported that among those older than 85, just over one-half had lived at their current residence for three decades or more; more than 90 percent of these homes were single-family detached homes.

Maintenance

While the age of a house does not necessarily reflect its physical condition, older houses typically need more frequent and more expensive repairs. Building materials become stressed with age. Older houses may be poorly insulated. Many housing units occupied by persons 65 or older have physical problems in one or more of six areas: plumbing, kitchen, maintenance of physical structure, public hall/common area, heating, and electrical systems.

The elderly and persons living alone are more likely to let maintenance work slide. The elderly constitute more than one-third of those who had not paid for any maintenance recently. Owners 65 and older have a greater likelihood of having severe or moderate housing problems than owners 35 to 64 years of age.

Physical Hazards

Features considered desirable by younger householders may be handicaps to the elderly. For example, the staircase in a two-story house may become a formidable obstacle to someone with osteoporosis or a neuromuscular problem. Narrow halls and doorways cannot be navigated in wheelchairs. High cabinets and shelves may be beyond the reach of an arthritis sufferer. Houses can be modified to meet the physical needs of the elderly, but not all older houses can be remodeled to accept such modifications, and installing them may be more costly than some elderly can afford.

The American Association of Retired Persons (AARP) believes that 85 percent of people over 55 prefer to remain in familiar surroundings, rather than move to alternative housing. As a result, those who are able redesign their homes to accommodate the changes that accompany aging — a concept known as "universal design." Its premise is that homes, from their initial blueprints or as modifications, should be equipped for people with disabilities — functional yet aesthetic.

Anticipating the increase in the elderly population in the coming years, some real estate developers are manufacturing experimental houses designed to meet the needs of the elderly and thus prolong independent living. Such houses include non-skid flooring, walls strong enough to support grab bars, light plugs at convenient heights, levers instead of knobs on doors and plumbing fixtures, and wide doors and hallways.

Simple adaptations include replacing doorknobs with levers that can be pushed downward with a fist or elbow, requiring no gripping or twisting; replacing light switches with flat, "touch" switches; placing closet rods at adjustable heights; installing stoves with front or side-mounted controls; and marking steps with bright colors. More complex renovations include replacing a bathroom with a wet room, a tiled space with a showerhead, waterproof chair, and sloping floor for a drain, large enough to accommodate a wheelchair; placing electrical receptacles higher than usual along walls; and widening passageways and doors for wheelchairs or battery-operated carts. Family and friends of disabled and elderly people also benefit from universal design.

Lack of Transportation

When an elderly person's vision and physical reflexes decline, driving a car can be difficult and perilous. Older people whose homes are far from shopping centers or public transportation may have to depend on others for transportation or delivery of the basic necessities, or they may simply have to do without. This is a particularly acute problem for the approximately 25 percent of the U.S. elderly population who live in rural areas. The rural elderly may be isolated not only from food and clothing stores, but from health and social services as well.

A Picture of Housing for the Elderly in One County

The University of Texas at Arlington (UTA; Arlington, Texas) undertook a study *(Dallas County Elderly Needs Assessment*, 1994) of the elderly residing in Dallas County, Texas. Among the findings were that homeowners were 78 percent of the elderly; two-thirds of those had no mortgages. Most (66 percent) had lived in the county for more than 30 years, 51 percent in their current residence for more than 20 years. Sixty-four percent said they wanted to stay in their own homes. Housing problems (availability and affordability) were concentrated in extremely poor and very low-income elderly households. Extremely poor elderly renters and homeowners alike were affected with severe cost burdens — at least one-third of them paid *half* or more of their income on housing, including utilities.

THE ROLE OF THE FEDERAL GOVERNMENT

In 1937, Congress passed the United States Housing Act of 1937 (PL 75-412) to create low-income public housing. Prior to 1956, only 10 percent of available units were occupied by persons 65 or older; today, the elderly occupy more than 40 percent of available low-income public housing units.

The federal government makes direct loans to private, non-profit developers to build housing designed specifically for the elderly and the handicapped. About one-half of the nation's low-income housing units are now more than 25 years old. Many were built during the 1930s and 1940s and are in need of major renovation.

Despite federal programs to provide decent, affordable housing, it is still beyond the reach of many millions of elderly. According to the National Council of Senior Citizens (a private advocacy group), the average time on a waiting list for elderly housing is three to five years, and only 1 in 7 elderly poor receives federal housing assistance. The Older Women's League estimates that for each vacancy in subsidized complexes, there are eight elderly people on a waiting list.

FUTURE TRENDS

The number of elderly persons living independently has increased significantly, and that trend is expected to continue into the next century. Those now approaching retirement age are more health-conscious than their parents, and they generally had a higher personal income during their working years. While many people still fail to plan adequately for their later years, the importance of such planning is being widely publicized by government agencies and private organizations. The "young-old" can still take steps to ensure a financially comfortable old age.

The declining birth rate which followed the baby boom has meant that there are fewer children with whom the future elderly can share housing. Because the extended family will become even less common than it is now, older people living alone will have to rely more on community services, including senior citizen centers, special transportation, meals, visiting nurses, or day care. A greater proportion of the elderly living alone use community services, a situation that is especially true of the poor.

While the number of elderly living independently will increase, so will the number of those who will become nursing home residents. Since 1980 the number of older Americans in need of long-term care has grown 14 percent, and the number is expected to increase steadily during the 1990s and double by 2020.

The near-universal desire of even the frail and chronically ill elderly to remain at home has fostered a number of alternatives that will enable them, when possible, to stay in familiar surroundings with at least some control of their lives. Among these approaches are adult day care, home repair services, and housekeeping and visiting nurse programs. Telephone reassurance programs telephone frail individuals daily to check their status. Some municipalities now provide free or low-cost transportation to elderly residents, including those with handicaps.

Technology also plays a part; electronic alarm systems and remote control appliances are increasingly marketed to the aging population. Foster families for the elderly have emerged. The goal of all of these programs is to enable as many elderly as possible to remain independent, in their own homes, and out of institutions, for as long as possible. (For a further discussion of health care, see Chapter IX.)

CHAPTER IV

WORKING — PAID AND UNPAID CONTRIBUTIONS

Senior citizens don't want handouts.... They want to continue to make a contribution to their fellow man. They want to continue to be a vital and living part of the American society. — Willard Wirtz, U.S. Secretary of Labor, 1968

Productivity is not the exclusive domain of the young. Genius, creativity, and dedication do not end on a person's sixty-fifth birthday. Older people have made and continue to make significant contributions in all areas.

Benjamin Franklin — writer, scientist, inventor, and statesman — helped draft the Declaration of Independence at the age of 70. Golda Meir was elected Prime Minister of Israel when she was 71. Thomas Alva Edison worked on such inventions as the light bulb, the microphone, and the phonograph until his death at the age of 81. Rear Admiral (Ret.) Grace Hooper, one of the early computer scientists and co-creator of the computer language COBOL, maintained an active speaking and consulting schedule up until her death in her 80s. Margaret Mead, the noted anthropologist, returned to New Guinea when she was 72 and exhausted a much younger television filming crew as they tried to keep up with her. Albert Einstein, who formulated the theory of relativity, was working on a unifying theory of the universe when he died at age 76. Pablo Picasso and Georgia O'Keefe created masterful paintings when they were each past 80 years of age. And in 1997, President George Bush celebrated his seventy-second birthday with a sky dive over the Arizona desert.

A CHANGING ECONOMY AND CHANGING ROLES

*America today possesses not only the fastest-growing, but the largest, best-educated, and most vigorous collection of older adults in our history. In fact, the senior population may represent the country's only **increasing** natural resource.* — Mark Freedman ("Seniors in National and Community Service: A Report Prepared for The Commonwealth Fund's Americans Over 55 At Work Program," 1994)

From Agricultural ...

In early America, there was little correlation between age and work. In that agricultural society, youngsters were put to work as soon as possible to contribute to the family upkeep. At the other end of the age scale, workers did not retire; they worked as long as they were physically able to do so. Then they were cared for by the younger members of the family. Older people were valued and respected for their accumulated knowledge and experience. They were an integral part of the interconnected family and labor systems.

... to Industrial

The Industrial Revolution took men away from the farm and into manufacturing jobs. The work was physically demanding, the hours long, and the tasks strictly structured. Women labored in factories and at home caring for the family. Older people found themselves without a place in the workforce. Their skills and experience were not relevant to new technologies, nor could they physically compete with the large number of young workers eager to take advantage of new economic opportunities.

As industrial workers matured, some of them were promoted to positions as supervisors and managers. Labor unions provided some job security through the seniority system ("first hired, last fired") for older workers who had been with the same company for many years. However, in an increasingly youth-oriented society, older workers were often pushed aside to make way for younger workers. The problem became so severe that Congress passed the Age Discrimination Act (PL 90-202) in 1967 and the Age Discrimination Act Amendment (PL 95-256) in 1978 prohibiting differential treatment of workers based solely on age. In 1987, Congress amended the act to abolish age-based mandatory retirement for most workers in the private sector as well as those in government employment (see Age Discrimination, below).

... to Service

The American economy continues its dramatic shift away from manufacturing and toward the service sector. Doctors, data entry persons, travel agents, auto mechanics, and teachers far outnumber coal miners, carpenters, and pipefitters. The number of agricultural employees continues to decline, manufacturing jobs are decreasing, and the service industry has doubled in the number of employees since 1970.

Many service jobs are ideally suited for older workers. They usually do not require heavy labor, and the cumulative experience of years of work is an advantage in almost all service fields. More than one-third of the jobs of older workers are in the service sector. Nonetheless, bias against older workers is still prevalent.

PARTICIPATION IN THE LABOR FORCE

In 1997, almost 3.9 million men and women over age 65 participated in the labor force (either by actively working or actively seeking work) compared to approximately 8.1 million people aged 55 to 59, and 4.6 million aged 60 to 64. Workers over age 65 were 11.6 percent of the U.S. elderly population. (See Table 4.1.)

Although older women outnumber older men in the general population, a greater percentage of men than women were in the labor force. Most men (67.6 percent) aged 55 to 64 were participants; by age 65, only 17.1 percent participated. Fifty-one percent of women aged 55 to 64 were in the labor force; by age 65, the percentage dropped to 8.6 percent.

Part-Time Work

Older people forced to leave their occupations sometimes feel unproductive and worthless. They may suffer emotional and financial hardship or become bored or lonely. It is increasingly common to find retired workers re-entering the workforce or remaining in the workforce by working part-time. In 1997, 25 percent of men and 43 percent of women 55 and older who were working had part-time jobs (Table 4.2).

For employers, hiring part-time older workers is often an attractive alternative to hiring younger, full-time workers, partly because of older workers' dependability and experience. Unfortunately, companies often pay older workers (or part-time workers, in general) lower wages and do not provide benefits such as health insurance, pensions, profit-sharing, etc.

Older persons receiving Social Security benefits may choose part-time work to supplement their incomes, although they lose part of their Social Security benefits if their earnings are too great. In 1997, the threshold for benefit retention for 62- to 64-year-old workers was raised to $8,640 annually (after which they lose $1 for every $2 they earn), and to $13,500 for workers 65 and older (after which they lose $1 for every $3 they earn).

RETIREMENT

Increasing longevity means that people spend more time in all phases of their lives — education, work, and retirement. In 1900, the average person spent only 1.2 years in retirement; by 1980, he was retired an average of 13.6 years. In 1997, the typical person 65 years of age could expect to live yet

TABLE 4.1

Employment status of the civilian noninstitutional population by age, sex, and race

(Numbers in thousands)

Age, sex, and race	1997									
	Civilian noninsti-tutional population	Civilian labor force								Not in labor force
		Total	Percent of population	Employed				Unemployed		
				Total	Percent of population	Agri-culture	Nonagri-cultural industries	Number	Percent of labor force	
TOTAL										
16 years and over	203,133	136,297	67.1	129,558	63.8	3,399	126,159	6,739	4.9	66,837
16 to 19 years	15,365	7,932	51.6	6,661	43.4	244	6,417	1,271	16.0	7,433
16 to 17 years	7,861	3,237	41.2	2,648	33.7	116	2,532	589	18.2	4,624
18 to 19 years	7,504	4,695	62.6	4,012	53.5	128	3,885	683	14.5	2,809
20 to 24 years	17,442	13,532	77.6	12,380	71.0	325	12,054	1,152	8.5	3,910
25 to 54 years	116,832	98,280	84.1	94,461	80.9	2,093	92,368	3,819	3.9	18,552
25 to 34 years	39,559	33,380	84.4	31,809	80.4	719	31,090	1,571	4.7	6,178
25 to 29 years	18,884	16,008	84.8	15,163	80.3	327	14,836	845	5.3	2,876
30 to 34 years	20,675	17,373	84.0	16,646	80.5	392	16,254	726	4.2	3,302
35 to 44 years	43,883	37,326	85.1	35,908	81.8	806	35,102	1,418	3.8	6,557
35 to 39 years	22,544	19,104	84.7	18,339	81.3	425	17,913	765	4.0	3,440
40 to 44 years	21,339	18,222	85.4	17,569	82.3	380	17,189	653	3.6	3,117
45 to 54 years	33,391	27,574	82.6	26,744	80.1	567	26,176	830	3.0	5,817
45 to 49 years	18,443	15,547	84.3	15,089	81.8	315	14,774	458	2.9	2,895
50 to 54 years	14,948	12,027	80.5	11,654	78.0	253	11,402	372	3.1	2,922
55 to 64 years	21,505	12,665	58.9	12,296	57.2	416	11,880	369	2.9	8,840
55 to 59 years	11,605	8,049	69.4	7,816	67.3	225	7,591	234	2.9	3,556
60 to 64 years	9,900	4,616	46.6	4,480	45.3	191	4,289	135	2.9	5,284
65 years and over	31,989	3,887	12.2	3,761	11.8	321	3,440	127	3.3	28,102
65 to 69 years	9,543	2,150	22.5	2,080	21.8	150	1,930	71	3.3	7,393
70 to 74 years	8,509	1,071	12.6	1,034	12.2	98	936	36	3.4	7,438
75 years and over	13,937	666	4.8	647	4.6	73	574	20	3.0	13,270
Men										
16 years and over	97,715	73,261	75.0	69,685	71.3	2,552	67,133	3,577	4.9	24,454
16 to 19 years	7,836	4,095	52.3	3,401	43.4	195	3,206	694	16.9	3,741
16 to 17 years	4,053	1,676	41.4	1,355	33.4	91	1,265	321	19.1	2,377
18 to 19 years	3,783	2,419	63.9	2,045	54.1	104	1,941	373	15.4	1,365
20 to 24 years	8,706	7,184	82.5	6,548	75.2	258	6,290	636	8.9	1,521
25 to 54 years	57,423	52,732	91.8	50,772	88.4	1,550	49,221	1,960	3.7	4,691
25 to 34 years	19,478	18,110	93.0	17,338	89.0	551	16,788	772	4.3	1,368
25 to 29 years	9,281	8,583	92.5	8,162	87.9	257	7,904	422	4.9	698
30 to 34 years	10,197	9,527	93.4	9,177	90.0	294	8,883	350	3.7	670
35 to 44 years	21,669	20,058	92.6	19,327	89.2	591	18,736	732	3.6	1,611
35 to 39 years	11,137	10,363	93.0	9,967	89.5	308	9,659	396	3.8	774
40 to 44 years	10,532	9,696	92.1	9,360	88.9	283	9,077	336	3.5	836
45 to 54 years	16,276	14,564	89.5	14,107	86.7	409	13,698	457	3.1	1,712
45 to 49 years	9,017	8,188	90.8	7,935	88.0	229	7,706	253	3.1	829
50 to 54 years	7,259	6,376	87.8	6,172	85.0	180	5,992	204	3.2	883
55 to 64 years	10,282	6,952	67.6	6,735	65.5	290	6,445	217	3.1	3,329
55 to 59 years	5,582	4,391	78.7	4,258	76.3	157	4,101	133	3.0	1,191
60 to 64 years	4,700	2,561	54.5	2,478	52.7	133	2,344	84	3.3	2,139
65 years and over	13,469	2,298	17.1	2,229	16.5	258	1,971	69	3.0	11,171
65 to 69 years	4,360	1,238	28.4	1,197	27.4	121	1,075	41	3.3	3,122
70 to 74 years	3,737	644	17.2	625	16.7	77	548	19	2.9	3,093
75 years and over	5,372	416	7.7	407	7.6	60	347	9	2.1	4,957
Women										
16 years and over	105,418	63,036	59.8	59,873	56.8	847	59,026	3,162	5.0	42,382
16 to 19 years	7,528	3,837	51.0	3,260	43.3	49	3,211	577	15.0	3,691
16 to 17 years	3,808	1,561	41.0	1,293	34.0	25	1,268	268	17.2	2,247
18 to 19 years	3,721	2,277	61.2	1,967	52.9	23	1,944	310	13.6	1,444
20 to 24 years	8,736	6,348	72.7	5,831	66.8	67	5,764	516	8.1	2,389
25 to 54 years	59,410	45,548	76.7	43,689	73.5	542	43,147	1,859	4.1	13,861
25 to 34 years	20,081	15,271	76.0	14,471	72.1	169	14,302	800	5.2	4,810
25 to 29 years	9,603	7,425	77.3	7,001	72.9	70	6,931	423	5.7	2,178
30 to 34 years	10,478	7,846	74.9	7,470	71.3	99	7,371	376	4.8	2,632
35 to 44 years	22,214	17,268	77.7	16,581	74.6	215	16,366	686	4.0	4,947
35 to 39 years	11,407	8,741	76.6	8,372	73.4	117	8,255	369	4.2	2,666
40 to 44 years	10,807	8,526	78.9	8,209	76.0	98	8,111	317	3.7	2,280
45 to 54 years	17,115	13,010	76.0	12,637	73.8	158	12,479	373	2.9	4,104
45 to 49 years	9,425	7,359	78.1	7,155	75.9	86	7,069	205	2.8	2,066
50 to 54 years	7,689	5,651	73.5	5,482	71.3	72	5,410	168	3.0	2,038
55 to 64 years	11,224	5,713	50.9	5,561	49.5	126	5,435	152	2.7	5,511
55 to 59 years	6,024	3,658	60.7	3,558	59.1	68	3,490	100	2.7	2,365
60 to 64 years	5,200	2,054	39.5	2,003	38.5	58	1,945	52	2.5	3,145
65 years and over	18,520	1,590	8.6	1,532	8.3	63	1,469	58	3.6	16,930
65 to 69 years	5,184	912	17.6	883	17.0	29	854	29	3.2	4,271
70 to 74 years	4,772	427	8.9	409	8.6	21	388	17	4.1	4,345
75 years and over	8,564	251	2.9	239	2.8	13	227	11	4.5	8,314

Source: *Employment and Earnings*, Bureau of Labor Statistics, Washington, DC, January 1998

TABLE 4.2

Persons at work in nonagricultural industries by age, sex, race, marital status, and usual full- or part-time status

(Numbers in thousands)

Age, sex, race, and marital status	December 1997							
	Total at work	Worked 1 to 34 hours				Worked 35 hours or more	Average hours	
		Total	For economic reasons	For noneconomic reasons			Total at work	Persons who usually work full time
				Usually work full time	Usually work part time			
TOTAL								
Total, 16 years and over	124,050	29,666	3,644	7,076	18,946	94,384	39.5	43.6
16 to 19 years	8,265	4,673	349	176	4,148	1,592	23.8	39.2
16 to 17 years	2,436	2,280	76	21	2,183	156	17.4	38.9
18 to 19 years	3,829	2,393	272	156	1,965	1,435	27.9	39.2
20 years and over	117,786	24,993	3,295	6,900	14,798	92,793	40.4	43.7
20 to 24 years	11,872	4,117	607	584	2,926	7,755	35.7	42.0
25 years and over	105,914	20,876	2,688	6,315	11,872	85,038	40.9	43.9
25 to 54 years	90,728	16,130	2,368	5,391	8,370	74,598	41.5	44.0
55 years and over	15,186	4,746	320	924	3,502	10,440	37.2	43.2
Men, 16 years and over	65,875	10,818	1,758	3,386	5,674	55,057	42.5	45.0
16 to 19 years	3,097	2,212	181	99	1,932	885	24.7	39.0
16 to 17 years	1,186	1,090	39	14	1,037	95	18.2	39.0
18 to 19 years	1,911	1,122	142	85	895	789	28.7	39.0
20 years and over	62,778	8,606	1,577	3,287	3,742	54,172	43.3	45.1
20 to 24 years	6,137	1,784	278	362	1,143	4,353	37.7	42.7
25 years and over	56,641	6,822	1,299	2,925	2,598	49,819	43.9	45.4
25 to 54 years	48,356	4,866	1,137	2,453	1,276	43,490	44.6	45.5
55 years and over	8,285	1,956	162	472	1,322	6,329	40.0	44.5
Women, 16 years and over	58,176	18,848	1,886	3,690	13,272	39,328	36.2	41.7
16 to 19 years	3,168	2,461	168	77	2,216	707	22.9	39.3
16 to 17 years	1,250	1,189	37	7	1,145	61	16.7	(1)
18 to 19 years	1,918	1,272	131	71	1,070	646	27.0	39.4
20 years and over	55,008	16,387	1,718	3,613	11,056	38,621	37.0	41.7
20 to 24 years	5,735	2,333	329	222	1,782	3,402	33.6	41.1
25 years and over	49,273	14,054	1,389	3,391	9,274	35,219	37.4	41.8
25 to 54 years	42,372	11,264	1,231	2,938	7,094	31,108	38.0	41.9
55 years and over	6,901	2,790	158	453	2,179	4,111	33.8	41.2
Race								
White, 16 years and over	104,645	25,502	2,810	5,975	16,717	79,142	39.6	43.9
Men	56,492	9,303	1,434	2,908	4,961	47,189	42.7	45.3
Women	48,152	16,199	1,376	3,067	11,756	31,954	36.0	41.9
Black, 16 years and over	13,716	2,899	656	794	1,448	10,817	38.9	41.8
Men	6,381	1,011	235	327	449	5,370	40.8	42.9
Women	7,335	1,888	421	467	1,000	5,447	37.2	40.7
Marital status								
Men, 16 years and over:								
Married, spouse present	40,563	4,616	776	2,119	1,721	35,947	44.4	45.8
Widowed, divorced, or separated	7,588	1,105	261	418	426	6,483	43.1	44.8
Single (never married)	17,723	5,097	721	849	3,527	12,626	37.6	43.1
Women, 16 years and over:								
Married, spouse present	31,446	10,063	757	2,079	7,227	21,383	36.2	41.4
Widowed, divorced, or separated	11,842	3,068	471	886	1,712	8,774	38.5	42.2
Single (never married)	14,887	5,717	658	725	4,334	9,171	34.4	41.9

1 Data not shown where base is less than 75,000.

NOTE: Beginning in 1997, data reflect revised population controls used in the household survey.

Source: *Employment and Earnings*, Bureau of Labor Statistics, Washington, DC, January 1998

another 17.3 years, probably in retirement, an increase from 3 percent to approximately 20 percent of one's life span. Retirement has become an institution in the life span of the American citizen.

The age of 65 has traditionally been considered "normal retirement age" since the Social Security legislation of 1935 set that age for receipt of Social Security benefits. However, many persons choose to leave the labor force before that time for a variety of reasons — health, the retirement of a spouse, the availability of Social Security or pension benefits, or the opportunity for leisure activities. Downturns in the economy, mergers, layoffs, down-sizing, and bankruptcies can also result in unplanned early retirement. Some companies have reduced staff by offering attractive retirement packages.

The result has been a declining retirement age, from around 68 in 1950 to 63 in 1995. Although the decline has leveled off in the last few years, some experts expect to see further decline after the turn of the century. However, some elderly, because of improved health, a later Social Security retirement age (from 65 to 67), and economic need caused by possible cuts in Social Security pension and health insurance benefits may feel they need and want to work longer. In addition, with fewer younger workers available, many businesses may need older workers.

Some labor economists feel that early retirements deprive the nation of skilled workers needed for robust growth. The government also loses the revenue that those workers would have contributed in income and payroll taxes. For those elderly who must work for economic reasons, forced retirement and unemployment are serious problems. Older workers often experience difficulty in being re-hired, and the duration of their unemployment is longer.

Work after Early Retirement

A worker's first retirement may not be his last. Early retirement is often triggered by the onset of pension benefits. These retirees may be back at work at another job within a year, either full- or part-time, although those jobs are unlikely to last more than two or three years.

The Bureau of Labor Statistics (*Monthly Labor Review*, "Work after Early Retirement: An Increasing Trend among Men," April 1995) reported that early pensioners returned to work at increasing rates from 1984 to 1993. The Bureau of Labor suggested this trend may be due to the decline in the real (inflation-adjusted) value of their pension benefits or other income and benefits, especially health insurance coverage, over that period. Such declines would encourage pensioners to work to supplement their income.

In addition, the continuing shift of employment opportunities into service-sector jobs may have opened more attractive opportunities for early pensioners. These jobs often provide more flexible schedules and require fewer physical demands than jobs in many other industries.

MYTHS AND MISPERCEPTIONS ABOUT OLDER WORKERS

Often, older workers are stereotyped by the common assumption that performance declines with age. Performance studies, however, show that older workers perform intellectually as well as or better than workers 30 or 40 years younger. They maintain their IQ levels, vocabulary, and creative thinking skills well into their sixties and sometimes beyond.

Many of today's jobs do not require physical stamina or strength; yet, older people are often seen as too frail or sickly to work. But corporate studies indicate that older workers have better attendance records and do as much work as younger employees. Poor health is cited as a reason for leaving a job in only a small number of workers over 50.

A concern about high health insurance costs and generally higher salaries of older workers, coupled with the notion of an older person's low productivity, may lead an employer to believe that it is not cost-effective to hire or retain older employees. However, in the majority of cases, this is not true. Very small companies may see higher insurance and benefit costs for older workers, but lower turnover rates, specialized skills, and job experience may more than offset these costs. Employee turnover is very costly for a company because the company puts time and money into training each new employee, and there is a learning period before a new employee becomes fully productive.

A Good Investment

A major study of American businesses, "America over 55 at Work Program," commissioned by the Commonwealth Fund from 1988-1993, concluded that older workers are good investments for employers. Older workers were found to have a rate of absenteeism 39 percent less than younger employees and a turnover rate 6 times lower. Firms that employed older workers tended to have half the loss in theft and damage and an 18 percent higher profit. The study also found that older workers could be trained in new technologies and were often better salespeople than younger workers. The report concluded that the employment of older people made good business sense. As John Challenger, spokesperson for a national out-placement firm summed up, "Companies are recognizing all the brain power and corporate memory they lost when older employees left."

A 1993 survey by the American Association of Retired Persons (AARP) and the Society for Human Resource Management concluded that older workers are underutilized and undervalued. Businesses indicated that although older workers offer numerous advantages to employers (Figures 4.1 and 4.2), 67 percent of respondents did not actively recruit older workers. What, then, explains the failure of

American industry to hire, train, and retain older workers?

Dr. Robert Atchley, of Miami University of Ohio's Scripps Gerontology Center, in "The Challenge of an Aging Work Force in an Aging Population" (1993), observed that the data has existed for a long time documenting the productivity of the older worker. He attributed the hesitancy of

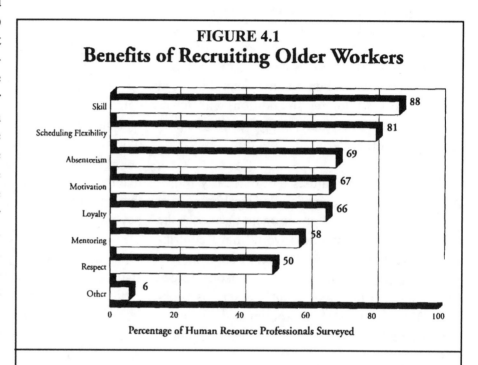

FIGURE 4.1
Benefits of Recruiting Older Workers

Percentage of Human Resource Professionals Surveyed

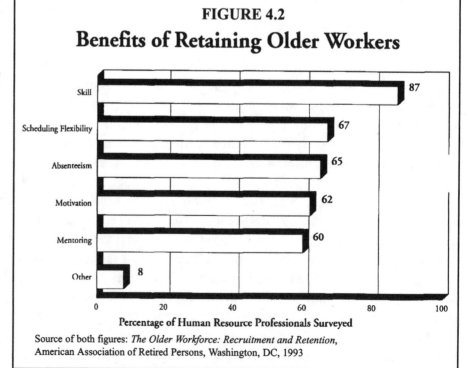

FIGURE 4.2
Benefits of Retaining Older Workers

Percentage of Human Resource Professionals Surveyed

Source of both figures: *The Older Workforce: Recruitment and Retention*, American Association of Retired Persons, Washington, DC, 1993

business to make use of older workers to a number of myths. Among those myths were the belief that older workers are 1) less productive, 2) sickly, 3) expensive in terms of insurance and other benefits, 4) not as bright as younger workers, and that 5) old age is unattractive (i.e. other employees do not like to be reminded of their own mortality).

The Myth of Lower Productivity

In fact, research overwhelmingly shows that experience is more predictive of performance than age. Sara Rix, in *Older Workers: Choices and Challenges* (1990), reported that the question, "Can older workers remain competitive?" is not the issue facing America, but rather, "How do you convince corporate America that older workers are and can remain competitive?"

The U.S Senate Special Committee on Aging found no decline in productivity; indeed, older employees performed as well or better than younger ones. Virtually every study reports that, except in those jobs requiring substantial physical exertion, older workers perform either as well as or better than younger workers. Dr. Atchley's study (above) concluded that productivity does not peak until the 50s and 60s. The "incompetence model" of aging focuses on the deficits some older people have relative to youth and contributes to self-fulfilling prophesies.

A congressionally mandated study conducted for the Equal Employment Opportunity Commission (EEOC) by researchers at Penn State University ("Alternatives to Chronological Age in Determining Standards of Suitability for Public Safety Jobs," 1992) reviewed more than 2,000 studies on various aspects of aging with the goal of determining whether age was correlated to job performance in public safety jobs, such as police and fire officers. Similar studies have been conducted on pilots and air traffic controllers to determine if mandatory retirement at a specific age was necessary to ensure public safety. The study concluded that chronological age was a poor predictor of job performance and limitation, even in situations where public safety was concerned, and recommended abolition of mandatory retirement. Other advantages to hiring older workers are their decreased time off for child-care responsibilities and a decreased need for supervision.

The Myth of Declining Health, Increased Absenteeism, and Injury

Aging is sometimes associated with wheelchairs, medication, dentures, and infirmity, especially in the minds of employers. In fact, absentee rates are lower for those 50-to-65 years of age than for the 33-to-44 year-old group. And, although, in the year of the study, older workers (55 and older) made up 13.6 percent of the labor force, they accounted for only 9.7 percent of workplace injuries. Also, numerous studies confirm that absenteeism among older workers is lower than among younger workers and that, although many people assume that a large segment of the elderly suffer from serious health problems, only one-fifth of older respondents report debilitation by health problems. Even those who claim to have chronic, controlled health issues are not necessarily limited or bothered by them.

The National Institute on Aging reports that many of the problems of old age are not due to old age at all, but rather to improper care of the body over a lifetime, in other words, to lifestyle. And overwhelmingly, studies show that older workers are more likely to be on the job even when ill than younger people and are generally more dedicated and committed to their jobs than younger workers.

Duke University's Center for Demographic Studies researchers, Kenneth Manton, Larry Corder, and Eric Stallard, periodically survey 20,000 Americans over 65. The survey reported, in "Estimates of Change in Chronic Disability and Institutional Incidence and Prevalence Rates in the U.S. Elderly Population" (1993 and 1995), that disability rates among the elderly declined during the 1980s and into the 1990s. The study showed that even as the number of elderly grew, the number of elderly requiring personal assistance declined 15 percent from 1982 to 1994. The study indicated a substantial possibility for increasing older peoples activity — that disability is not an inevitable part of aging.

Higher Benefit Costs

While the costs of some benefits, primarily insurance, increase as a person ages, most increased costs of benefits associated with age are linked more to seniority and salary. Nonetheless, the Andrus Gerontology Center at the University of Southern California found that male workers 50 and older were more expensive in their health insurance claims than male workers under 50. On the other hand, female employees over 50 were less expensive than female workers under 50, primarily due to the high costs associated with maternity and child-rearing. That study revealed an overall higher rate of insurance claims for workers over 50. On the other hand, older workers generally do not have as many dependents and are often already covered by other health or pension plans, including Medicare.

The Myth That Older Workers Are Expensive to Train

Employers sometimes believe that the elderly are more expensive to train because 1) they are not as bright as young people and 2) they have fewer years to return the employer's investment in training costs.

First, of Americans over the age of 65, only 10 percent show any significant loss of memory, and fewer than half of those are seriously impaired. Most of those losses in mental capacity happen to the very old, not to those in their 60s and 70s, and are due not to age itself but to depression, drug effects, treatable illnesses, or lack of exercise.

Research suggests that older employees value and, therefore, focus not on bits of information but on overall relationships. Older employees bring to their jobs a lifetime of learning that does not have to be taught and which is valuable to themselves,

their co-workers, and their employers. They have an "organizational" memory — they understand why organizations have evolved in the ways they have. Psychological skills, such as the ability to adapt and find life satisfaction, do not vary by age. Although older workers are somewhat more resistant to change, they can and do adapt; in fact, their greater life experiences have nurtured greater long-term resiliency.

Second, older employees tend to stay at their jobs longer than younger workers. Employees over the age of 45 rarely change jobs unless forced to do so by external circumstances. Training and retraining older workers is a fiscally sound investment for employers.

The Belief That Old People Are Unattractive

America is a youth-oriented culture, and many people shun the physical appearances and reminders of aging — wrinkles, baldness, and assumed sexlessness. Many prospective hirees report that they have been hired only after they colored their hair. Physical attractiveness pays. Researchers suggest that managers, employers, and co-workers do not like to be reminded of their own mortality.

Webster's Ninth New Collegiate Dictionary defines stereotype as a "standardized mental picture that is held in common by members of a group and that represents an oversimplified opinion, affective attitude, or judgment." Age researcher Noreen Hale (*The Older Worker*, San Francisco, Jossey-Bass, 1990) contended that "while inaccurate, stereotypes about older workers impel younger workers and the elderly themselves to become fearful of growing old. They can even foster ageism." The nation's preoccupation with youth undermines the contribution of experience and knowledge of older workers.

AGE DISCRIMINATION

The 1967 Age Discrimination in Employment Act (ADEA, PL 90-202) and the 1978 amendment were enacted to promote the employment of older workers based on their ability and to ban discrimination against workers between 40 and 65 years of age. The law made it illegal for employers to discriminate because of age in hiring, discharging, and compensating employees. It also prohibited companies from coercing older workers into accepting incentives to early retirement. In 1987, the act was amended to lift the 65-year-old age limit, making it illegal to discriminate against any worker over 40 years of age and eliminating mandatory retirement at any age.

In 1990, the Supreme Court (*Public Employees Retirement System of Ohio v. Betts*, [492 US 158]) spelled out the terms under which employee benefits may be provided to older workers. In the case before the court, an employee had been denied disability retirement benefits and was forced instead to accept a less generous early retirement benefit because of her age. The court ruled that employers may not withhold benefits from older workers although they may adjust levels of benefits to offset the higher cost of providing those benefits to older workers.

Although age discrimination in the workplace is against the law, it still exists. Some workers begin to experience negative attitudes about their age when they are in their 50s, and by the time they reach 60, age discrimination may be obvious. There are many ways an employer (and fellow employees) can exert pressure on an older employee to retire or resign. Age discrimination may be overt, but it can also be covert, subtle, or even unintentional.

The Pressure to Retire

Corporations base employment decisions not only on how much an employee contributes to the company, but on how much salary and benefits the company must pay the employee *relative to the cost of other employees*. Since salary tends to increase with longevity on the job, older workers usually receive higher wages than younger ones. Thus, if two employees are equally productive, but the older one has a higher salary, a company has an economic incentive to encourage the older worker to take early retirement or to lay him or her off.

Employees in this situation find themselves in a difficult position. Early retirement benefits are almost always less than regular retirement benefits, and they may not provide enough financial support to allow a retiree to live comfortably without working. Finding a new job is more difficult for an older person than for a younger one, and older persons are usually unemployed for longer periods of time than are younger ones. If they refuse to accept early retirement, they may find themselves without jobs at all, perhaps with no pension and no severance pay.

A 1990 federal law, the Older Workers Benefit Protection Act (PL 101-433), which strengthens the Age Discrimination in Employment Act, provides that an employee's waiver of the right to sue for age discrimination, a clause sometimes included in severance packages, is invalid unless "voluntary and knowing."

Suing the Company

Anyone choosing to file an age discrimination suit can expect to face extensive legal fees. In addition, employers are reluctant to hire someone who has filed a discrimination suit against a former employer. Workers caught in this position can suffer emotional and financial damage which may adversely affect them for the rest of their lives.

Nonetheless, more older workers are choosing to sue their employers. Three main classes of issues affecting older workers are at issue: (1) whether "over-qualification" can be grounds (or pretext) for refusing to hire an older person, (2) whether a senior worker's higher salary can be used as a basis for discharge, and (3) what pre-conditions can employers demand from older workers prior to hiring (for example, hiring an older worker with special exemptions from benefits).

However, a number of sources report that an aging population, coupled with low unemployment, strong demand for experienced workers, and managers who are themselves older are making age less of an issue in the marketplace. The Equal Employment Opportunity Commission (EEOC) reported that since 1993, age discrimination complaints have fallen 21 percent and are expected to decline another 35 percent by 2000, providing the economy stays strong. "An increasing percentage of people over 50 is going to have the mix of skills that companies are looking for," reported Michael Karpeles, a Chicago employment-law attorney. He pointed to a factor in their favor: the technology gap between younger and older workers is narrowing as PCs become easier to use.

FEARS ABOUT RETIREMENT

A 1995 Gallup poll of American workers reported that Americans are generally pessimistic about their readiness for retirement and that they are, to a large degree, justified in their fears. Forty-four percent of Americans polled appear to be financially prepared for retirement; the rest are saving less than they could, or should, or are earning too little to save.

While 56 percent of those polled believed that their standard of living will remain the same after retirement, one-third expected their standard of living will be worse than it is today (Figure 4.3). Skepticism about Social Security benefits is nearly universal, with only 16 percent expecting to get all

the benefits they earned and only 29 percent expecting these benefits to be a major source of their retirement income. Only 33 percent were counting on a company pension as a major source of income. Fifty-three percent of workers were concerned they will not be able to retire when they want to. The apprehension was greatest among younger workers and those with the smallest incomes. Those in government jobs were somewhat less concerned than those employed in the private sector or self-employed.

Retirees Speak Out

A 1995 Employee Benefit Research Institute study found that America's retirees thought that retirement was difficult. On average, they believed their lifestyle declined after they left employment. While 18 percent of respondents claimed they had a "very comfortable" lifestyle while working, only 13 percent described their retired life as "very comfortable." Twenty percent of the retirees reported they were "just making ends meet," and 10 percent said they were struggling.

On the other hand, many older persons have worked most of their adult lives and are ready for a period of leisure and freedom. A combination of Social Security benefits, pensions, savings, and investments make retirement possible for many older people who wish to quit working, or must, when they reach retirement age.

HISTORICAL TRENDS AND THE FUTURE OF OLDER WORKERS

The number of men 55 and older participating in the civilian (non-military) labor force has declined in recent years. In 1950, 87 percent of men aged 55 to 64 and over 45 percent of those aged 65 and older participated; by 1997, the percentages dropped to 66 percent and 17 percent, respectively.

On the other hand, the number of women between the ages of 55 and 64 in the labor force increased substantially during the same period, from about 27 percent in 1950 to 49 percent in 1997. The number of women 65 years and older who

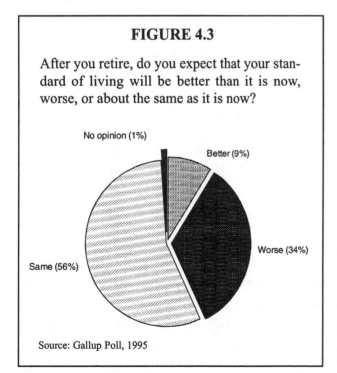

FIGURE 4.3

After you retire, do you expect that your standard of living will be better than it is now, worse, or about the same as it is now?

No opinion (1%)

Better (9%)

Worse (34%)

Same (56%)

Source: Gallup Poll, 1995

worked dropped slightly from 9.7 percent in 1950 to 8.5 percent in 1995.

The U.S. Bureau of Labor Statistics (BLS) predicts that as America's population grows older, so will its workforce. By 2000, the median age of the labor force will increase from about 36 to 39 years. During the early years of the twenty-first century, as the baby boomers mature, the median age will increase dramatically. At the same time, the number of workers between the ages of 16 and 24 will decline.

The role of the older worker in America's future is difficult to predict. As fewer young people enter the labor force, industry may have no choice but to retain or hire older workers. There is a general feeling that today's young workers are less skilled and less educated than their mature counterparts, making older workers more desirable employees. In addition, as the age for receiving Social Security benefits is raised and private pensions become more rare, more elderly may need to work longer.

Why Aging Boomers Will Continue to Work

Many sources believe baby boomers are likely to stay in the labor force longer than their parents did. More-educated workers tend to have longer work lives, and boomers are the most educated generation in U.S. history. A study of workers in Wisconsin, "Older Workers in the 21st Century: Active and Educated, a Case Study" (*Monthly Labor Review*, June, 1996), found a clear association between educational attainment and labor force participation. Although labor force participation among older adults has declined for many years, recent evidence suggests that the trend has slowed and may be reversing, and some experts have projected a modest rise by 2005 and an even greater rise over the following decades. Among explanations offered for the decline in labor force participation among older adults in past decades are:

- Restructuring of the economy has cut the number of blue-collar workers, whose productivity is most likely to decline with advancing age, and

- Job growth is concentrated in white-collar and service occupations, in which age matters less.

Among the factors that will likely cause growth in the proportions of older workers are:

- The proportions of women of all ages in the labor force has been increasing, thus creating a larger pool of older women to work;

- Divorce rates among boomers are higher, so many will not have a spouse's pension income to rely on;

- Higher-educated workers tend to command higher salaries, making a monthly Social Security check a poor substitute for a paycheck. (A typical college-educated worker sacrifices more income by retiring than does a worker who failed to finish high school. Higher education thus creates a financial incentive to remain in the labor force.)

- Intangible benefits, such as greater job satisfaction, and tangible factors, such as cleaner and safer work conditions, serve to bolster labor force participation among better-educated workers.

VOLUNTEERING — THE UNPAID CONTRIBUTION

In recent decades, these needs [of religious and service organizations] have become harder to fill because the women who used to do volunteer work as part of their traditional "at home" roles are instead entering the paid work force in record numbers. To offset this loss in potential volunteers, one particularly promising and growing group comprises the older, retired members of society. Because Americans are retiring at younger ages, and are in better health and better educated than earlier cohorts of retirees, they are very likely to have the time, skills, and energy to contribute to society through volunteer work.—A. Regula Herzog and James N.Morgan,

One of the reasons some older people become depressed and frustrated when they retire from the work force is they sense that they are no longer making meaningful contributions — that they are not an important part of society. But every day, millions of older Americans participate through volunteer work. Older persons make ideal volunteers. They have time in a world where time is at a premium; they have wisdom and experience that years of living can bring; they have compassion from having encountered many of the same problems with which they are helping others cope.

Volunteering by older people is a relatively new phenomenon. Historically, the elderly were seen as the segment of society most in need of care and support. However, as medical technology enables people to live longer, healthier lives and stereotypes about aging crumble, the elderly are now recognized as a valuable asset for every type of volunteer activity. Increased education and affluence among the elderly suggest they may be more able and available for volunteer work.

The Gallup Organization reported, in *Giving and Volunteering in the United States: 1996* (Independent Sector, Washington, DC, 1994), that in 1995, approximately 44.7 percent of persons age 65 to 74 years of age were volunteers; among those over 75 years of age, 33.7 percent did volunteer work. These volunteers worked an average of slightly more than 4 hours per week. Not only does volunteer work benefit society, it also gives the volunteer worker a sense of worth and purpose.

Who Volunteers?

Older people do not usually do volunteer work merely because they have nothing else to do. The strongest influence on volunteer activity is a person's general activity. People with higher levels of education (and consequently, often a higher income) are more likely to be volunteers at all ages, including old age, as are those who report general

TABLE 4.3			
Income	Volunteer rate		
	Total	Men	Women
Under $10,000	9.2	7.5	10.0
$10,000 to $29,999	15.6	12.9	18.0
$30,000 to $49,999	23.4	20.9	26.0
$50,000 or more	27.0	25.1	29.1

Source: "Volunteers in the U.S. Who Donates Their Time," *Monthly Labor Review*, Washington, DC, February 1991

satisfaction with their lives.

The Commonwealth Fund, in its "Americans Over 55 at Work Program" (1994), reported that every fourth older American — 13.7 million in all — volunteers. The proportions of men and women volunteering are nearly equal: 27 percent of women and 25 percent of men. Another 6 million older Americans are willing and able to volunteer, but are not doing so currently.

Volunteering often continues until a very old age. Twenty-three percent of people 75 and older are still volunteering. Further, 90 percent of volunteers believe their work contributes a great deal to their organization, and most feel their own lives are enriched by their volunteer work. Among those who volunteer, 71 percent are satisfied with their lives, compared to 58 percent of those who do not volunteer.

A factor closely linked to volunteer work is income level. In general, the higher one's income, the more likely he or she is to engage in volunteer work. As Table 4.3 demonstrates, the volunteer rate increased from 9.2 percent of those below the annual income level of $10,000 to 27 percent among persons earning $50,000 or more a year.

Well-off persons are better able to donate their time because volunteering often requires some out-of-pocket expenses that the poorer person cannot afford. In the future, the increasing number of baby-boom elderly with greater discretionary income will likely lead to a rise in the participation of the elderly in volunteer work.

The typical elderly volunteer works 6.5 hours per week. The time donated annually by older Americans to voluntary causes is equivalent to 1.1 million full-time employees, nearly 46 times the number of paid staff of the American Red Cross. At the hourly wages paid to workers doing similar jobs, the volunteer activities of older workers are worth $17 billion per year. In comparison, the total annual budget of the Red Cross is approximately $1.4 billion.

Volunteer Programs

Volunteer activities take many forms. Many older volunteers work through their churches and community centers or help friends and neighbors on a regular basis. Others work with established government and private programs. In 1998, 527 Americans aged 50 and older (8 percent of the total number of Peace Corps volunteers) were serving as Peace Corps volunteers in 93 countries throughout the world. Senior volunteers assignments are similar to those of younger volunteers. Age is no handicap to bringing assistance and new knowledge to those needing help, wherever they may be.

Thousands of senior citizens provide volunteer service through national and local non-government programs. In some cities, retired physicians and nurses donate their time to run clinics. Senior volunteers helped the City of Virginia Beach's police department expand its services by maintaining and purging files, checking suspects through the national Crime Information Center, and collecting, collating, and coding reports.

Some metropolitan communities around the country have implemented programs in which senior citizens earn credit for volunteer work. These service credits are earned by performing services for others, ranging from child care to hospital visits. Credits are redeemed when the volunteer needs assistance, which is provided by another volunteer (who in turn receives service credits). Volunteers are thus rewarded for their service, yet there is no expense for either government or private agencies.

The Future of Senior Volunteering

There are indications that more older adults are looking for opportunities to serve. The U.S. Administration on Aging reported that 14 million Americans over 65 (37 percent of the senior population) might be willing to come forward if asked, while 4 million current volunteers say they would like to volunteer more time. Forty percent of those interviewed say the government should be doing more to promote service opportunities. Some older persons cannot afford the minimal cost associated with volunteering, even with the reimbursement for expenses offered by some programs. As the value of older volunteers receives wider recognition, perhaps resources will become available to help more of them in their desire to help others.

CHAPTER V

EDUCATION AND VOTING BEHAVIOR

EDUCATION LEVELS OF OLDER AMERICANS

At the turn of the last century, most children were not educated beyond the eighth grade. Today's elderly over age 85 reflect the limited educational opportunities of children born and reared during the early 1900s. After World War I, the number of young people graduating from high school began to increase, a change reflected in the education level of today's younger elderly. Tomorrow's elderly will mirror the rapid growth in education that occurred after World War II and will have even higher levels of educational attainment.

In 1995, 69 percent of Americans 65 to 74 years old and 57 percent of those 75 years or older had completed at least four years of high school, compared to 87.1 percent of people in the 25- to 34 year-old age. Only 14 percent of Americans 65 to 74 years of age and 11 percent of those 75 years and older had completed four or more years of college, considerably less that the 25 percent of the 25- to 34-year-old group. (See Table 5.1.) Figure 5.1 shows the gradual climb in the

TABLE 5.1

Summary Measures of the Educational Attainment of the Population, Ages 25 and Over: March 1995

(Numbers in thousands)

Age, sex, race, region, residence, and Hispanic origin	Number of persons	Percentage with		
		High school graduate or more	Some college or more	Bachelor's degree or more
All persons	166,438	81.7	47.8	23.0
Age group:				
25 to 34 years old	41,388	87.1	53.2	25.0
35 to 44 years old	42,335	88.4	55.0	26.6
45 to 54 years old	30,693	86.2	53.8	21.9
55 to 64 years old	20,755	77.2	39.9	19.0
65 to 74 years old	18,214	68.9	32.5	14.2
75 years or older	13,053	56.8	26.6	11.2
Sex:				
Male	79,463	81.7	49.8	26.0
Female	86,975	81.6	45.9	20.2
Race:				
White	141,113	83.0	49.0	24.0
Black	18,457	73.8	37.5	13.2
Other	6,869	75.4	49.5	28.5
Hispanic origin:[1]				
Hispanic	14,171	53.4	27.1	9.3
Non–Hispanic	128,707	85.9	51.1	25.4
Marital status:				
Never married	23,926	83.3	52.2	28.2
Married spouse present	105,558	84.6	50.3	25.1
Married spouse absent	6,339	68.8	36.0	12.3
Separated	4,546	71.2	35.7	10.6
Widowed	13,343	59.1	25.8	9.3
Divorced	17,273	84.0	47.1	17.3
Region:				
Northeast	33,580	83.4	46.3	26.3
Midwest	38,534	83.9	46.4	21.7
South	58,380	78.4	45.5	21.2
West	35,945	82.9	54.2	24.2
Metropolitan residence:				
Metropolitan area	132,752	82.9	50.3	25.0
Nonmetropolitan area	33,686	76.9	37.8	14.8

[1]May be of any race.
Source: U.S. Bureau of the Census, Current Population Survey.

Source: *Educational Attainment in the United States: 1995*, U.S. Bureau of the Census, Washington, DC, 1996

number of years of education completed by Americans from 1940 to 1995. By the year 2000, the average person over age 65 is expected to have completed 12.4 years of school.

Continuing to Learn

Recent years have shown a growing number of elderly going back to school — a "graying of the campus." Adult education means more than it ever has. Retired people are the major participants in what was once termed "adult education," that is, in courses that do not lead to a formal degree. A number of the elderly now have the time and funds to seek learning for personal and social reasons. Some universities allow the elderly to audit courses without charge. They are attending numerous courses sponsored by community, senior citizen, and recreation facilities. Increas-

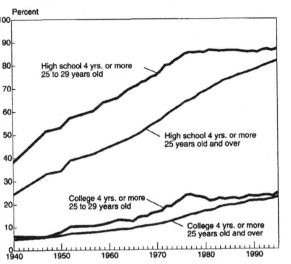

FIGURE 5.1
Percent of Persons Who Have Completed High School or College: Selected Years 1940 to 1995

Source: U.S. Bureau of the Census, Current Population Survey.

Source: *Educational Attainment in the United States: 1995*, U.S. Bureau of the Census, Washington, DC, 1996

TABLE 5.2
Type of employer involvement and number of courses taken by adult education participants [1]
17 years old and older, by selected characteristics of participants: 1991

Characteristics of participants	Adult education participants in the past year, in thousands	Type of employer involvement (percent of adult education participants)						Percentage distribution of the number of adult education courses taken in the past year		
		Any type	Given at place of work	Employer paid some portion	Employer provided course	Employer required course	Employer provided time off	One	Two or three	Four or more
1	2	3	4	5	6	7	8	9	10	11
Total	57,391	64	32	51	38	30	48	43	34	21
Age										
17 to 24 years	7,125	54	28	39	36	26	39	46	30	22
25 to 34 years	17,530	68	31	55	40	36	50	43	34	20
35 to 44 years	17,083	70	35	56	40	30	53	38	36	23
45 to 54 years	8,107	71	39	59	44	32	55	41	36	22
55 to 64 years	4,516	64	30	48	36	27	45	50	32	16
65 years and over	3,031	18	8	12	9	9	12	60	27	9
Sex										
Men	25,923	73	35	58	42	34	56	42	37	19
Women	31,469	57	29	46	35	27	41	44	31	22
Racial/ethnic group										
White, non-Hispanic	47,401	65	32	53	39	30	49	42	35	21
Black, non-Hispanic	4,586	59	36	48	41	38	44	41	31	24
Hispanic	4,032	58	30	39	33	31	43	56	27	14
Other races, non-Hispanic	1,371	56	28	36	30	20	40	39	27	28
Highest level of education completed										
Less than high school diploma	3,437	35	17	21	19	21	19	72	17	8
High school diploma	31,602	62	31	50	36	31	45	47	32	18
Associate degree	2,461	78	47	66	51	39	63	32	40	25
Bachelor's degree or higher	19,891	71	34	57	44	30	56	33	39	26
Labor force status										
In labor force	49,242	72	36	58	43	34	54	41	35	22
Employed	47,143	74	37	60	44	35	56	40	36	22
Unemployed	2,099	35	12	13	12	19	18	56	23	16
Not in labor force	8,149	16	7	11	9	8	10	60	26	12
Annual family income										
$10,000 or less	3,843	39	18	25	24	23	29	59	20	15
$10,001 to $15,000	3,178	52	27	37	24	27	37	53	32	13
$15,001 to $20,000	3,308	57	28	42	35	29	39	46	37	15
$20,001 to $25,000	4,063	67	34	46	37	34	48	48	32	17
$25,001 to $30,000	5,445	58	30	48	38	29	39	44	34	19
$30,001 to $40,000	9,043	68	35	57	43	35	50	42	32	24
$40,001 to $50,000	9,313	67	34	55	42	33	50	45	32	20
$50,001 to $75,000	11,235	72	35	61	43	32	58	39	37	22
More than $75,000	7,963	68	30	54	37	24	53	32	41	26

[1] Adult education is defined as all non-full-time education activities such as part-time college attendance, classes or seminars given by employers, and classes taken for adult literacy purposes, or for recreation and enjoyment.

NOTE.—Data are based upon a sample survey of the civilian noninstitutional population. Because of rounding and survey item nonresponse, details may not add to totals.

SOURCE: U.S. Department of Education, National Center for Education Statistics, "Participation in Adult Education," unpublished data. (This table was prepared July 1991.)

TABLE 5.3

Participants in adult education 17 years old and older, by selected characteristics of participants: 1991

[Numbers in thousands]

Characteristics of participants	Number of adults in population [1]	Ever a participant in adult education [2]		Participated in adult education [2] in past 3 years		Participated in adult education [2] in past year	
		Number	Percent of population	Number	Percent of population	Number	Percent of population
1	2	3	4	5	6	7	8
Total	181,800	97,397	54	69,361	38	57,391	32
Age							
17 to 24 years	21,688	9,240	43	8,756	40	7,125	33
25 to 34 years	47,244	27,325	58	22,773	48	17,530	37
35 to 44 years	38,565	25,043	65	19,581	51	17,083	44
45 to 54 years	25,375	14,755	58	9,351	37	8,107	32
55 to 64 years	19,967	10,101	51	5,150	26	4,516	23
65 years and over	28,960	10,934	38	3,750	13	3,031	10
Sex							
Men	82,154	42,163	51	29,945	36	25,923	32
Women	99,646	55,234	55	39,415	40	31,469	32
Racial/ethnic group							
White, non-Hispanic	143,144	80,099	56	56,715	40	47,401	33
Black, non-Hispanic	20,141	8,213	41	5,552	28	4,586	23
Hispanic	13,804	6,905	50	5,396	39	4,032	29
Other races, non-Hispanic	4,711	2,180	46	1,698	36	1,371	29
Highest level of education completed							
Less than high school diploma ...	28,306	7,337	26	4,127	15	3,437	12
High school diploma	110,384	58,135	53	39,403	36	31,602	29
Associate degree	5,034	3,949	78	3,191	63	2,461	49
Bachelor's degree or higher	38,076	27,976	73	22,640	59	19,891	52
Labor force status							
In labor force	125,440	73,513	59	58,078	46	49,242	39
Employed	115,620	69,421	60	55,093	48	47,143	41
Unemployed	9,820	4,092	42	2,985	30	2,099	21
Not in labor force	56,361	23,884	42	11,283	20	8,149	14
Annual family income							
$10,000 or less	27,504	10,706	39	5,766	21	3,843	14
$10,001 to $15,000	15,465	7,014	45	4,426	29	3,178	21
$15,001 to $20,000	16,117	6,335	39	4,183	26	3,308	21
$20,001 to $25,000	16,092	7,666	48	5,343	33	4,063	25
$25,001 to $30,000	17,973	9,309	52	6,570	37	5,445	30
$30,001 to $40,000	26,110	14,922	57	10,313	39	9,043	35
$40,001 to $50,000	21,303	13,270	62	10,526	49	9,313	44
$50,001 to $75,000	24,540	16,629	68	12,971	53	11,235	46
More than $75,000	16,695	11,546	69	9,263	55	7,963	48

[1] Persons 17 years of age and over on the date of the survey.
[2] Adult education is defined as all non-full-time education activities such as part-time college attendance, classes or seminars given by employers, and classes taken for adult literacy purposes, or for recreation and enjoyment.

NOTE.—Data are based upon a sample survey of the civilian noninstitutional population. Because of rounding and survey item nonresponse, details may not add to totals.

SOURCE: U.S. Department of Education, National Center for Education Statistics, "Participation in Adult Education," unpublished data. (This table was prepared July 1991.)

ingly, the elderly are also attending two- and four-year institutions for undergraduate and graduate degrees as well as auditing courses for non-credit.

The reasons for returning for additional schooling have changed as well. While the elderly once might have taken courses only for pleasure, today's older students may be in school for more practical reasons as well. Many older people are retraining for new careers or to remain competitive in existing occupations. Homemakers "displaced" by divorce or widowhood are often seeking careers. Table 5.2 shows that among persons 65 years of age and older, in 1991 (the last data available), 38 percent participated in adult education at some time, and 13 percent had participated in the past three years. Table 5.3 shows that among those 65 and older, in the year preceding the 1991 study, 18 percent of persons participating in adult education did so with employer involvement of some kind (offering classes at job site, paying for courses, requiring training, giving time off for courses).

VOTING BEHAVIOR

Americans are more likely to vote as they get older. Retirement often means more leisure time to

TABLE 5.4

(Numbers in thousands)

Characteristics	Voting-age population	Registered		Voted	
		Number	Percent	Number	Percent
GENDER AND AGE					
Both sexes	193,651	127,661	65.9	105,017	54.2
18 - 20 yrs	10,785	4,919	45.6	3,366	31.2
21 - 24 yrs	13,865	7,099	51.2	4,630	33.4
25 - 44 yrs	83,393	51,606	61.9	41,050	49.2
45 - 64 yrs	53,721	39,489	73.5	34,615	64.4
65 yrs and over	31,888	24,547	77.0	21,356	67.0
Male	92,632	59,672	64.4	48,909	52.8
18 - 20 yrs	5,372	2,294	42.7	1,521	28.3
21 - 24 yrs	6,901	3,417	49.5	2,140	31.0
25 - 44 yrs	41,005	24,453	59.6	19,211	46.8
45 - 64 yrs	25,945	18,829	72.6	16,530	63.7
65 yrs and over	13,408	10,680	79.7	9,507	70.9
Female	101,020	67,989	67.3	56,108	55.5
18 - 20 yrs	5,413	2,625	48.5	1,845	34.1
21 - 24 yrs	6,964	3,681	52.9	2,490	35.8
25 - 44 yrs	42,388	27,153	64.1	21,840	51.5
45 - 64 yrs	27,776	20,662	74.4	18,085	65.1
65 yrs and over	18,480	13,867	75.0	11,849	64.1

Source: *Voting and Registration: 1996*, U.S. Bureau of the Census, Washington, DC, 1997

devote to community affairs such as politics. In addition, dependence on Social Security funds by many older people gives them a major personal stake in how the government is run. In 1998, 46 percent of Americans aged 50 and over — 32 million people — are members of the American Association of Retired Persons (AARP), sometimes considered the most powerful lobby on Capitol Hill because of its forceful, non-partisan political activities.

The AARP does not endorse any particular candidate but questions candidates on issues such as health care, Social Security and Medicare, long-term care, pension reform, and age discrimination. A candidate's position on each issue is made available to members of AARP, making these older citizens an informed and potentially formidable force in a candidate's bid for election.

Voting participation increases with age. The U.S. Census Bureau found that in the 1996 presidential election, among those 21 to 24 years old, 33.4 percent reported voting. Among the 25- to 44-year-old group, 49.2 percent reported voting; and among those 45 to 64 years of age, 64.4 percent voted. Of those persons over 65, 67 percent voted, twice the participation rate of the youngest voters. (See Table 5.4.)

Although fewer people voted in the 1994 congressional elections (when there was no presidential election), as is traditionally the case, the results were similar, with increased voting among the older Americans. In the 1994 congressional elections, 76 percent of persons older than 65 registered to vote, and 61 percent actually voted, the highest percent of all age groups. (See Figure 5.2.)

71

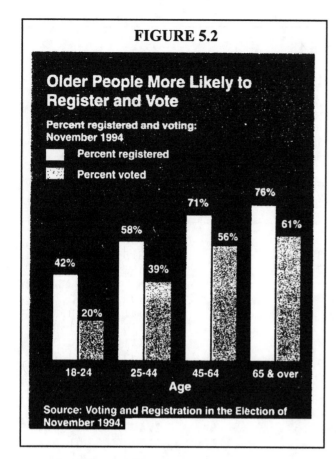

FIGURE 5.2

Older People More Likely to Register and Vote

Percent registered and voting:
November 1994

☐ Percent registered

▨ Percent voted

Source: Voting and Registration in the Election of November 1994.

With the growing number of elderly and their increasing education and financial resources, voting participation will likely increase. Older Americans are expected to become an even more powerful voting bloc as the aging population swells.

Political Party Affiliation

The Center for Political Studies, a political think-tank, has found differences in political party affiliation based on age. Those persons 64 years and older show a firmer identification with the two major American political parties — Democratic and Republican — than younger Americans. Only half of those younger than 64 years reported attachment to one of those two parties, with a considerable population considering themselves "independent." Among the older citizens, fully three-quarters considered themselves either Democrat or Republican.

This may reflect either a greater flexibility among younger voters or less firmly committed opinions and shorter voting histories. It may also indicate a true shift in attitudes towards political parties among American voters. Voters may become more committed to a particular political party as they age, simply due to maturation. On the other hand, today's younger people may simply have fundamentally different attitudes towards political parties; as they age, they may remain less connected to either of the two major political parties, a trend that could have important political implications.

CHAPTER VI

GENERAL HEALTH AND HEALTH PROBLEMS

One of the fears many people have about growing older is facing the possible loss of mental and physical abilities. Although the human body progressively declines with age, the rate and amount of decline are individual processes. One person may be afflicted with arthritis and senility at age 65, while another is vigorous and active at 90. Nonetheless, overall, older people have more health problems and require more health care than younger ones.

LIFE EXPECTANCY

Life expectancy for all Americans has increased dramatically since the turn of the century. The average life span in the United States in 1900 was no more than 40 years. This low figure was based upon a high incidence of infant and early childhood mortality. A person surviving childhood could expect to live more than 40 years. By current estimates, someone born in 1996 will live almost twice that long, 76.1 years, up from 75.8 in 1995.

Women Live Longer Than Men

In this century, women have lived longer than men and probably will continue to do so, although the gap is narrowing. The National Center for Health Statistics reported that, in 1996, a man could, on

---

TABLE 6.1

Death rates for selected causes of death: United States, 1994–95

[Data are based on the National Vital Statistics System]

Cause of death	Age-adjusted death rate 1994	Age-adjusted death rate 1995	Crude death rate 1994	Crude death rate 1995	Rank 1994	Rank 1995
	Deaths per 100,000 resident population					
All causes	507.4	503.9	875.4	880.0	. . .	. . .
Diseases of heart	140.4	138.3	281.3	280.7	1	1
Ischemic heart disease	91.4	89.5	184.9	183.2	. . .	. . .
Cerebrovascular diseases	26.5	26.7	58.9	60.1	3	3
Malignant neoplasms	131.5	129.9	205.2	204.9	2	2
Respiratory system	40.1	39.7	59.4	59.5	. . .	. . .
Breast[1]	21.3	21.0	32.7	32.6	. . .	. . .
Chronic obstructive pulmonary diseases	21.0	20.8	39.0	39.2	4	4
Pneumonia and influenza	13.0	12.9	31.3	31.6	6	6
Chronic liver disease and cirrhosis	7.9	7.6	9.8	9.6	10	10
Diabetes mellitus	12.9	13.3	21.8	22.6	7	7
Human immunodeficiency virus infection	15.4	15.6	16.2	16.4	8	8
Unintentional injuries	30.3	30.5	35.1	35.5	5	5
Motor vehicle crashes	16.1	16.3	16.3	16.5	. . .	. . .
Suicide	11.2	11.2	12.0	11.9	9	9
Homicide and legal intervention	10.3	9.4	9.6	8.7	11	12
Firearm injuries	15.1	13.9	14.8	13.7	. . .	. . .

. . . Category not applicable.
[1]Female only.

NOTES: Code numbers for cause of death are based on the International Classification of Diseases, Ninth Revision, described in Appendix II, table V. Categories for the coding and classification of human immunodeficiency virus infection were introduced in the United States beginning with data year 1987.

SOURCE: Centers for Disease Control and Prevention, National Center for Health Statistics. Vital statistics of the United States, vol II, mortality, part A, for data years 1994–95. Washington: Public Health Service; Data computed by the Division of Health and Utilization Analysis from data compiled by the Division of Vital Statistics and table 1.

average, expect to live 73 years and a woman, 79 years. Life expectancy for Whites (76.8 years) continued to exceed that of Blacks (70.3 years).

Reasons for Increased Life Expectancy

During the first half of the century, increased longevity was a result of reducing or eliminating many diseases that killed infants and children and improved methods of delivering babies, so that more people survived to middle age. In recent years, increased life expectancy is attributed not only to declining infant mortality, but also to decreasing mortality from chronic diseases among the middle-aged and elderly due to new medical knowledge, healthier diet and exercise habits, and life-sustaining technology. In other words, old people are living to be older.

LEADING CAUSES OF DEATH

Seven out of every 10 people die from heart disease, cancer, or stroke. The leading causes of death and the death rate from each cause in 1995 are shown in Table 6.1. (Malignant neoplasms refer to cancer, and cerebrovascular diseases include strokes.)

"Still Number One" — Heart Disease

Coronary heart disease (CHD) kills more Americans than any other disease. The American Heart Association reported that CHD caused 481,287 deaths in the United States in 1995 — 50.9 percent male and 49.1 percent female. More than 13.9 million people alive today have a history of heart attack, angina, or both. This year, approximately 1.1 million Americans will have heart attacks, and about one-third of them will die. About 85 percent of people who die of heart attacks are age 65 or older. Blacks are more likely to suffer heart-related diseases and deaths than

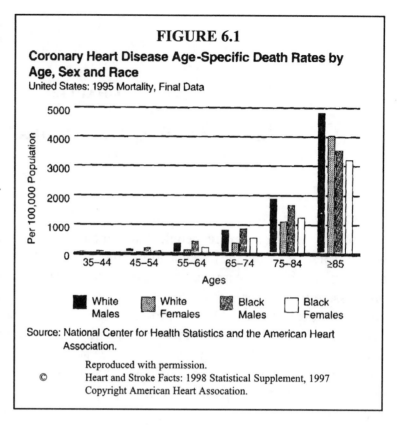

FIGURE 6.1

Coronary Heart Disease Age-Specific Death Rates by Age, Sex and Race

United States: 1995 Mortality, Final Data

Source: National Center for Health Statistics and the American Heart Association.

Whites. In 1995, CHD death rates were 124.4 per 100,000 for White males and 133.1 per 100,000 for Black males. White females had a CHD death rate of 60.3 per 100,000 and Black females, 81.6 per 100,000. Studies show that the risk of death from heart disease is much greater among the least-educated than for the most-educated people.

Women have less coronary heart disease than men until they reach age 65, at which point their numbers approach those of men. The risk of dying from heart disease increases greatly after age 65, and the death rate more than doubles for each age group between 65 and 85. (See Figure 6.1.)

Although heart disease is still the number one killer, the past four decades have shown a marked decline in death rates for heart disease. Over just the past 15 years, the death rate for coronary heart disease has declined 40 percent. Several factors account for the decline, primarily better control of hypertension and cholesterol and changes in exercise and nutrition. Also important is the expanding use of trained mobile emergency personnel (paramedics) in most urban areas. The

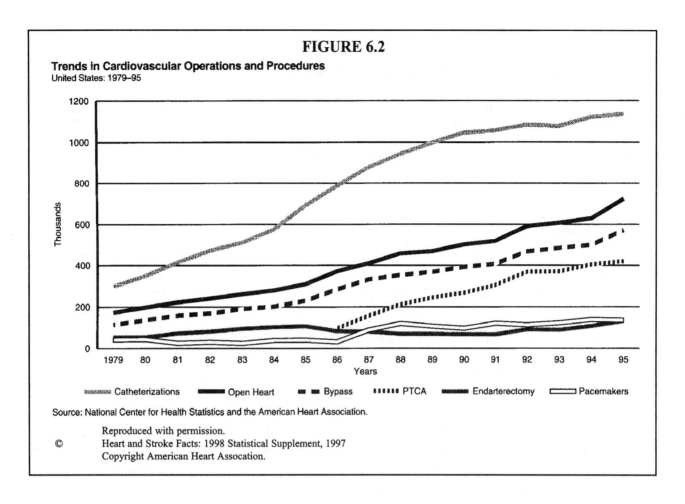

FIGURE 6.2

Trends in Cardiovascular Operations and Procedures
United States: 1979–95

Y-axis: Thousands (0, 200, 400, 600, 800, 1000, 1200)
X-axis: Years (1979, 80, 81, 82, 83, 84, 85, 86, 87, 88, 89, 90, 91, 92, 93, 94, 95)

Legend: Catheterizations — Open Heart — Bypass — PTCA — Endarterectomy — Pacemakers

Source: National Center for Health Statistics and the American Heart Association.

generalized use of CPR (cardiopulmonary resuscitation) and new emergency medications also increase the likelihood of one's surviving an initial heart attack.

Increased use of procedures such as heart transplant, cardiac catheterization, coronary by-pass surgery, pacemakers, and angioplasty have also contributed to extending the lives of those afflicted with heart disease (Figure 6.2). As importantly, these procedures usually improve the quality of life of the individual who typically suffers less pain and debility after the procedure. In 1998, the cost of cardiovascular disease, including coronary heart disease, congestive heart failure, high blood pressure, and "other" heart diseases, is estimated at $175.3 billion. This includes direct costs, such as the cost of physicians and other professionals, hospital and nursing home services, medications, and home health; and indirect costs, such as lost productivity resulting from illness and death. (See Table 6.2.)

Most recent studies indicate that post-menopausal women not only suffer from heart disease as frequently as their male counterparts, but those with the disease are more than twice as likely to die from an initial heart attack than men. The reasons for this are not known at this time. Some observers have suggested, however, that because of the misconception that women do not experience the disease as frequently, their complaints are not taken as seriously as those of men. Also, physiologic factors, such as hormone effects and small blood vessel size, which may increase difficulty during surgical procedures, may play a role in women's succumbing to heart disease. Research on heart disease has historically been done on male subjects, but a growing number of studies include women.

Cancer

The likelihood of developing cancer, the second leading cause of death among the elderly,

TABLE 6.2

Estimated Direct and Indirect Costs of Cardiovascular Diseases and Stroke
United States: 1998

	Heart Disease**	Coronary Heart Disease	Stroke	Hypertensive Disease	Congestive Heart Failure	Total Cardiovascular Disease*
Direct Costs						
Hospital/Nursing Home	73.8	39.3	23.3	6.8	14.5	119.9
Physicians/Other Professionals	13.3	7.5	2.1	7.4	1.4	25.9
Drugs	6.1	2.9	0.3	7.5	1.0	14.8
Home Health/Other Medical Durables	4.7	1.4	2.7	1.4	2.0	10.4
Total Expenditures*	**$97.9**	**$51.1**	**$28.3**	**$23.3**	**$18.8**	**$171.1**
Indirect Costs						
Lost Productivity/Morbidity	15.7	6.6	5.1	4.8	NA	25.2
Lost Productivity/Mortality*	61.7	37.9	9.9	3.6	1.3	77.9
Grand Total*	**$175.3**	**$95.6**	**$43.3**	**$31.7**	**$20.2**	**$274.2**

* Totals may not add up due to rounding and overlap.

** This category includes coronary heart disease, congestive heart failure and part of hypertensive disease as well as other "heart" diseases.

\# Lost future earnings of persons who will die in 1998 discounted at 2.5 percent.

NA indicates not available.

Source: Direct costs were calculated by Thomas A. Hodgson, chief economist and acting director, Division of Health and Utilization Analysis, OAEHP, NCHS, CDC. Estimates of indirect costs were made by Thomas J. Thom, statistician in the division of Epidemiology and Clinical Applications, NHLBI.

increases every decade after the age of 30. In 1995, among those 65 to 74, there were 306.1 cancer deaths per 100,000 persons, for those 75 to 84, 372.7 per 100,000, and for those 85 and over, 294.0 per 100,000 persons (Table 6.3). Success in the cure of certain tumors (Hodgkin's disease and certain forms of leukemia) has been offset by the rise in rates of other cancers, such as breast and lung cancers. Progress in treating cancer has largely been related to screenings, early diagnoses, and new drug therapies.

Strokes

Strokes ("brain attacks" or cerebrovascular disease) are the third leading cause of death and the primary cause of disability among the elderly. Strokes killed 157,991 people in 1995 — 39 percent males and 61 percent females. About 4 million stroke survivors are alive today. The incidence of stroke is strongly related to age; over 55 years of age, the incidence of stroke more than doubles each successive decade of age (Figure 6.3). The American Heart Association calculated the costs of stroke in 1998 at $43.3 billion, which includes direct costs of physicians, hospitals, nursing services, and medications, as well as indirect costs, such as lost productivity.

GENERAL HEALTH OF OLDER AMERICANS

The National Center for Health Statistics (NCHS) reported that, in 1994, 25.6 percent of noninstitutionalized people 65 to 74 years old and 31.3 percent of those older than 75 described their health as fair or poor. (See Table 6.4.) The likelihood of being disabled increases with age. The Bureau of the Census reports that, in 1994, 34.1 percent of those 65 to 74 had some degree of functional disability. One-tenth of those 65 to 74 had limitations so severe as to make them unable to carry on any major activity. Among those over 75, 44.1 percent suffered limitations due to chronic conditions, and 10.7 percent were limited in their major activities. (See Table 6.5.)

Chronic conditions are the burden of old age. At the start of the century, acute conditions (severe illnesses of limited duration, such as infections)

TABLE 6.3

Death rates for malignant neoplasms of respiratory system, according to sex, detailed race, Hispanic origin, and age: United States, selected years 1950–95

[Data are based on the National Vital Statistics System]

Sex, race, Hispanic origin, and age	1950[1]	1960[1]	1970	1980	1985	1990	1992	1993	1994	1995	1993–95[2]
All persons	Deaths per 100,000 resident population										
All ages, age adjusted	12.8	19.2	28.4	36.4	39.1	41.4	40.8	40.8	40.1	39.7	40.2
All ages, crude	14.1	22.2	34.2	47.9	53.5	58.9	59.3	59.8	59.4	59.5	59.6
Under 25 years	0.1	0.1	0.1	0.1	0.1	0.1	0.1	0.1	0.1	0.1	0.1
25–34 years	0.9	1.1	1.0	0.8	0.8	0.8	0.7	0.7	0.7	0.7	0.7
35–44 years	5.1	7.3	11.6	9.6	8.2	7.2	7.1	6.6	6.5	6.4	6.5
45–54 years	22.9	32.0	46.2	56.5	53.1	48.8	44.8	42.9	40.9	39.8	41.1
55–64 years	55.2	81.5	116.2	144.3	159.8	166.5	159.8	158.9	153.5	148.2	153.5
65–74 years	69.3	117.2	174.6	243.1	270.3	298.1	302.9	306.1	305.9	306.1	306.0
75–84 years	69.3	102.9	175.1	251.4	292.4	344.1	357.0	363.3	367.4	372.7	367.9
85 years and over	64.0	79.1	113.5	184.5	205.0	252.9	268.2	280.8	278.7	294.0	284.7
Male											
All ages, age adjusted	21.3	34.8	50.6	59.7	60.7	61.0	58.5	58.1	56.5	55.3	56.6
All ages, crude	23.1	38.5	57.0	71.9	75.6	78.3	76.6	76.8	75.4	74.6	75.6
Under 25 years	0.2	0.1	0.1	0.1	0.1	0.1	0.1	0.1	0.1	0.1	0.1
25–34 years	1.3	1.7	1.5	1.0	0.9	1.0	0.8	0.9	0.8	0.8	0.8
35–44 years	8.1	11.4	17.0	12.6	10.6	9.1	8.6	8.3	8.0	7.6	8.0
45–54 years	39.3	54.7	72.1	79.8	71.0	63.0	57.7	54.6	51.9	49.9	52.1
55–64 years	94.2	150.2	202.3	223.8	233.6	232.6	217.0	216.0	206.8	196.1	206.3
65–74 years	116.3	221.7	340.7	422.0	432.5	447.3	439.8	441.2	434.5	432.4	436.0
75–84 years	105.1	188.5	354.2	511.5	558.9	594.4	587.5	584.8	576.7	573.4	578.2
85 years and over	95.4	132.2	215.3	386.3	457.3	538.0	545.5	559.7	556.1	567.6	561.2
Female											
All ages, age adjusted	4.6	5.2	10.1	18.3	22.5	26.2	27.1	27.2	27.3	27.5	27.3
All ages, crude	5.2	6.2	12.6	25.2	32.6	40.4	42.8	43.7	44.2	45.1	44.3
Under 25 years	0.1	0.1	0.1	0.1	0.1	0.0	0.0	0.1	*	0.0	0.0
25–34 years	0.6	0.6	0.6	0.6	0.7	0.6	0.6	0.6	0.6	0.7	0.6
35–44 years	2.3	3.4	6.5	6.8	5.8	5.4	5.6	5.0	4.9	5.1	5.0
45–54 years	6.7	10.1	22.2	34.8	36.2	35.3	32.5	31.6	30.4	30.1	30.7
55–64 years	15.4	17.0	38.9	74.5	94.5	107.6	108.4	107.3	105.3	104.8	105.8
65–74 years	26.7	26.2	45.6	106.1	145.3	181.7	195.3	199.2	203.6	205.0	202.6
75–84 years	38.8	36.5	56.5	98.0	135.7	194.5	216.0	226.3	236.4	245.1	236.0
85 years and over	42.0	45.2	56.5	96.3	104.2	142.8	160.8	173.9	171.8	187.5	177.8
White male											
All ages, age adjusted	21.6	34.6	49.9	58.0	58.7	59.0	56.7	56.3	54.8	53.7	54.9
All ages, crude	24.1	39.6	58.3	73.4	77.6	81.0	79.5	79.7	78.5	77.8	78.7
45–54 years	39.1	53.0	67.6	74.3	65.5	57.9	52.9	49.5	47.4	46.0	47.6
55–64 years	95.9	149.8	199.3	215.0	223.3	222.5	208.0	208.5	199.4	188.2	198.7
65–74 years	119.4	225.1	344.8	418.4	425.2	438.2	431.7	432.4	427.0	426.1	428.5
75–84 years	109.1	191.9	360.7	516.1	561.7	593.6	585.0	579.6	571.8	569.2	573.5
85 years and over	102.7	133.9	221.8	391.5	463.8	540.4	549.2	559.8	552.3	565.3	559.2
Black male											
All ages, age adjusted	16.9	36.6	60.8	82.0	87.7	91.0	86.7	86.0	82.8	80.5	83.1
All ages, crude	14.3	31.1	51.2	70.8	75.5	77.8	74.7	74.7	72.5	71.2	72.8
45–54 years	41.1	75.0	123.5	142.8	133.1	125.0	114.9	113.5	104.2	96.4	104.4
55–64 years	78.8	161.8	250.3	340.3	373.2	377.5	346.4	331.1	322.2	315.0	322.7
65–74 years	65.2	184.6	322.2	499.4	565.9	613.4	599.9	608.2	581.1	573.9	587.6
75–84 years	- - -	126.3	290.6	499.6	579.0	669.9	683.6	711.2	708.1	695.3	704.7
85 years and over	- - -	110.3	154.4	337.7	409.7	535.7	552.6	596.8	623.2	607.3	609.2
American Indian or Alaskan Native male[3]											
All ages, age adjusted	- - -	- - -	- - -	23.2	28.4	29.7	31.7	31.0	31.1	32.7	31.6
All ages, crude	- - -	- - -	- - -	15.7	19.6	21.1	23.1	23.1	23.0	25.1	23.7
45–54 years	- - -	- - -	- - -	*	*	26.6	28.7	26.6	22.6	28.4	25.9
55–64 years	- - -	- - -	- - -	80.0	95.7	106.8	134.9	100.2	119.8	114.3	111.5
65–74 years	- - -	- - -	- - -	221.2	234.6	206.7	208.7	233.4	290.8	258.7	261.1
75–84 years	- - -	- - -	- - -	*	281.8	371.4	371.4	418.6	220.1	368.6	335.1
85 years and over	- - -	- - -	- - -	*	*	*	*	*	*	*	222.3

Source: *Health, United States, 1996-97*, National Center for Health Statistics, Hyattsville, MD, 1997

were predominant and often deadly. With the development of antibiotics and cures for many acute infectious diseases, people are living much longer, and chronic conditions are now the prevalent health problem for the elderly.

More than 4 out of 5 persons ages 65 and over have at least one chronic (long-lasting or often recurring) illness, and many have multiple chronic conditions. Leading chronic conditions of people with disabilities are arthritis, back problems, heart disease, lung or respiratory disease, and hypertension (Table 6.6). Older men are more likely than women to have acute illnesses that are life threatening, while older women are more likely to have chronic conditions that cause physical limitation over a long term.

The elderly use professional medical equipment and supplies, dental care, prescription drugs, and vision aids more than people under age 65 and are hospitalized more than younger people. The average length of hospitalization for an elderly person has declined over the years from 12.1 days per stay in 1964 to 8.4 days in 1990 and 7.8 days in 1994, but it is still significantly longer than for younger people (Table 6.7). Shorter stays are partly due to the federal government's introduction of DRGs (Diagnosis Related Groups — categories of illnesses that prescribe/allow for set duration of treatment. (See Chapter IX.) DRGs encourage hospitals to release patients as quickly as possible. Shorter stays are also due to the increasing use of outpatient procedures instead of hospital admission for those procedures.

The aging of the American population increases demand for physician care. In 1994, those over age 65 contacted physicians 11.3 times

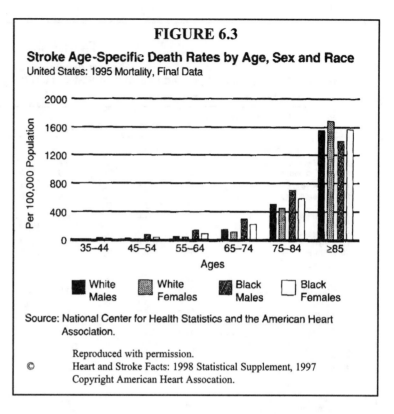

FIGURE 6.3

Stroke Age-Specific Death Rates by Age, Sex and Race
United States: 1995 Mortality, Final Data

Source: National Center for Health Statistics and the American Heart Association.

per year, far more often than for younger people (Table 6.8). Experts predict that in the year 2000, older Americans will visit the doctor almost 296 million times, and by 2030, the number will reach an estimated 556 million medical visits per year (Table 6.9).

SOCIOECONOMIC DIFFERENCES

Income or socioeconomic status (SES) is directly related to the onset of chronic illness and

---

TABLE 6.4

Respondent-assessed health status, according to selected characteristics: United States, 1987–94

[Data are based on household interviews of a sample of the civilian noninstitutionalized population]

Characteristic	Percent with fair or poor health							
	1987	1988	1989	1990	1991	1992	1993	1994
Total[1,2]	9.5	9.4	9.1	8.9	9.3	9.7	9.7	9.6
Age								
Under 15 years.........................	2.4	2.7	2.4	2.4	2.5	2.8	2.8	2.9
Under 5 years	2.6	3.4	2.6	2.9	2.6	2.9	3.3	2.9
5–14 years	2.3	2.4	2.3	2.2	2.4	2.8	2.6	2.9
15–44 years	5.4	5.5	5.6	5.4	5.8	6.4	6.6	6.4
45–64 years	17.4	17.1	16.1	16.0	16.7	17.2	17.1	16.6
65 years and over	30.8	29.4	28.5	27.7	29.0	28.7	28.0	28.0
65–74 years..........................	28.2	26.6	26.3	25.1	26.0	25.7	25.0	25.6
75 years and over	34.9	33.8	32.0	31.7	33.6	33.2	32.4	31.3

Source: *Health, United States, 1996-97*, National Center for Health Statistics, Hyattsville, MD, 1997

TABLE 6.5

Limitation of activity caused by chronic conditions, according to selected characteristics: United States, 1990 and 1994

[Data are based on household interviews of a sample of the civilian noninstitutionalized population]

Characteristic	Total with limitation of activity		Limited but not in major activity		Limited in amount or kind of major activity		Unable to carry on major activity	
	1990	1994	1990	1994	1990	1994	1990	1994
	Percent of population							
Total[1,2]	12.9	14.3	4.1	4.4	5.0	5.6	3.9	4.4
Age								
Under 15 years	4.7	6.4	1.2	1.6	3.1	4.1	0.4	0.7
Under 5 years	2.2	3.1	0.6	0.8	1.0	1.6	0.6	0.7
5–14 years	6.1	8.1	1.6	2.0	4.1	5.4	0.4	0.7
15–44 years	8.5	10.1	2.6	3.1	3.5	4.0	2.4	3.0
45–64 years	21.8	22.6	5.7	5.5	7.5	7.9	8.6	9.2
65 years and over	37.5	38.2	15.4	15.6	11.9	11.9	10.2	10.7
65–74 years	33.7	34.1	13.2	13.2	9.9	10.0	10.6	10.8
75 years and over	43.3	44.1	18.8	18.9	14.9	14.5	9.6	10.7
Sex and age								
Male[1]	12.9	14.3	3.8	4.2	4.7	5.3	4.4	4.8
Under 15 years	5.5	7.6	1.4	1.8	3.6	5.0	0.5	0.8
15–44 years	8.4	10.1	2.3	2.8	3.5	3.9	2.7	3.4
45–64 years	21.4	21.3	4.7	4.6	6.6	6.9	10.1	9.9
65–74 years	34.0	34.7	13.0	13.3	8.4	8.5	12.7	12.8
75 years and over	38.8	40.7	20.3	21.6	10.2	10.2	8.3	8.9
Female[1]	13.0	14.3	4.3	4.6	5.3	5.7	3.4	4.0
Under 15 years	3.9	5.1	1.0	1.4	2.5	3.1	0.4	0.6
15–44 years	8.7	10.1	2.9	3.5	3.6	4.0	2.2	2.6
45–64 years	22.2	23.9	6.6	6.4	8.4	8.8	7.2	8.6
65–74 years	33.5	33.5	13.4	13.2	11.1	11.2	8.9	9.2
75 years and over	46.0	46.2	17.9	17.3	17.7	17.1	10.4	11.7
Race and age								
White[1]	12.8	14.0	4.2	4.4	5.0	5.5	3.6	4.0
Under 15 years	4.7	6.0	1.3	1.5	3.0	3.9	0.4	0.6
15–44 years	8.5	10.0	2.7	3.3	3.6	4.1	2.2	2.7
45–64 years	21.2	21.9	5.8	5.6	7.6	7.8	7.9	8.5
65–74 years	33.2	33.2	13.4	13.3	9.8	9.8	10.0	10.2
75 years and over	42.9	43.5	19.2	19.0	14.7	14.2	9.0	10.3
Black[1]	15.5	18.0	3.8	4.2	5.3	6.7	6.5	7.1
Under 15 years	5.3	8.5	1.2	1.9	3.4	5.6	0.7	1.0
15–44 years	9.4	11.4	2.2	2.6	3.4	4.1	3.9	4.8
45–64 years	28.1	30.7	5.7	5.3	7.7	9.5	14.8	15.8
65–74 years	41.6	44.4	12.4	13.8	11.5	13.1	17.6	17.6
75 years and over	50.9	52.5	16.2	18.5	17.6	18.1	17.0	15.9

Source: *Health, United States, 1996-97*, National Center for Health Statistics, Hyattsville, MD, 1997

disability in later years. The more educated and affluent elderly are more likely to be healthy longer. Americans of the lowest SES experience more chronic illness such as cancer, heart attacks, strokes, and lung disease. These illnesses are not as common in upper-SES elderly until after the age of 75. The likelihood of experiencing an acute condition was also greater at the lower SES levels. Table 6.10 shows the health status of the elderly by income level and the incidence of both acute and chronic conditions.

The number of chronic conditions suffered by an older person also varies by SES. Those in the highest SES group reported fewer simultaneous chronic conditions and less limitation of activity than those in the lowest SES.

Possible explanations for the health differences among elderly of different SES include the following:

• A higher incidence of risk behaviors (smoking, high-fat diet, more sedentary lifestyle) among the lower SES;

• Greater occupational stresses and hazards in the work environments of the lowest SES;

• Acute and chronic stress among the lower SES;

• Decreased access to medical care among the lower SES.

79

CHRONIC PHYSICAL PROBLEMS OF THE ELDERLY

Physical ailments can strike anyone at any age, but some illnesses and conditions are more common among the elderly. Chronic conditions account for most deterioration experienced with aging and are the major cause of high use of medical resources. Figure 6.4 shows the prevalence of the top 10 conditions suffered by the aging.

Arthritis

Arthritis is an "umbrella term" for a family of more than 100 separate diseases that affect the body's connective tissue. In common usage, it refers to inflammation of the joints. Arthritis is not a disease solely of the elderly, but its prevalence increases with age. Arthritis affects 1 out of 7 people; for those over 65, almost half will experience some form of this joint disease, although impairment ranges from mild occasional stiffness to crippling.

The greatest consequence of arthritis is loss of mobility and deformity in the affected tissues or joints. Patients diagnosed with osteoarthritis (a degenerative joint disease) generally experience some loss in ability to perform daily functions, such as household chores, shopping, running errands, and leisure activities. Patients with

rheumatoid arthritis (inflammation of primarily the joint lining) often experience a loss in every activity, and the losses are more severe. Arthritis ranks second only to heart disease as a cause of disability payments.

Osteoporosis

Osteoporosis, a bone disorder associated with decrease in bone mass and resulting susceptibility to fracture, has only recently been recognized as a fairly common condition of old age, especially among women. About 25 million Americans, 80 percent of them women, have some form of osteoporosis. According to the National Osteoporosis Foundation, osteoporosis is the leading cause of bone fractures — approximately

---

TABLE 6.6

Physical Conditions That Cause Disabilities
Conditions most frequently cited by persons 15 years old and over with a functional, ADL, or IADL limitation as a cause of the limitation(s): 1991-92

Condition	Number with condition (millions)
Arthritis or rheumatism	7.2
Back or spine problems	5.7
Heart trouble	4.6
Lung or respiratory trouble	2.8
High blood pressure	2.2
Stiffness or deformity of extremity	2.0
Diabetes	1.6
Blindness or vision problems	1.5

Source: "Americans with Disabilities," *Statistical Brief*, Bureau of the Census, Washington, DC, 1994

TABLE 6.7

Discharges, days of care, and average length of stay in short-stay hospitals, according to selected characteristics: United States, 1964, 1990, and 1994

[Data are based on household interviews of a sample of the civilian noninstitutionalized population]

Characteristic	Discharges			Days of care			Average length of stay		
	1964	1990	1994	1964	1990	1994	1964	1990	1994
	Number per 1,000 population						Number of days		
Total[1,2]	109.1	91.0	87.5	970.9	607.1	549.4	8.9	6.7	6.3
Age									
Under 15 years	67.6	46.7	40.7	405.7	271.3	237.2	6.0	5.8	5.8
Under 5 years	94.3	79.9	67.7	731.1	496.4	423.7	7.8	6.2	6.3
5–14 years	53.1	29.0	26.4	229.1	150.8	138.4	4.3	5.2	5.2
15–44 years	100.6	62.6	60.6	760.7	340.5	326.8	7.6	5.4	5.4
45–64 years	146.2	135.7	121.9	1,559.3	911.5	711.5	10.7	6.7	5.8
65 years and over	190.0	248.8	268.8	2,292.7	2,092.4	2,086.2	12.1	8.4	7.8
65–74 years	181.2	215.4	230.1	2,150.4	1,719.3	1,648.7	11.9	8.0	7.2
75 years and over	206.7	300.6	324.2	2,560.4	2,669.9	2,711.6	12.4	8.9	8.4

Source: *Health, United States, 1996-97*, National Center for Health Statistics, Hyattsville, MD, 1997

TABLE 6.8

Physician contacts, according to selected patient characteristics: United States, 1987–94

[Data are based on household interviews of a sample of the civilian noninstitutionalized population]

Characteristic	1987	1988	1989	1990	1991	1992	1993	1994
	Physician contacts per person							
Total[1,2]	5.4	5.3	5.3	5.5	5.6	5.9	6.0	6.0
Age								
Under 15 years	4.5	4.6	4.6	4.5	4.7	4.6	4.9	4.6
Under 5 years	6.7	7.0	6.7	6.9	7.1	6.9	7.2	6.8
5–14 years	3.3	3.3	3.5	3.2	3.4	3.4	3.6	3.4
15–44 years	4.6	4.7	4.6	4.8	4.7	5.0	5.0	5.0
45–64 years	6.4	6.1	6.1	6.4	6.6	7.2	7.1	7.3
65 years and over	8.9	8.7	8.9	9.2	10.4	10.6	10.9	11.3
65–74 years	8.4	8.4	8.2	8.5	9.2	9.7	9.9	10.3
75 years and over	9.7	9.2	9.9	10.1	12.3	12.1	12.3	12.7
Sex and age								
Male[1]	4.6	4.6	4.8	4.7	4.9	5.1	5.2	5.2
Under 5 years	6.7	7.3	7.5	7.2	7.6	7.1	7.5	7.0
5–14 years	3.4	3.4	3.7	3.3	3.5	3.5	3.8	3.5
15–44 years	3.3	3.3	3.4	3.4	3.4	3.7	3.6	3.7
45–64 years	5.5	5.2	5.2	5.6	5.8	6.1	6.1	6.3
65–74 years	8.1	7.9	8.5	8.0	8.6	9.2	9.3	10.1
75 years and over	9.2	9.6	9.9	10.0	11.6	12.2	11.7	11.6
Female[1]	6.0	6.0	5.9	6.1	6.3	6.6	6.7	6.7
Under 5 years	6.7	6.8	5.9	6.5	6.6	6.7	6.9	6.5
5–14 years	3.1	3.3	3.3	3.2	3.2	3.3	3.4	3.3
15–44 years	5.8	6.0	5.9	6.0	5.9	6.2	6.4	6.2
45–64 years	7.2	6.9	7.0	7.1	7.4	8.2	8.1	8.3
65–74 years	8.6	8.8	7.9	9.0	9.7	10.1	10.4	10.5
75 years and over	10.0	9.0	9.9	10.2	12.7	12.1	12.8	13.4
Race and age								
White[1]	5.5	5.5	5.5	5.6	5.8	6.0	6.0	6.1
Under 5 years	7.1	7.6	7.1	7.1	7.4	7.3	7.5	7.1
5–14 years	3.5	3.6	3.8	3.5	3.7	3.7	3.9	3.7
15–44 years	4.7	4.8	4.8	4.9	4.9	5.0	5.1	5.1
45–64 years	6.4	6.1	6.2	6.4	6.6	7.2	7.0	7.4
65–74 years	8.4	8.3	8.0	8.5	9.4	9.6	9.7	10.5
75 years and over	9.7	9.3	9.7	10.1	12.1	12.0	12.2	12.4
Black[1]	5.1	4.8	4.9	5.1	5.2	5.9	6.0	5.7
Under 5 years	5.1	4.6	5.3	5.6	6.0	5.6	6.2	5.2
5–14 years	2.3	2.2	2.3	2.2	2.1	2.3	2.4	2.5
15–44 years	4.2	4.2	3.9	4.2	4.0	5.3	4.7	4.8
45–64 years	7.3	6.6	6.3	7.1	7.5	7.8	8.7	7.7
65–74 years	8.6	9.1	10.0	9.2	7.3	10.9	11.5	9.3
75 years and over	10.8	8.7	12.7	10.4	15.7	13.7	13.1	16.3

Source: *Health, United States, 1996-97*, National Center for Health Statistics, Hyattsville, MD, 1997

1.5 million new fractures each year — in the elderly, with associated medical charges (including rehabilitation and treatment facilities) estimated at $10 billion. As the number of elderly grows, experts estimate these costs will increase to $60 billion per year by 2000 and $200 billion per year by 2040.

Osteoporosis develops slowly over a person's lifetime. After the mid-20s, bone tissue gradually thins out and is not replaced by new bone as quickly as in earlier years. When osteoporosis advances to the point where 35 to 40 percent of a person's bone density has been destroyed, the vertebrae (bones of the spine) begin to collapse, causing the spine to curve outward in a "dowager's hump." Bone fractures and broken hips become more common, some resulting in permanent damage and even premature death. The disease is difficult to diagnose in its early stages because X-rays can detect only bone loss of more than 30 percent. The recent introduction of photon densitometry, which can measure very small losses in bone density, enables earlier diagnosis, although such bone scans are not routinely performed.

Osteoporosis affects half of all women over age 50. Women are far more susceptible to osteoporosis than men, especially women who are fair-skinned, small boned, of northern European, Chinese, or Japanese descent, and who have reduced estrogen levels due to menopause or removal of the ovaries. After menopause, women lose bone mass rapidly as loss of estrogen ac- accelerates calcium de- depletion in the body. At age 65, bone loss rate slows down again.

Hip fractures are the most serious consequence of osteoporosis. About 20 percent result in death, and 25 percent result in severe handicaps. (Figure 6.5 shows the outcomes of osteoporosis-related hip fractures.) Two-thirds of such fractures require institutional care.

The disease can be prevented or its effects diminished by measures taken earlier in life. Doctors recommend that women over the age of 40 take between 1,000 and 1,500 milligrams of calcium daily by eating calcium-rich food, such as milk, yogurt, cheese, tofu, dark leafy green vegetables, salmon, sardines, and shellfish, or by calcium supplements. It is also important to maintain adequate levels of vitamin D, which helps the body absorb and use calcium and magnesium. Most people get sufficient vitamin D from exposure to sunlight, but the skin loses much of its ability to produce the vitamin as one ages.

Regular exercise, especially walking, jogging, and bicycle riding, also aids in preventing osteoporosis. The risk is increased by smoking, heavy drinking, high caffeine and protein intake, and lack of regular exercise. The newest experimental therapies involve the intake of sodium fluoride, calcitonin, and various drugs. Estrogen replacement therapy during, after, and sometimes just prior to menopause is now recognized as having the additional side effect of maintaining bone density in women.

TABLE 6.9

PROJECTED PHYSICIAN VISITS AND PERCENT CHANGE IN VISITS FOR YEARS 2000 AND 2030
(number of people and visits in thousands)

Year	Age		
	65+	65 to 74	75+
2000			
Noninstitutionalized population	34,882	18,243	16,639
Total physician contacts	295,613	147,480	148,133
% change in contacts, 1989-2000	14.2	1.0	31.1
2030			
Noninstitutionalized population	65,604	35,988	29,616
Total physician contacts	555,717	290,932	264,785
% change in contacts, 1989-2030	114.6	99.3	134.4

SOURCE: U.S. Administration on Aging. Unpublished projections based on physician visit rates from the 1989 National Health Interview Survey and population projections from the U.S. Bureau of the Census.

Source: *Aging America: Trends and Projections*, Department of Health and Human Services, Washington, DC, 1991

In 1995, scientists at the University of Texas Southwestern Medical Center at Dallas confirmed that a new slow-release form of chloride and calcium can reduce spinal fractures and build bone in elderly women with severe osteoporosis by 70 percent.

Diabetes

The elderly are quite susceptible to Type II, or non-insulin dependent, diabetes. This form of diabetes, also called adult-onset diabetes, accounts for over 85 percent of all diabetic cases. (Type I diabetes, also known as insulin-dependent diabetes, generally begins in childhood.) In 1995, diabetes killed 59,254 Americans and was the seventh most common cause of death (Table 6.1). Many more people died from heart disease or strokes resulting from diabetes. An estimated 8.7 million Americans have diabetes, although some experts believe that half the victims do not yet know they have the disease.

Frequent complications of diabetes are nerve damage in the legs and feet, sometimes resulting in amputations, and eye problems that can result in blindness. Both forms of the disease require the daily, sometimes even hourly, monitoring of blood sugar and insulin levels and can often be controlled with a diet and weight reduction program. Currently there are new methods for administering insulin, such as implants and pumps, and home blood sugar self-test kits are now easily available for diabetic patients. Oral medications are now widely used.

Diabetes seems to be on the increase. Although much of the increase can be attributed to the growth in the number of older Americans, some experts believe additional factors have contributed to the rise. The Centers for Disease Control and Prevention (CDC) study, "Trends in the Prevalence and Incidence of Self-Reported Diabetes Mellitus — United States, 1980 -1994," investigated the prevalence of this disease. The survey found that diabetes increased with increasing age (Figure 6.6) and that the prevalence and incidence of the disease have risen since 1980 (Table 6.11). From 1980 to 1994, the crude prevalence rate increased 17 percent, from 25.2 to 29.8 per 1,000 population. The age-adjusted rate increased 15 percent. Experts suggest several factors, including increased obesity, heredity, and environmental factors, have contributed to this increase.

Prostate Problems

Prostate problems in men increase significantly after age 50. Often the prostate becomes enlarged and blocks the urethra, the canal through which urine leaves the body, making urination difficult. This condition can often be relieved with surgery. Occasionally, cancer develops in the prostate gland, but, if found and treated early, it is generally not life-threatening, since prostate cancer progresses very slowly and remains localized for a long time. Recent introduction of screening men with the PSA (prostatic specific antigen) blood test aids in diagnosing cancer in the prostate.

Urinary Problems

An estimated 9 percent of noninstitutionalized persons aged 65 and over have problems controlling urination. The problem increases with age, with an estimated 986,000 persons 65 to 74 years old and 1.2 million persons 75 years and older having some urinary difficulty. The problem appears to be more common in women than men.

Urinary problems often have a serious emotional impact. People with urinary problems are more likely to report their health as fair to poor and to report deterioration of their health. About three-fourths of those with urinary problems suffer some limitation in at least some activity.

Urinary incontinence, the inability to control bladder function, is not a disease, but rather a symptom of other dysfunctions. Nor is incontinence a natural consequence of aging. Specialists report that many people do not report their problems with incontinence because they are not aware that help

TABLE 6.10

Selected Measures of the Health Status of the Elderly, by Family Income, 1990

Measure of health status	Under $10,000	$10,000 to $19,999	$20,000 to $34,999	$35,000 or more
Incidence of acute conditions per 100 persons	112.2	112.0	99.4	94.8
Number of selected chronic conditions per 1,000 persons				
Hearing impairment	384.2	316.6	326.7	292.8
Hernia of abdominal cavity	67.4	56.1	72.4	38.2
Diabetes	117.7	91.9	83.4	93.5
Heart disease	317.3	345.5	274.4	312.7
Hypertension	426.9	375.6	398.7.	353.6

Source: National Center for Health Statistics, unpublished data from the National Health Interview Survey, and National Center for Health Statistics, Current Estimates from the National Health Interview Survey, 1990, Series 10, No. 181 (Washington, D.C.: U.S. Government Printing Office, 1991), pp. 88-91.

Source: *Elderly Americans — Health, Housing, and Nutrition Gaps between the Poor and Nonpoor*, U.S. General Accounting Office, Washington, DC, 1992

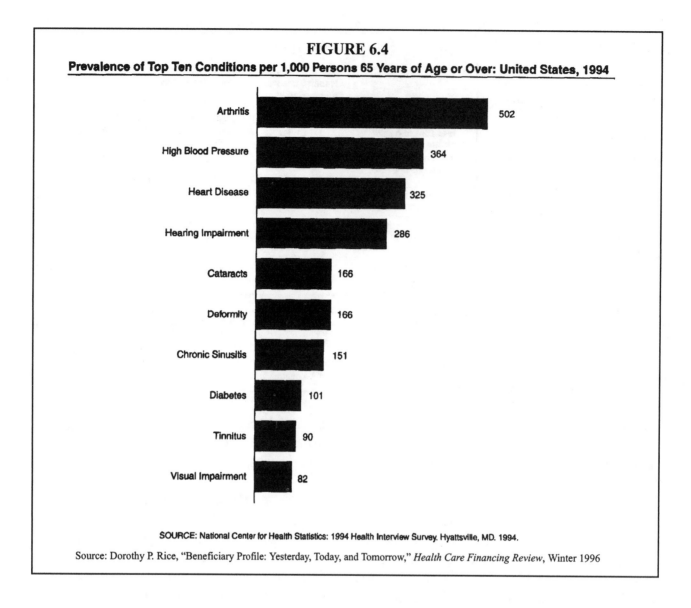

FIGURE 6.4

Prevalence of Top Ten Conditions per 1,000 Persons 65 Years of Age or Over: United States, 1994

Arthritis	502
High Blood Pressure	364
Heart Disease	325
Hearing Impairment	286
Cataracts	166
Deformity	166
Chronic Sinusitis	151
Diabetes	101
Tinnitus	90
Visual Impairment	82

SOURCE: National Center for Health Statistics: 1994 Health Interview Survey. Hyattsville, MD. 1994.

Source: Dorothy P. Rice, "Beneficiary Profile: Yesterday, Today, and Tomorrow," *Health Care Financing Review*, Winter 1996

is possible. The aggressive marketing of absorbent undergarments has had the effect of indicating to the elderly that their problem is a normal complication of aging, discouraging many people from seeking help. Doctors estimate that 85 to 90 percent of sufferers could be successfully treated.

Malnutrition

Poor nutritional status is a primary concern for the elderly. Nutritionally inadequate diets can contribute to or exacerbate diseases, hasten the development of degenerative diseases associated with aging, and delay recovery from illness. *Prevention Magazine*, in its 1996 index of health behaviors, found that those over 50 years of age (42 percent scoring high) were more likely than younger persons to try to eat healthfully (Table 6.12; these were self-reported scores).

Even with the emphasis in recent years on good nutrition as a major factor contributing to good health, an estimated 30 to 60 percent of all elderly people maintain eating habits that provide them with less than the recommended daily level of nutrients and protein, and a quarter of the elderly suffer from some form of malnutrition. If they are inactive, their bodies become less capable of absorbing and using nutrients in the foods they do eat, and certain medications increase the body's needs for particular nutrients. Many hospital stays are for conditions preventable by proper eating.

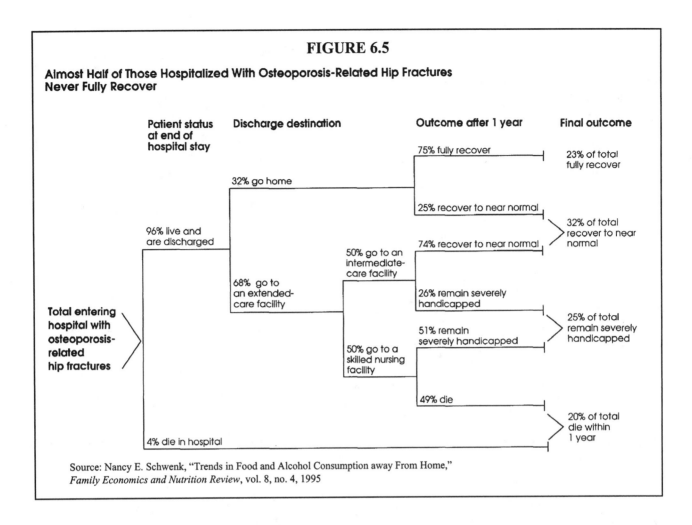

FIGURE 6.5

Almost Half of Those Hospitalized With Osteoporosis-Related Hip Fractures Never Fully Recover

Source: Nancy E. Schwenk, "Trends in Food and Alcohol Consumption away From Home," *Family Economics and Nutrition Review*, vol. 8, no. 4, 1995

The American Dietetic Association believes that few doctors are trained to recognize malnutrition, despite knowing that well-nourished elderly people become ill less often, and recover from illness and injury quicker, and are less expensive to treat.

An individual's eating habits can be affected by many factors — loneliness, depression, poverty, poor appetite, or lack of transportation. Meals provided by community service organizations, whether they are dinners served at a senior center or home-delivered meals, are one of the most important services offered to the elderly. However, experts on nutrition for the elderly increasingly believe the traditional solutions to the problems of hunger and malnutrition, such as Meals on Wheels, may not recognize the whole problem. Chronic illnesses often depress appetites. In addition, medications can suppress hunger and cause loss of senses that make the older person lose interest in food. In other words, even if one brings food to the elderly, they will not necessarily eat.

Sometimes, elderly people are simply too poor to eat properly. The Tufts University Center on Hunger, Poverty, and Nutrition Policy reported that, in 1990, about 3.27 million, or 10.5 percent of Americans 65 and older, experienced hunger. In addition, studies show that the protein needs of older people are significantly higher than the daily protein intake recommended by federal agencies.

Living Alone Affects Dietary Quality

Many elderly people, especially women, live alone. The U.S. Department of Agriculture reported in 1995 that the diets of adults living alone were significantly lower in nutrient intakes than the diets of multi-person households. Of those living alone, younger age groups were as likely, or more than likely, as those over 65 not to get adequate nutrients. Women older than 75 and men older than 65 were deficient in some nutrients (Tables 6.13 and 6.14).

Hearing Loss

Hearing loss is a very common problem among the elderly, afflicting 60 to 80 percent of the 65 and older population, approximately 8.7 million elderly. Forty-three percent of Americans with hearing trouble are 65 and older. Elderly men are much more likely to be hearing-impaired than are elderly women. There are many causes of hearing loss, the most common being age-related changes in the ear's mechanism. People suffering from hearing loss may withdraw from social contact and are sometimes mislabeled as confused or even senile. They are often reluctant to admit hearing problems, and sometimes hearing loss is so gradual that even the afflicted person may not be aware of it for some time.

Treatment is available for increasing numbers of patients, if they seek help. Many physicians are unaware of the services now available to the hearing impaired, whose options are increasing. Among the solutions now offered are high-tech hearing aids, amplifiers for doorbells and telephones, infrared amplifiers, even companion

FIGURE 6.6

Prevalence* of self-reported diabetes, by age group — United States, 1980–1994

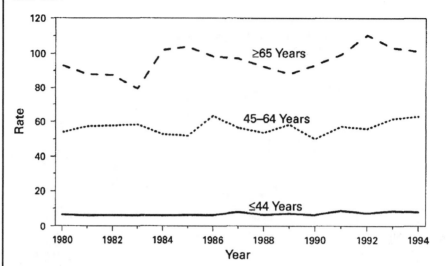

*Rate per 1000 population.

Source: "Trends in Prevalence and Incidence of Self-Reported Diabetes Mellitus — United States, 1980-1994," *Morbidity and Mortality Weekly Report*, October 31, 1997

dogs trained to respond to sounds for the owner. The National Center for Health Statistics reported that, in 1991, of those elderly with hearing problems, 34 percent had hearing loss so severe they could hear only shouted words. Elderly Whites were significantly more likely than non-Whites to have hearing trouble.

TABLE 6.11

Prevalence and incidence of self-reported diabetes mellitus, by year — United States, National Health Interview Survey, 1980–1994

Year	Prevalence			Incidence		
	No. existing cases*	Crude rate[†]	Age-adjusted rate[†]	No. existing cases*	Crude rate[§]	Age-adjusted rate[§]
1980	5528	25.4	25.5	541	2.5	2.5
1981	5645	25.1	25.3	501	2.2	2.2
1982	5729	25.2	25.4	713	3.1	3.2
1983	5613	24.5	24.7	690	3.0	3.0
1984	6004	25.9	26.0	645	2.8	2.8
1985	6134	26.2	26.2	679	2.9	2.9
1986	6563	27.8	27.8	644	2.7	2.7
1987	6609	27.7	27.6	715	3.0	3.0
1988	6162	25.6	25.4	678	2.8	2.8
1989	6467	26.6	26.3	677	2.8	2.8
1990	6212	25.2	24.8	521	2.1	2.1
1991	7206	29.0	28.5	672	2.7	2.7
1992	7365	29.3	28.5	613	2.4	2.4
1993	7783	30.6	29.7	865	3.4	3.3
1994	7744	29.8	29.3	965	3.7	3.7

*In thousands.
[†]The number of persons who reported having diabetes per 1000 population.
[§]The number of persons who reported having had diabetes diagnosed within the previous 12 months per 1000 population.

Source: "Trends in Prevalence and Incidence of Self-Reported Diabetes Mellitus — United States, 1980-1994," *Morbidity and Mortality Weekly Report*, October 31, 1997

Vision Changes

Almost no one escapes changes in vision as he or she grows older. Ninety-five percent of people 65 and older wear glasses. By age 40, a person often notices a change in what may have been perfect vision. It becomes increasingly difficult to read small print or thread a needle at the usual distance. For many, night vision declines. This is often caused by a condition called presbyopia (tired eyes) and is a very common occurrence. People who were previously nearsighted may actually find some improvement in eyesight as they become slightly farsighted.

Eye Diseases

Much more serious than simple loss of visual clarity are cataracts, glaucoma, and problems affecting the retina, which frequently occur in elderly people.

Cataracts

Cataracts occur when the crystalline structure of the eye lens breaks down. The lens becomes clouded, limiting the amount of light reaching the optic nerve and distorting images. Most cataracts develop slowly over time, but they can eventually cause almost total blindness. In recent years there has been a huge increase in lens replacement operations in which the clouded lens is removed and a plastic lens is substituted.

Glaucoma

Glaucoma is the leading cause of blindness in the United States.

TABLE 6.12

NUTRITION INDEX SCORES BY KEY DEMOGRAPHIC GROUPS

	High* %	Medium %	Low %	N #
ALL ADULTS	28	42	30	(630)
GENDER				
Male	19	43	38	(311)
Female	36	40	24	(319)
AGE				
18 - 29	19	47	34	(135)
30 - 39	20	41	39	(170)
40 - 49	28	38	34	(123)
50+	42	40	18	(191)
STRENUOUS EXERCISE				
3 or more days per week	34	43	24	(251)
Less than 3 days per week	24	40	36	(369)

* Nutrition index scores are based on the number of dietary and nutritional guidelines respondents "try a lot" to follow (listed in Table 2-2). Those who try a lot on six to nine items are scored "high"; three to five items are scored as "medium," and zero to two items are scored as "low."

Source: *The Prevention Index — A Report Card on the Nation's Health*, Rodale Press, Inc., Emmaus, PA, 1996

TABLE 6.13

Nutrient intakes: Women living alone as compared with women living with others

Nutrient	All ages	19 - 34	35 - 54	55 - 64	65 - 74	75+
Food energy	L	L	–	–	–	–
Carbohydrate	–	–	–	–	–	–
Protein	L	L	–	L	–	L
Fat	L	L	–	L	–	–
Saturated fat	L	L	L	–	–	–
Vitamin A	H	–	–	H	–	–
Carotenes	–	–	–	–	–	–
Vitamin C	–	–	–	–	–	–
Vitamin E	–	–	–	–	–	–
Thiamin	L	L	–	–	–	–
Riboflavin	–	L	–	–	–	–
Niacin	L	L	–	–	–	–
Vitamin B-6	–	L	–	–	–	–
Vitamin B-12	–	–	–	–	–	–
Folate	–	–	–	–	–	–
Phosphorus	L	L	–	–	–	–
Calcium	L	L	–	–	–	–
Magnesium	–	–	–	–	–	–
Iron	–	L	–	–	–	–
Zinc	L	L	–	L	–	–
Cholesterol	–	–	–	–	–	–
Fiber	–	–	–	–	–	–
Sodium	L	L	–	–	–	L

L = significantly lower; H = significantly higher. From weighted mean 3-day intakes; significant at $p < .05$. Blank cells indicate no statistically significant relation.

Source: Gerrior, S.A., Guthrie, J.F., Fox, J.J., Lutz, S.M., Keane, T.P., and Basiotis, P.P., 1994, How Does Living Alone Affect Dietary Quality? U.S. Department of Agriculture, Agricultural Research Service, Home Economics Research Report No. 51.

Source: "How Does Living Alone Affect Dietary Quality?" *Family Economics and Nutrition Review*, vol. 8, no. 4, 1995

Experts estimate that three million Americans have the most common form of the disease, called open-angle glaucoma, and some 80,000 are blind as a result of it. Although glaucoma can affect people of any age, it is most common in people older than 60. It is caused by incomplete drainage of fluids out of the eyeball, causing pressure to build up inside the eyeball. It usually presents no early symptoms, but if undetected in its early stages, it can result in irreversible blindness. There is no cure for glaucoma and no way to restore vision lost. Routine glaucoma tests are especially important for older people. Medication (eye drops or pills) can generally manage the condition. At later stages, laser therapy and surgery are effective in stopping further damage.

Problems of the Retina

The retina is a thin lining of nerves on the back of the eye. Over time, it can become torn or detached, jeopardizing vision. If treated in time by laser therapy, tears and separations can almost always be repaired. *Senile macular degeneration* is a condition in which the macula, a specialized part of the retina responsible for sharp central and reading vision, is damaged. Symptoms include blurred vision, a dark spot in the center of the vision field, and vertical line distortion.

Diabetic retinopathy occurs when the small blood vessels that flourish in the retina do not perform properly. Blood vessels can leak fluid that distorts vision, and sometimes blood is released into the center of the eye causing blindness. Diabetic retinopathy is a major cause of blindness.

HEALTH AND WORK

Poor health is the single most important reason nonworking elderly left their last jobs. A 1993 University of Michigan study of nearly 13,000 persons over the age of 50 found that persons leaving work for health reasons were about four times more likely than working persons to have

TABLE 6.14

Nutrient intakes: Men living alone as compared with men living with others

Nutrient	Age (years)					
	All ages	19 - 34	35 - 54	55 - 64	65 - 74	75+
Food energy	L	–	–	–	–	–
Carbohydrate	–	–	–	–	–	–
Protein	L	–	–	–	–	L
Fat	L	–	–	–	–	–
Saturated fat	L	L	–	–	–	–
Vitamin A	–	–	–	–	–	–
Carotenes	–	–	–	–	L	–
Vitamin C	–	–	L	–	–	–
Vitamin E	–	–	L	–	L	–
Thiamin	–	–	L	–	–	–
Riboflavin	–	–	–	–	–	–
Niacin	–	–	–	–	–	–
Vitamin B-6	–	–	–	–	–	–
Vitamin B-12	–	L	–	–	–	–
Folate	–	–	–	–	–	–
Phosphorus	L	–	–	–	–	L
Calcium	L	–	L	–	–	L
Magnesium	–	–	–	–	–	–
Iron	–	–	–	–	–	–
Zinc	–	–	H	–	–	L
Cholesterol	–	–	–	–	–	–
Fiber	–	–	–	–	L	–
Sodium	L	–	L	L	–	–

L = significantly lower; H = significantly higher. From weighted mean 3-day intakes; significant at $p < .05$. Blank cells indicate no statistically significant relation.

Source: Gerrior, S.A., Guthrie, J.F., Fox, J.J., Lutz, S.M., Keane, T.P., and Basiotis, P.P., 1994, How Does Living Alone Affect Dietary Quality? U.S. Department of Agriculture, Agricultural Research Service, Home Economics Research Report No. 51.

Source: "How Does Living Alone Affect Dietary Quality?" *Family Economics and Nutrition Review*, vol. 8, no. 4, 1995

chronic lung disease or heart conditions. They were about five times more likely to have had a stroke, about three times more likely to have diabetes, and about twice as likely to have back problems. (See Table 6.15.)

ORGANIC MENTAL DISEASES OF THE ELDERLY — DEMENTIA*

As equally devastating as the decline of a once-healthy body is the deterioration of the mind. As with other disorders, mental impairments can occur in persons of any age, but certain types of illnesses are much more prevalent in the elderly. In this area more than any other, the differences between individuals can vary dramatically. Some people may show no decline in mental ability until far into old age. Others experience occasional forgetfulness. A few are robbed of all their mental faculties before they reach 60.

Older people with mental problems were once labeled as "senile." Only in recent years have researchers found that physical disorders can cause progressive deterioration of mental and neurological functions. These disorders produce symptoms collectively known as "dementia." Symptoms of dementia include loss of language functions, inability to think abstractly, inability to care for oneself, personality change, emotional instability, and loss of a sense of time or place.

It is important to note that occasional forgetfulness and disorientation are normal signs of the aging process. True dementia is a disease and is not the inevitable result of growing older. Many disorders may cause or simulate dementia.

Alzheimer's Disease

The most prevalent form of dementia is Alzheimer's disease, named after the German

TABLE 6.15
Health and Work
(% with selected health conditions)

Health Condition	Left Last Job for: Health Reasons	Left Last Job for: Other Reasons	Currently Working
Men			
Chronic Lung Disease	25	9	6
Heart Condition	46	18	13
Stroke	15	4	2
Back Problems	57	34	32
Diabetes	25	13	9
Women			
Chronic Lung Disease	23	9	7
Heart Condition	30	11	8
Stroke	9	3	2
Back Problems	61	38	33
Diabetes	23	9	9

Source: University of Michigan Health and Retirement Study, 1993. Funded by the National Institute on Aging.

neurologist Alois Alzheimer, who, in 1906, discovered the "neurofibrillary tangles" now associated with the disease. Alzheimer's is a degenerative disorder of the brain and nervous system; there is no known cause, cure, or treatment.

Just a dozen years ago, Alzheimer's was still a relatively obscure disease that received little study and still less publicity. Symptoms were generally attributed to aging and the victims diagnosed as senile. If Alzheimer's were separately identified, it would be the eleventh leading killer of adults today. Today, Alzheimer's is the subject of intense research and is very much in the public consciousness. Unfortunately, many people have become familiar with the disease because a relative or loved one has been diagnosed with Alzheimer's.

Prevalence

As the population ages, Alzheimer's is becoming more of a concern. As many as 10 percent of people over the age of 65 with memory problems or other mental impairment probably

---

*For information on mental illness among the elderly, see Chapter VII.

suffer from Alzheimer's. Up to 3 percent of people between 65 and 74, 19 percent of those between 75 and 84, and 47 percent of those over 85 are likely to have the disease. The National Institute on Aging estimates that 4 million people now suffer from Alzheimer's in the United States, and by 2050 the number may reach 14 million. This increase is likely due to the growing number of older persons, improved diagnosis, and increased awareness of the condition. In addition, some research suggests that the prevalence has increased as well.

Death rates increase with age — those 85 and older were 19 times more likely to get the disease than those 65 to 74 (Figure 6.7). Deaths from Alzheimer's, once somewhat greater for men than women, are now about the same. The death rate for the disease is somewhat greater for the White than for the Black population. Figure 6.8 shows the death rates for Alzheimer's from 1979 to 1995.

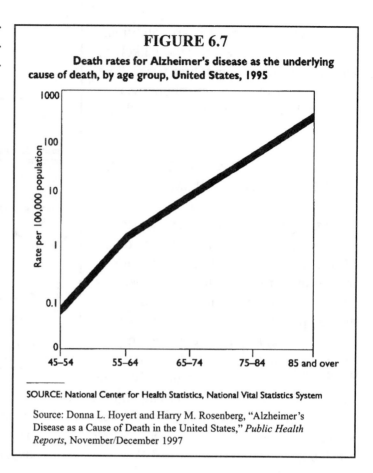

FIGURE 6.7

Death rates for Alzheimer's disease as the underlying cause of death, by age group, United States, 1995

SOURCE: National Center for Health Statistics, National Vital Statistics System

Source: Donna L. Hoyert and Harry M. Rosenberg, "Alzheimer's Disease as a Cause of Death in the United States," *Public Health Reports*, November/December 1997

An accurate count of the number of patients is difficult because of the stigma attached to the disease. Scientists report that when they try to trace the inheritance of Alzheimer's in families, they often meet denial and resistance among family members to admitting the presence of the disease.

Symptoms

The diagnosis of Alzheimer's disease can be positively confirmed only after death. An autopsy of the brain of an Alzheimer's victim reveals abnormal tangles of nerve fibers (neurofibrillary tangles), tips of nerve fibers embedded in plaque, and a significant shortage of the enzymes that produce the neurotransmitter acetylcholine. Researchers are now looking for a diagnostic test for Alzheimer's in living subjects.

The symptoms of living victims usually begin with mild episodes of forgetfulness and disorientation. Most victims develop the disease between the ages of 55 and 80. As the disease progresses, memory loss increases and mood changes are frequent, accompanied by confusion, irritability, restlessness, and speech impairment. Eventually, the victim may lose all control over his or her mental and bodily functions. Alzheimer's victims survive an average of 8 to 10 years after the first onset of symptoms; some live an additional 25 years.

Suspected Causes

Despite intensified research in recent years, little is known about the cause (or causes) of Alzheimer's. One thing is certain — it is *not* a normal consequence of aging. It is, rather, a disease that either strikes older people almost exclusively, or more likely, its symptoms appear and become more pronounced as a person grows older.

There are several theories on the cause(s) of Alzheimer's. Some theories currently being pursued by researchers are

- A breakdown in the system that produces acetylcholine;

- A slow-acting virus that has already left the body before symptoms appear;

- A genetic (hereditary) origin.

Current research is focusing largely on heredity. Several studies have implicated two specific genes on the chromosomes of Alzheimer's patients. Other studies of twins suggest a strong role of heredity in the development of the disease. Recent research has confirmed a link between Alzheimer's and a high level of certain proteins in cerebrospinal fluid. The protein is not believed to cause the disease but may be a "marker" in diagnosing the disease. Other research suggests that it may be possible to use brain scans to detect mental deterioration years before symptoms become apparent, which would allow the possibility for earlier treatment.

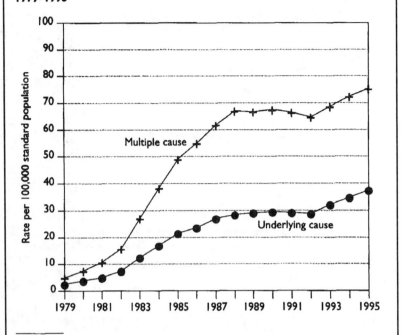

FIGURE 6.8

Age-adjusted death rates per 100,000 standard population for Alzheimer's disease as an underlying cause of death or one of multiple causes of death, decedents ages 65 years and older, United States, 1979–1995

NOTE: Rates for Alzheimer's disease as one of multiple causes includes deaths for which the disease is listed as the underlying cause and deaths for which it is mentioned as one of the causes.

SOURCE: National Center for Health Statistics, National Vital Statistics System

Source: Donna L. Hoyert and Harry M. Rosenberg, "Alzheimer's Disease as a Cause of Death in the United States," *Public Health Reports*, November/December 1997

Caring for the Alzheimer's Patient

There are many victims of Alzheimer's besides the person with the disease. While medications, such as tranquilizers, may reduce some symptoms and occasionally slow the progression of the disease, eventually most Alzheimer's patients need constant care and supervision. Some nursing homes and health care facilities are not equipped to provide this kind of care, and, if they accept Alzheimer's patients at all, they will accept only those in the very earliest stages. A growing number of nursing homes are promoting their instituions as designed to care for Alzheimer's patients, but they may be beyond the means of many families, and many children of parents with Alzheimer's desire (or feel a moral obligation) to care for them at home as long as possible.

No matter how willing and devoted the caregiver, the time, patience, and resources required to provide care over a long period of time are immense, and the task can become overwhelming. Recent studies show that the stress of caring for an Alzheimer's patient can affect the caregiver's immune system, making him or her more vulnerable than normal to infectious diseases. Most observers believe that the public services that could benefit these patients are underused. Once again, the stigma of the illness may prevent people from seeking available help.

Alzheimer's and Environment

The major challenges to caregivers of Alzheimer's patients are often the memory loss, disorientation, and wandering. Their crises are usually related to confusion states, not acute medical need. Traditional nursing home care is not

91

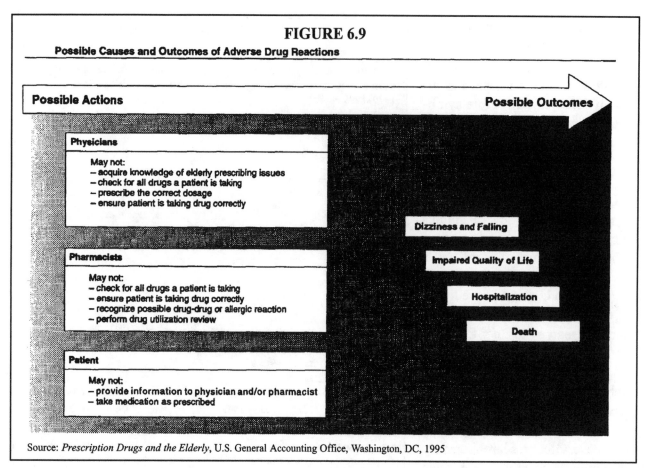

FIGURE 6.9

Possible Causes and Outcomes of Adverse Drug Reactions

Possible Actions → **Possible Outcomes**

Physicians

May not:
– acquire knowledge of elderly prescribing issues
– check for all drugs a patient is taking
– prescribe the correct dosage
– ensure patient is taking drug correctly

Pharmacists

May not:
– check for all drugs a patient is taking
– ensure patient is taking drug correctly
– recognize possible drug-drug or allergic reaction
– perform drug utilization review

Patient

May not:
– provide information to physician and/or pharmacist
– take medication as prescribed

Dizziness and Falling

Impaired Quality of Life

Hospitalization

Death

Source: *Prescription Drugs and the Elderly*, U.S. General Accounting Office, Washington, DC, 1995

designed to deal with such disorientation and wandering, but is rather oriented to immediate physical nursing. Nor do Alzheimer's patients, at least in the early stages of the disease, require nursing care in the classical sense.

Experiments with Alzheimer's patients are currently being done with design and architecture. Some authorities suggest that home and institution design can reduce the confusion of these patients and keep them relaxed, safe, and independent as long as possible. The keeping of mementos and familiar objects from one's past, involvement in household chores, and rooms designed with toilets in sight are parts of the experiments being carried out. Alzheimer's is becoming an enormous social problem with great social and financial costs. Continued research is vital to understanding the management of this disease.

The Government's Role

The prevalence of dementia (especially Alzheimer's disease), the profound emotional and financial burden of caring for its victims, and the predicted increase in the older population are putting pressure on the federal government to provide more assistance in caring for current victims and to increase funding for research to find the causes and a cure.

Millions of dollars are currently being spent for Alzheimer's research. This figure is dwarfed by the estimated billions of dollars the disease costs in terms of care and lost productivity of caregivers as well as patients. As the nation's population ages, federally funded health systems will likely be severely strained.

DRUG USE AMONG THE ELDERLY

In 1997, the National Council on the Aging (NCOA) reported that, in addition to other regular medications they may take, nearly 1 in 5 Americans over age 60 regularly takes medication for chronic pain. According to the NCOA, one senior in 20 suffers from the side effects caused by pain medication. Seniors typically take up to seven medications per day.

Unique Effect on Elderly

In recent decades, the pharmaceutical (drug) industry has revolutionized the treatment of disease. New medications are released into the market weekly, many for treatment of conditions common to the elderly. Unfortunately, little is known about the unique physiological response of the older body to many chemicals and medications. As a person ages, the body often responds differently to chemicals than it did at a younger age. Medication taken in incorrect dosages, in combination with other drugs, or on complicated schedules can confuse an elderly person and may result in drug mismanagement. The outcome is often overdose, drug reaction, unsuccessful treatment, or even death.

A major Congressional study (*Prescription Drugs and the Elderly*, U.S. General Accounting Office, July 1995) reported that 3 percent of all hospital admissions are caused by adverse drug reactions. However, the percentage is much higher for the elderly, 17 percent, almost six times greater than the general population. This inappropriate use of medications adds about $20 billion to the nation's hospital bills.

The study also reported that less severe reactions to prescribed drugs, including drowsiness, loss of coordination, and confusion, can go unnoticed or be discounted by health professionals or family as normal effects of aging. They can lead to falls or car accidents. An estimated 32,000 elderly people suffer hip fractures every year as a result of falls, and about 16,000 elderly drivers have traffic accidents while suffering from adverse drug reactions. Figure 6.9 shows the possible causes and outcomes of adverse drug reactions.

Indiscriminate Use of Drugs

A second problem for the elderly in drug therapy involves the indiscriminate use of drugs. Patients may be sedated almost routinely when a non-drug therapy may be appropriate. For example, sleep difficulties may be managed not only with medication but by exercise and the elimination of caffeine and naps. The elderly often find it difficult to sleep, and many people think they need sleeping pills. They may be unaware that the pills can cause side effects that resemble psychosis or dementia, especially when taken for long periods of time.

TABLE 6.16

WEIGHT STATUS BY KEY DEMOGRAPHIC GROUPS

	Overweight %	Within Range %	Underweight %	N #
ALL ADULTS, AGE 25+ AND CLASSIFIABLE	68	19	13	(1159)
GENDER				
Male	76	14	10	(571)
Female	60	23	17	(588)
RACE				
White	66	20	14	(953)
Black	77	12	19	(107)
AGE				
18 - 29	58	20	22	(238)
30 - 49	68	22	10	(508)
50 - 64	79	8	13	(194)
65+	69	19	12	(203)
STRENUOUS EXERCISE				
3 or more days per week	70	18	12	(231)
Less than 3 days per week	64	22	14	(254)
Never	79	9	12	(95)
MODERATE EXERCISE				
3 or more days per week	62	24	13	(271)
Less than 3 days per week	71	14	14	(203)
Never	74	12	14	(86)

Source: *The Prevention Index — A Report Card on the Nation's Health*, Rodale Press, Inc., Emmaus, PA, 1996

A number of studies show that sleeping pills are not only overused by many old people but are also abused — taken for too long and in alarmingly high doses. Another problem with sleep in the elderly is that many elderly use it as an escape from boredom. Dr. Philip Westbrook, director of the Sleep Disorders Center at Cedars-Sinai Medical Center in Los Angeles, reported that "the real problem is that they don't have anything to do when they're awake, so they want to be asleep." Some ask their doctors for sleeping pills to prolong the time when they are asleep.

Not Taking Prescribed Drugs

A third medication problem of the elderly is intentional noncompliance. Hospitals report that intentional noncompliance is the second most common factor in drug-related hospitalizations. Elderly persons suffering from depression, resignation, those who have misunderstood their doctor, or those who may be attempting suicide, might willfully disregard medication instructions.

Research is now increasing in the study of the elderly. Geriatrics (see below) has become an accepted, although still not widely populated, medical specialty. Research in this field will likely help to develop more effective and safer treatment for the elderly.

GETTING — AND STAYING — HEALTHY

Because of increased educational efforts and general media coverage of health topics, older people, as well as younger, are becoming more aware of personal habits and lifestyles that may contribute to poor health and accelerate the aging process, particularly over a long period of time. Many older people are making a conscious effort

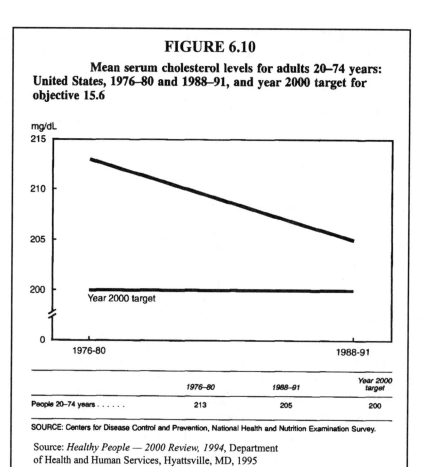

FIGURE 6.10

Mean serum cholesterol levels for adults 20–74 years: United States, 1976–80 and 1988–91, and year 2000 target for objective 15.6

	1976–80	1988–91	Year 2000 target
People 20–74 years	213	205	200

SOURCE: Centers for Disease Control and Prevention, National Health and Nutrition Examination Survey.

Source: *Healthy People — 2000 Review, 1994*, Department of Health and Human Services, Hyattsville, MD, 1995

to change what may be lifelong bad habits and acquire new ones that can improve their physical and mental conditions.

Among the health practices useful in helping older people to improve and maintain health are keeping mentally and physically active, proper nutrition, proper use of drugs and alcohol, living in a safe environment, eliminating smoking, and participating in screening programs and tests.

Experts believe that the elderly take better care of themselves than younger people do. They are less likely to smoke, drink, or experience stress than younger people. The elderly have better eating habits than their younger counterparts. They are, however, less likely to exercise.

Weight

The proportion of adults who are overweight increases with age. Experts believe that 69 percent of persons over the age of 65 are overweight

TABLE 6.17

Current cigarette smoking by persons 18 years of age and over, according to sex, race, and age: United States, selected years 1965–94

[Data are based on household interviews of a sample of the civilian noninstitutionalized population]

Sex, race, and age	1965	1974	1979	1983	1985	1987	1990	1991	1992	1993	1994
All persons	Percent of persons 18 years of age and over										
18 years and over, age adjusted	42.3	37.2	33.5	32.2	30.0	28.7	25.4	25.4	26.4	25.0	25.5
18 years and over, crude	42.4	37.1	33.5	32.1	30.1	28.8	25.5	25.6	26.5	25.0	25.5
All males											
18 years and over, age adjusted	51.6	42.9	37.2	34.7	32.1	31.0	28.0	27.5	28.2	27.5	27.8
18 years and over, crude	51.9	43.1	37.5	35.1	32.6	31.2	28.4	28.1	28.6	27.7	28.2
18–24 years	54.1	42.1	35.0	32.9	28.0	28.2	26.6	23.5	28.0	28.8	29.8
25–34 years	60.7	50.5	43.9	38.8	38.2	34.8	31.6	32.8	32.8	30.2	31.4
35–44 years	58.2	51.0	41.8	41.0	37.6	36.6	34.5	33.1	32.9	32.0	33.2
45–64 years	51.9	42.6	39.3	35.9	33.4	33.5	29.3	29.3	28.6	29.2	28.3
65 years and over	28.5	24.8	20.9	22.0	19.6	17.2	14.6	15.1	16.1	13.5	13.2
White:											
18 years and over, age adjusted	50.8	41.7	36.5	34.1	31.3	30.4	27.6	27.0	28.0	27.0	27.5
18 years and over, crude	51.1	41.9	36.8	34.5	31.7	30.5	28.0	27.4	28.2	27.0	27.7
18–24 years	53.0	40.8	34.3	32.5	28.4	29.2	27.4	25.1	30.0	30.4	31.8
25–34 years	60.1	49.5	43.6	38.6	37.3	33.8	31.6	32.1	33.5	29.9	32.5
35–44 years	57.3	50.1	41.3	40.8	36.6	36.2	33.5	32.1	30.9	31.2	32.0
45–64 years	51.3	41.2	38.3	35.0	32.1	32.4	28.7	28.0	28.1	27.8	26.9
65 years and over	27.7	24.3	20.5	20.6	18.9	16.0	13.7	14.2	14.9	12.5	11.9
Black:											
18 years and over, age adjusted	59.2	54.0	44.1	41.3	39.9	39.0	32.2	34.7	32.0	33.2	33.5
18 years and over, crude	60.4	54.3	44.1	40.6	39.9	39.0	32.5	35.0	32.2	32.7	33.7
18–24 years	62.8	54.9	40.2	34.2	27.2	24.9	21.3	15.0	16.2	19.9	18.7
25–34 years	68.4	58.5	47.5	39.9	45.6	44.9	33.8	39.4	29.5	30.7	29.8
35–44 years	67.3	61.5	48.6	45.5	45.0	44.0	42.0	44.4	47.5	36.9	44.5
45–64 years	57.9	57.8	50.0	44.8	46.1	44.3	36.7	42.0	35.4	42.4	41.2
65 years and over	36.4	29.7	26.2	38.9	27.7	30.3	21.5	24.3	28.3	27.9	25.6
All females											
18 years and over, age adjusted	34.0	32.5	30.3	29.9	28.2	26.7	23.1	23.6	24.8	22.7	23.3
18 years and over, crude	33.9	32.1	29.9	29.5	27.9	26.5	22.8	23.5	24.6	22.5	23.1
18–24 years	38.1	34.1	33.8	35.5	30.4	26.1	22.5	22.4	24.9	22.9	25.2
25–34 years	43.7	38.8	33.7	32.6	32.0	31.8	28.2	28.4	30.1	27.3	28.8
35–44 years	43.7	39.8	37.0	33.8	31.5	29.6	24.8	27.6	27.3	27.4	26.8
45–64 years	32.0	33.4	30.7	31.0	29.9	28.6	24.8	24.6	26.1	23.0	22.8
65 years and over	9.6	12.0	13.2	13.1	13.5	13.7	11.5	12.0	12.4	10.5	11.1
White:											
18 years and over, age adjusted	34.3	32.3	30.6	30.1	28.3	27.2	23.9	24.2	25.7	23.7	24.3
18 years and over, crude	34.0	31.7	30.1	29.4	27.7	26.7	23.4	23.7	25.1	23.1	23.7
18–24 years	38.4	34.0	34.5	36.5	31.8	27.8	25.4	25.1	28.5	26.8	28.5
25–34 years	43.4	38.6	34.1	32.2	32.0	31.9	28.5	28.4	31.5	28.4	30.2
35–44 years	43.9	39.3	37.2	34.8	31.0	29.2	25.0	27.0	27.6	27.3	27.1
45–64 years	32.7	33.0	30.6	30.6	29.7	29.0	25.4	25.3	25.8	23.4	23.2
65 years and over	9.8	12.3	13.8	13.2	13.3	13.9	11.5	12.1	12.6	10.5	11.1
Black:											
18 years and over, age adjusted	32.1	35.9	30.8	31.8	30.7	27.2	20.4	23.1	23.9	19.8	21.1
18 years and over, crude	33.7	36.4	31.1	32.2	31.0	28.0	21.2	24.4	24.2	20.8	21.7
18–24 years	37.1	35.6	31.8	32.0	23.7	20.4	10.0	11.8	10.3	8.2	11.8
25–34 years	47.8	42.2	35.2	38.0	36.2	35.8	29.1	32.4	26.9	24.7	24.8
35–44 years	42.8	46.4	37.7	32.7	40.2	35.3	25.5	35.3	32.4	31.5	28.2
45–64 years	25.7	38.9	34.2	36.3	33.4	28.4	22.6	23.4	30.9	21.3	23.5
65 years and over	7.1	8.9	8.5	13.1	14.5	11.7	11.1	9.6	11.1	10.2	13.6

NOTES: Estimates for 1992 and beyond are not strictly comparable with those for earlier years, and estimates for 1992 and 1993 are not strictly comparable with each other due to a change in the definition of current smoker in 1992 and the use of a split sample in 1992. See discussion of current smoker in Appendix II.

SOURCE: Centers for Disease Control and Prevention, National Center for Health Statistics, Division of Health Interview Statistics: Data from the National Health Interview Survey; data computed by the Division of Health and Utilization Analysis from data compiled by the Division of Health Interview Statistics.

(Table 6.16). The increasing share of Americans who are overweight is due largely to the fact that the population is aging. As the median age goes up, so does the weight. Among the reasons people gain weight as they age are that they tend to exercise less, they may care less about their appearance, and metabolism seems to slow down as people age so that their bodies burn fewer calories.

Cholesterol

Cholesterol is believed to be linked to the risk of heart disease. In 1994, the Centers for Disease Control and Prevention reported that increasingly more Americans are having their cholesterol levels checked and that the mean serum cholesterol level has declined (Figure 6.10). The U.S. Department of Health, in its *Healthy People Review 2000*, which makes recommendations for better health, set the target cholesterol rate for American adults by the year 2000 at 200, still lower than today's mean.

Smoking

Per capita tobacco consumption has declined by 40 percent in the United States in the past 40 years. Since 1965, the percent of people who smoke has declined. In 1994, fewer people over 65 (13.2 percent of males and 11.1 for females) smoked than all other age groups. (See Table 6.17.)

TABLE 6.18

PARTICIPATION IN MODERATE PHYSICAL ACTIVITY BY KEY DEMOGRAPHIC GROUPS

	Three or More Days a Week %	Less than Three Days a Week %	Never %	Don't Know %	N #
ALL ADULTS	45	36	16	3	(627)
GENDER					
Male	47	37	14	2	(309)
Female	44	36	17	3	(318)
AGE					
18 - 29	57	32	9	2	(125)
30 - 49	51	38	10	1	(260)
50+	32	38	25	5	(236)
EDUCATION					
College graduate	49	43	7	2	(173)
Some college	51	36	12	1	(154)
No college	41	35	21	3	(298)
INCOME					
Over $50,000	49	39	10	2	(149)
$35,001 - $50,000	50	35	15	*	(106)
$25,001 - $35,000	49	39	11	1	(96)
$25,000 or less	41	35	22	2	(188)

Source: *The Prevention Index — A Report Card on the Nation's Health*, Rodale Press, Inc., Emmaus, PA, 1996

Exercise

Regular physical activity often comes closer to being a fountain of youth than anything modern medicine can offer. It is almost never too late to start. Researchers have documented many improvements in the health and well-being of older Americans who take up exercise. The major areas of benefit are:

• Heart disease and stroke — Exercise can halve the risk of heart disease or stroke by lowering blood pressure, raising the level of protective cholesterol (HDL), reducing clot formation, controlling diabetes, and countering weight gain.

• Cancer — Exercise lowers the risk of cancer of the colon, one of the leading causes of cancer deaths. In animals, exercise protects against breast cancer.

• Osteoporosis — At any age at which exercise is begun, it can increase bone density and reduce

fractures. In addition, older people who become active experience improvements in balance, strength, coordination, and flexibility, which all help prevent falls that often result in debilitating fractures.

• Diabetes — Active people are less likely to develop diabetes than sedentary people. Physical activity increases the sensitivity of cells to insulin, which lowers blood sugar and the need for insulin.

• Weight — Exercise helps maintain normal weight or foster weight loss. Most importantly, exercise helps people lose fat and gain muscle. Even in those of normal weight, exercise can counter age-related loss of muscle mass and the deposition of body fat, especially abdominal fat, which has been found to be heart-damaging.

• Immunity — Exercise increases the circulation of immune cells that fight infections and tumors. Physically fit people get fewer respiratory infections and colds than people who are not fit.

TABLE 6.19

Percentage* of respondents who reported no leisure-time physical activity,† by month and selected characteristics — United States, Behavioral Risk Factor Surveillance System, 1994§

Characteristic	Jan	Feb	Mar	Apr	May	Jun	Jul	Aug	Sep	Oct	Nov	Dec	Percentage point range
Sex													
Men	32.5	32.6	26.9	25.7	24.3	23.4	24.9	23.8	25.9	25.5	28.7	30.4	9.2
Women	37.9	37.2	33.0	29.2	27.7	26.0	28.7	29.6	29.4	31.9	31.8	36.2	11.9
Age group (yrs)													
18–29	25.2	22.8	21.1	18.6	18.0	18.9	20.2	20.2	22.1	19.1	25.3	26.4	8.4
30–44	34.0	34.2	28.5	24.3	22.9	20.8	22.3	24.7	24.3	27.3	27.8	33.0	13.4
45–64	40.8	39.3	34.1	32.4	30.6	27.4	32.4	28.2	30.6	32.8	32.4	33.9	13.4
65–74	41.1	42.5	37.3	34.0	33.3	35.0	32.9	34.7	34.7	36.0	33.2	43.9	11.0
≥75	46.0	55.8	46.1	46.5	43.8	42.8	45.6	45.0	44.5	47.9	45.7	43.3	13.0¶
Race/Ethnicity													
White, non-Hispanic	34.4	32.7	27.5	26.0	24.3	22.4	25.0	24.4	26.5	26.7	27.6	31.4	12.0
Black, non-Hispanic	43.5	46.4	45.6	37.1	31.3	33.9	35.6	41.0	30.8	38.5	40.2	44.0	15.6
Hispanic	39.5	43.7	38.2	34.9	40.0	39.5	34.9	35.0	39.4	42.1	43.2	41.6	8.8
Other**	28.3	35.5	27.3	21.3	26.7	23.5	28.7	32.4	28.0	26.0	34.6	33.2	14.2
Total	**35.3**	**35.0**	**30.0**	**27.5**	**26.1**	**24.7**	**26.8**	**26.9**	**27.8**	**28.9**	**30.3**	**33.5**	**10.6**

*95% confidence intervals ranged from ±1.4% to ±10.6%.
†Defined as no participation in exercise, recreation, or physical activities other than regular job duties (e.g., running, calisthenics, golf, gardening, or walking for exercise.)
§n=105,853.
¶When February is excluded, the range is 5.1 percentage points.
**Numbers for other racial groups were too small for meaningful analysis.

Source: "Monthly Estimates of Leisure-Time Physical Inactivity — United States, 1994," *Morbidity and Mortality Weekly Report*, May 9, 1997

• Arthritis — Nearly everyone over 65 has some arthritic symptoms. Studies show that moderate exercise reduces pain and the need for medication.

• Depression — Exercise has long been known to help people overcome clinical depression. With the elderly, the benefits are greatest when they are brought in contact with others in the process.

• Gastrointestinal bleeding — Regular activity significantly reduces gastrointestinal hemorrhage in older people, probably by improving circulation to the digestive tract.

• Memory — Even brief periods of exercise can result in immediate improvements in memory in older adults. Exercise also fosters clearer thinking and faster reaction time by helping to speed the transmission of nerve messages.

• Sleep — In older adults who are sedentary, regular exercise, like walking, improves sleep quality and decreases the time it takes to fall asleep.

Despite these benefits, those over the age of 50 are much less likely than other age groups to exercise (Table 6.18). Thirty-two percent of the elderly exercised moderately three days a week or more, compared to 51 percent of those 30 to 49, and 57 percent among those 18 to 29. Fully one-quarter of those over 50 never exercised.

In 1997, the Centers for Disease Control and Prevention (CDC) reported that leisure-time physical activity declined with age. Among those 65 to 74, between approximately 33 and 44 percent of people reported no leisure-time activity. Among those older than 75, between 43 and 56 percent had no such activity. (See Table 6.19.) One of the national health objectives for the year 2000 is to reduce to 22 percent the proportion of elderly who engage in no leisure-time physical activity. Most older people who do exercise engage in low-impact exercises such as walking and swimming.

Social Ties

Contact with other people seems to be a significant factor in lowering mortality rates

97

among persons aged 70 and older, while being married seems to improve longevity for those between 38 and 59. The importance of social ties may increase with age partly because they compensate for the loss of spouses.

THE ECONOMICS OF HEALTH AND THE ELDERLY

The increasing numbers of elderly is focusing attention on the economic costs of health among the growing older population. The National Institute of Medicine (an advisory panel of the Federal Government) reports that each year the United States spends $600 million on research into the ailments of aging.

The cost of treating health problems of the old exceeds $162 billion a year. Unless ways are found to prevent or treat certain illnesses, the cost of caring for the disabled elderly will likely double in the next decade. Americans 65 years and older make up 13 percent of the population but account for 44 percent of all days in the hospital. The Alliance for Aging Research reports that people 65 and over (12.5 percent of the population) consume 30 percent of all health resources. By 2030, they will be 20 percent of the population and will likely utilize 50 percent of all health resources. The National Institute of Medicine believes that by delaying the time an elderly person enters a nursing home by only one month, the nation could save three billion dollars a year.

THE GROWTH OF GERIATRIC MEDICINE

The United States faces an acute shortage of doctors trained to treat older patients (geriatricians).

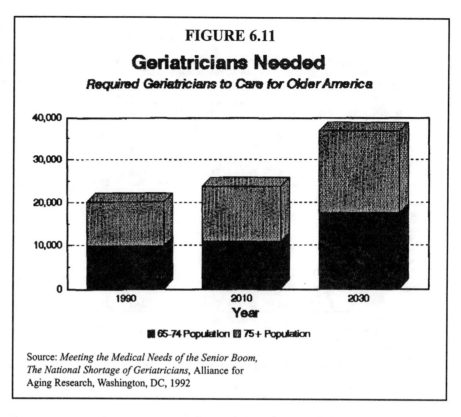

FIGURE 6.11

Geriatricians Needed
Required Geriatricians to Care for Older America

■ 65-74 Population ▨ 75+ Population

Source: *Meeting the Medical Needs of the Senior Boom, The National Shortage of Geriatricians*, Alliance for Aging Research, Washington, DC, 1992

This shortage will reach serious proportions as the post-World War II baby boom generation reaches retirement age. Currently, the United States has only one-fifth the numbers of geriatricians needed. Based on conservative estimates, at least 20,000 geriatricians are needed to provide appropriate care for the current population of over 30 million older Americans. By 2030, more than 65 million Americans will be over 65, and more than 36,000 geriatricians will be needed (Figure 6.11).

While the demand for geriatrics information grows and specialists and medical students want training in that area, most medical schools have no qualified staff to train them. Only doctors who have completed fellowships in geriatrics are eligible for certification. At this time, only about 100 geriatricians are graduated each year from all U.S. medical schools. The Alliance for Aging research reports that the United States has only one-fourth the number of academic physician-scientists needed to train doctors in geriatrics.

CHAPTER VII

MENTAL ILLNESS AND ALCOHOL ABUSE

As the nation ages, older Americans — along with their physical and mental well-being — have become topics of increasing interest. Mental illness and alcohol abuse are two major areas of concern that are receiving increased attention from the medical profession.

MENTAL HEALTH IS IMPORTANT

Mental health problems can be as debilitating as physical problems. Mental illness in the elderly may be functional, organic, or a combination of the two. Functional causes can include emotional stress, neuroses, or psychoses. Organic factors may include cerebral arteriosclerosis, chemical imbalances, or tumors. Most functional disorders are curable, while an estimated 15 percent of organic disorders are not. Many are manageable with therapy or medication. (Physical and organic mental illness is discussed in Chapter VI.)

Geriatric medicine, the study of the health problems of older people, is a relatively new field, and research is just beginning in this area. More information is needed on the normal mental ranges and capabilities of older people and the relationship between physiological changes and brain functions, as well as between physical illness and mental confusion. As the number of older people in the United States continues to increase, especially as the population of baby-boomers ages, the demand for geriatric research and resources for physical and mental health care will also grow.

PERSPECTIVES OF A LIFETIME MAY CHANGE AS PEOPLE GROW OLDER

Few personal problems disappear with old age, and many become more acute. Marital problems, which may have been controlled because one or both of the spouses were away at work, may erupt when a couple spends more time together in retirement. A possible "identity crisis" and reduced income due to retirement can aggravate a tense situation and put a strain on both husband and wife, especially if one of them becomes ill.

Old age is often a period of regrets, of "if onlies" and "could have beens," which can lead to mutual recriminations. With the median age of retirement for Americans falling and the life expectancy rising, married couples can now expect to spend many years together in retirement. Most elderly couples manage the transition, but some have problems.

Along with psychological adjustments to aging, the physical effects of aging must also be confronted. If good health habits and necessary medical treatment have not been maintained in early life, a person's health may decline more rapidly, and disease may worsen the situation. Hearing loss is common, and close correlations have been found between loss of hearing and depression. Vision loss often occurs, which limits reading, watching television, driving, and mobility. Loss of sight or hearing can cause perceptual disorientation, which, in turn, may lead to depression, paranoia, fear, and alienation.

A constant awareness of death can also become a problem during retirement years. Although most of the elderly in good health resolve their concerns with death, some acknowledge denial and fear. How well one accepts the inevitability of death can be a major factor in shaping that person's aging years.

The National Opinion Research Center of the University of Chicago, in its General Social Survey (GSS), periodically surveys attitudes of Americans. The 1994 survey found that work often lost its appeal for workers as they age. Fifty percent of those 55 to 59 reported that they would quit working if they could live comfortably the rest of their lives. Among those 60 to 64 years old, 38 percent said they would quit if they could; 15 percent of those over 65 claimed they want to quit work. Fifty-one percent of those 50 to 59 said they found life exciting, although their enjoyment seems to decline after the age of 60. Thirty-four percent of those 60 to 64 and 37 percent of those older than 65 claimed life was exciting.

Marital Satisfaction

Married people seem to remain healthier than those persons who are alone. Research suggests that marriage is correlated with longer and more satisfied lives, especially for men. And, in general, marital satisfaction increases with age. For the most part, frequent disagreements decrease with age. Adults older than 60 are less likely than other age groups to disagree on money, vacation plans, sex, children, and housekeeping, issues that have likely been resolved early in their relationships. They do, however, disagree on immediate daily concerns, such as which programs to watch on television, just as frequently as younger people.

OLDER AMERICANS CONSIDER THEMSELVES "SURVIVORS"

Because many of today's elderly grew up during the adversity of the Great Depression of 1929 and the early 1930s, most of them do not consider themselves disadvantaged or unable to handle hardship. Instead, many older Americans consider themselves "survivors." This attitude is generally confirmed by studies of older Americans that show that only a small number of the elderly believe they need counseling or consider loneliness to be a very serious problem. The psychological stress of retirement and physical decline may be of concern to some retirees, but not for the majority.

In fact, the fifties, not the sixties and seventies, are more likely to be reported as the years of confrontation with one's mortality and values. Bernice Neugarten, a psychologist at the University of Chicago, reported that the physical and career shifts that occur when people are in their fifties cause many people to become introspective. By the time they enter their sixties and seventies, many have resolved these conflicts.

The loss of work and the decline in social status that often accompany the loss of employment are two of the major causes of stress during old age. In a work-oriented society, these losses can create feelings of uselessness and lack of self-worth. Such a sense of worthlessness, if not replaced with something meaningful to the individual, can lead to depression, lowered resistance to disease, and lack of motivation. For those living in poverty, these feelings are compounded by poor housing, often in dangerous surroundings, inadequate diets, and financial worries caused by fixed incomes, making the elderly poor more susceptible to mental problems.

DEPRESSION

Depression is a common disorder. Although many younger people are willing to admit to themselves that they are depressed and to seek treatment, most elderly are not.

The medical community reports that although people over 60 are more likely to suffer from depression than any other age group including teenagers, they are the least likely to recognize or acknowledge that they are depressed. The

National Institute of Mental Health estimates that 3 percent of Americans over 65 are clinically depressed, while 7 to 12 percent of the elderly suffer from milder forms of depression that impair their quality of life.

A 1997 study, *Screening for Depression in Elderly Primary Care Patients* (J. M. Lyness, et al), found that 9 percent of elderly patients tested had major depressive disorder (MDD) and another 8 suffered minor depression. Neuropsychiatrist Dr. Martiece Carson, of the University of Oklahoma Health Sciences Center, estimates that in nursing homes, the situation is far worse, with 20 to 40 percent of patients being very depressed. Experts believe that a large proportion of the elderly population is undiagnosed and untreated.

Although many elderly persons are routinely treated by doctors for other conditions, many doctors fail to recognize that they are depressed, either because the doctors do not ask or because the elderly do not divulge it — many in their generation still attach a stigma to psychiatric problems. Studies of elderly people who committed suicide as a result of depression have found that three-quarters visited a doctor within a week of their deaths, but in only one-quarter of those cases did the doctor recognize that the patient was depressed.

Some people have a lifelong tendency toward depression that does not become obvious until late in life when the condition may be triggered by circumstances such as retirement, serious illness, or the loss of a loved one — situations common to aging. Older people face many real-life problems that can compound a biological tendency to depression. While it is natural for a person to feel depressed after a traumatic loss, when it lingers for months or years, it may be due to a physical or emotional disorder.

Often a physical illness itself causes depression in the elderly by altering the chemicals in the brain. Among the illnesses that can touch off depression are diabetes, hypothyroidism, kidney or liver dysfunction, heart disease, and infections. In people with these ailments, treating the underlying disease usually eliminates the depression. Sometimes medications, including over-the-counter drugs, prescribed for other conditions precipitate depression.

In 1995, scientists reported that depression in the elderly nearly tripled the risk of a stroke and underscored the need to treat the medical depression, not just to raise their spirits, but also in order to better protect them from other diseases. Other studies have found that elderly people with depression fared worse in recovering from heart attack, hip fractures, and severe infections like pneumonia. They also had more difficulty regaining functions like walking after being stricken by diseases of all kinds.

Depression, in some elderly people, causes them to willfully disregard medical needs, to take medications incorrectly, and to eat poorly. Experts believe these may be "covert" acts of suicide. In addition, depression interferes with the functioning of the immune system. Treatment works in about 80 percent of cases where patients receive appropriate therapy and take their medications.

TROUBLE WITH COPING — SUICIDE

Loss of a loved one is a major cause of depression and suicide for older people. During the first year after the death of a spouse, the risk of suicide for the remaining partner is 2.5 times greater than the general population; in the second year after a loss, the risk is 1.5 times as great.

Suicide Rates

Americans 65 and older make up about 13 percent of the population but account for about 20 percent of all suicides. In 1995, suicide was the third-leading cause of injury-related deaths among older U.S. residents, following deaths from accidental falls and motor vehicle crashes.

TABLE 7.1

Death rates for suicide, according to sex, detailed race, Hispanic origin, and age: United States, selected years 1950-95

[Data are based on the National Vital Statistics System]

Sex, race, Hispanic origin, and age	1950[1]	1960[1]	1970	1980	1985	1990	1992	1993	1994	1995	1993-95[2]
All persons	Deaths per 100,000 resident population										
All ages, age adjusted	11.0	10.6	11.8	11.4	11.5	11.5	11.1	11.3	11.2	11.2	11.2
All ages, crude	11.4	10.6	11.6	11.9	12.4	12.4	12.0	12.1	12.0	11.9	12.0
Under 1 year	...	...	...	...	...	...	...	...	...	...	...
1-4 years	...	...	...	...	...	...	...	...	...	...	...
5-14 years	0.2	0.3	0.3	0.4	0.8	0.8	0.9	0.9	0.9	0.9	0.9
15-24 years	4.5	5.2	8.8	12.3	12.8	13.2	13.0	13.5	13.8	13.3	13.5
25-44 years	11.6	12.2	15.4	15.6	15.0	15.2	14.8	15.1	15.3	15.3	15.2
25-34 years	9.1	10.0	14.1	16.0	15.3	15.2	14.5	15.1	15.4	15.4	15.3
35-44 years	14.3	14.2	16.9	15.4	14.6	15.3	15.1	15.1	15.3	15.2	15.2
45-64 years	23.5	22.0	20.6	15.9	16.3	15.3	14.7	14.6	14.0	14.1	14.2
45-54 years	20.9	20.7	20.0	15.9	15.7	14.8	14.7	14.5	14.4	14.6	14.5
55-64 years	27.0	23.7	21.4	15.9	16.8	16.0	14.8	14.6	13.4	13.3	13.8
65 years and over	30.0	24.5	20.8	17.6	20.4	20.5	19.1	18.9	18.1	18.1	18.4
65-74 years	29.3	23.0	20.8	16.9	18.7	17.9	16.5	16.3	15.3	15.8	15.8
75-84 years	31.1	27.9	21.2	19.1	23.9	24.9	22.8	22.3	21.3	20.7	21.4
85 years and over	28.8	26.0	19.0	19.2	19.4	22.2	21.9	22.8	23.0	21.6	22.5

Source: *Health, United States, 1996-97*, National Center for Health Statistics, Washington, DC, 1997

The suicide rate among the elderly began to increase in 1981, a reversal of a half-century decline. In 1995, the rate of suicide for those over 65 was 18.1 per 100,000 persons, compared to a rate of 11.2 per 100,000 for the general population. (See Table 7.1.) Men older than 65 (36.3 per 100,000 persons) have, by far, the highest suicide rates of all age groups, with those older than 85 most likely to kill themselves (63.1 per 100,000 persons). The increase in suicide among the elderly since 1981 is not an international trend, but peculiar to the United States.

The Centers for Disease Control and Prevention (CDC) reported that from 1980 to 1992, firearms were the most common method of suicide used by both men (74 percent) and women (31 percent) over 65, although a considerable proportion of women (25 percent) killed themselves with overdoses of drugs (Figure 7.1). Suicides were highest among divorced/widowed men (76.4 per 100,000) — 2.7 times that of married men.

Why Suicide among the Elderly?

Suicide figures for the elderly are not always reliable since many suicides are "passive." Persons who are sick, lonely, abandoned, or financially troubled have been known to starve themselves, not take medication, or mix medications dangerously. Also, the deaths counted as suicides are only those where suicide is named on the official death certificate. Other suicides may be attributed to secondary causes on death certificates. One in 6 elderly depressives succeed in committing suicide, in contrast to 1 in 100 in the general population.

The upward trend in suicide among the elderly perplexes health care experts who note that the elderly today are generally more financially secure and healthier than in past generations. Experts suggest that the technological advances being made to extend life (or postpone death) may have resulted in longer but less satisfying lives for many seniors. In particular, older males, who have the highest suicide rates, may become depressed at the loss of job, income, and power status when they retire.

Some mental health professionals have noted that the concept of "rational suicide" is gaining popularity. The elderly, who are faced with the possibility of extending their lives by medical technologies, are weighing the costs, and more of them are rejecting the option to extend life. Recently, as society's attitude toward suicide has changed, there has been a rise in the right-to-die movement, living wills, Dr. Jack Kevorkian and his assisted suicides, and the 1991 publication of a suicide manual.

The Centers for Disease Control (CDC) suggests that some of the increase in suicide rates is associated with increased firearms use. The CDC also predicts that, because older persons constitute the fastest-growing group in the United States, the number of suicides in this age group will likely continue to increase, especially with the lessening stigma attached to suicide.

Risk Factors

Risk factors for suicide among the elderly differ from those of younger persons. The elderly at risk for suicide often have a higher incidence of alcohol abuse and depression, are socially isolated, and use suicide methods that are more likely to succeed. In addition, older persons make fewer attempts per completed suicide, have a higher male-to-female ratio than other age groups, have often visited a health care provider shortly before their suicide, and have more physical illnesses and affective disorders. (For more information see *Death and Dying — Who Decides?*, Information Plus, Wylie, Texas, 1996.)

TREATMENT OF MENTAL ILLNESS

While most mental illness among older people can be treated, an estimated 80 percent will never receive treatment. The trend has been to shift the elderly out of the mental health system and into nursing homes, although few nursing homes or intermediate care facilities are equipped to recognize or treat mental illness among the elderly.

FIGURE 7.1

Percentage of suicides among persons aged ≥65 years, by sex and method* — United States, 1980–1992

Legend:
- Firearm (E955)
- Hanging (E953)
- Inhalation (E951-952)
- Overdose (E950)
- Other (E954, 956-959)

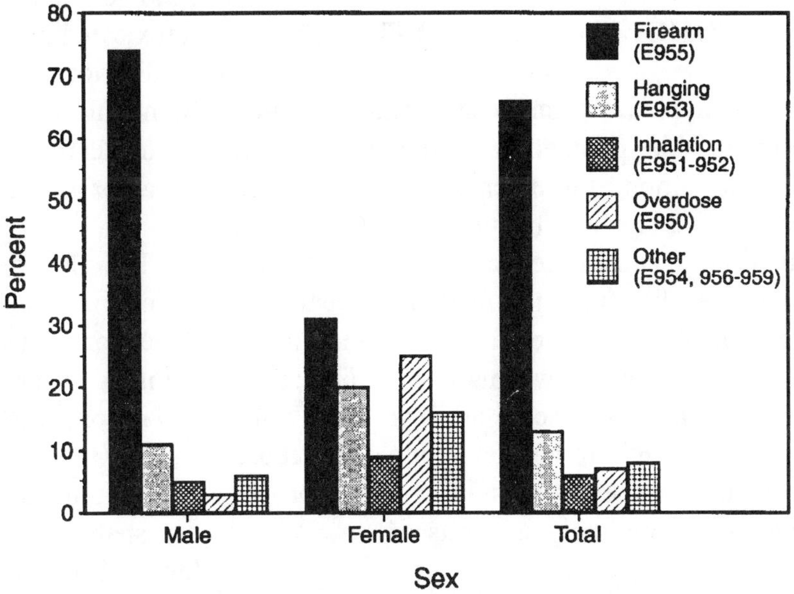

*Identified through *International Classification of Diseases, Ninth Revision*, codes on death certificates.

Source: "Suicide among Older Persons — United States, 1980-1992," *Morbidity and Mortality Weekly Report*, vol. 45, no. 1, January 12, 1996

Consequently, older people placed in nursing homes often receive little or no help with mental health problems.

Mental health experts estimate that 20 to 50 percent of all people labeled "senile" have conditions that are either preventable or reversible if detected and treated early. Today, 50 percent of American medical schools have geriatric courses, but since they are elective courses (not mandatory), only 2 percent of medical students take them. Only about 100 geriatricians are graduated each year.

In addition, many experienced doctors find older people difficult to treat because their ailments are often more complicated, and their healing process is slower and therefore less satisfying for the doctor, compared to the treatment of younger patients. This unfamiliarity and discomfort in treating the elderly may help explain why the proportion of mental health services targeted at treating the elderly is only half that of the general population. (See Chapter VI for a discussion of dementia and Alzheimer's disease.)

ALCOHOLISM AND ITS EFFECTS

Alcohol is the primary substance of abuse among the older population. Studying the rate of alcoholism among the older population is often more difficult than investigating that of the general population. Because older people are less likely to be employed full-time, job-related problems due to alcohol abuse are not frequent. Since many elderly are widowed, fewer marital conflicts result from alcohol. Older people are less likely to be arrested or brought to hospitals for alcohol abuse treatment, and once brought in, the proper diagnosis is more likely to be missed.

On the other hand, older Americans are also less likely to drink than younger Americans. Table 7.2 shows that a greater percentage of those over 50 (60 percent) report that they do not drink than other age groups and that among those elderly who drink, only 3 percent claim to be heavy drinkers. The percentage of drinkers begins to decline at age 50 and drops sharply after 60. While about 7 out of 10 persons 18 to 29 years old claim to be current drinkers, only 4 out of 10 people over age 65 report being current drinkers.

Several factors may contribute to the overall reduction in alcohol consumption by the elderly. Older people may suffer negative reactions from alcohol, and the expense may also limit their ability to purchase alcohol. Since elderly women outnumber elderly men, and women are less likely to drink than men, the total number of elderly abstainers is greater.

However, the House of Representatives Select Committee on Aging believes that drinking levels are higher among the elderly than reported. The committee contends that almost 60 percent of older Americans drink daily, and 15 percent of those are heavy drinkers (drink four or more drinks per day). One-third or more of elderly problem drinkers began drinking heavily with increasing age, when life changes and losses became common. As their metabolism slows, they often become more sensitive to alcohol and get intoxicated more easily. They may also be taking medications that do not mix well with alcohol. Sometimes, children of the alcoholic and even health care professionals may interpret their behavior as senility or choose to ignore it.

The National Institute of Alcohol and Alcoholism estimates that 10 to 15 percent of older Americans abuse alcohol, although among those admitted to nursing homes, psychiatric facilities, and hospitals, 20 percent may abuse alcohol.

Retirement, loss of a spouse, and loneliness can spark drinking. Figure 7.2 shows the stress levels of elderly problem and nonproblem drinkers and the social resources available to help them. As shown, problem drinkers have few resources available. Children of elderly alcoholics may interpret the behavior as senility or choose to ignore it, assuming that older parents might as well ease the pain of their remaining days.

Characteristics of Alcoholism among Older People

There are three types of older drinkers, distinguished by the lengths and the patterns of their drinking histories. The first group are those over 60 who have been drinking most of their lives. This group has been termed "survivors" or "early onset problem drinkers." They have beaten the statistical odds by living to an old age despite heavy drinking. These are the persons likely to show numerous medical problems, such as cirrhosis of the liver or brain damage, and psychological problems, such as depression.

The second group has histories of "bout" drinking between periods of relative sobriety. These are called "intermittents" because they may revert to heavy alcohol use under the stress and loneliness of aging.

The third group has been characterized as "reactors" or "late onset problem drinkers." The stress of later years, particularly the loss of work or a spouse, may bring about heavy drinking. These people show few of the physical consequences of prolonged drinking and fewer disruptions of their lives. More than two million American men and women over the age of 60 are believed to suffer from alcoholism. About two-thirds have had long-standing alcohol addictions; in the remaining one-third, alcohol abuse develops late in life.

HEALTH-RELATED CONSEQUENCES OF ALCOHOLISM

Older people generally show a decreased tolerance to alcohol. Consumption of a given amount of alcohol by an elderly person will usually produce a higher blood-alcohol level than it would in a younger individual. Chronic medical problems such as cirrhosis, may be present, but the need to detoxify (rid the body of poison) and to treat alcohol-withdrawal problems is less common. One possible explanation may be that those who have heavily abused alcohol do not survive into old age in great numbers.

Alcohol-induced organic brain syndrome (OBS) is characterized by confusion and disorientation. In elderly alcoholics it can be confused with, or complicated by, a diagnosis of "senility" (infirmity of body and mind associated with old age). A National Institute on Alcohol and Alcoholism (NIAA) program (1992) diagnosed 61 percent of elderly alcoholics as having OBS. Mortality for alcoholics with OBS is higher than those without OBS.

Since elderly people take more medication than other age groups, they are more susceptible to drug/alcohol interactions. Alcohol can reduce the effectiveness and safety of many medications and sometimes result in coma or death. Adverse consequences of alcohol consumption in older people are not restricted to problem drinkers. Older individuals with medical problems, including diabetes, heart disease, liver disease, and

TABLE 7.2

ALCOHOL USE BY KEY DEMOGRAPHIC GROUPS

	Heavy %	Moderate %	Never Drink %	Undesignated %	N #
ALL ADULTS	11	50	37	2	(1257)
GENDER					
Male	18	51	30	1	(620)
Female	6	50	43	1	(637)
RACE/ETHNICITY					
White	11	52	36	1	(1035)
Black	9	42	47	2	(118)
Hispanic	16	43	40	1	(82)
AGE					
18 - 29	23	51	26	1	(260)
30 - 39	11	57	30	2	(553)
40 - 49	7	46	47	*	(212)
50+	3	35	60	2	(215)
EDUCATION					
College graduate	8	66	24	2	(361)
Other college	10	60	29	1	(296)
High school graduate	13	46	40	1	(445)
Less than high school graduate	14	28	57	1	(138)
INCOME					
Over $50,000	12	61	26	1	(305)
$35,001 - $50,000	11	61	28	*	(221)
$25,001 - $35,000	14	52	32	1	(199)
$25,000 or less	12	40	47	1	(369)
REGION					
East	11	52	35	2	(247)
Midwest	14	51	34	1	(332)
South	10	43	46	1	(480)
West	10	59	29	2	(198)
COMMUNITY SIZE					
Urban	10	49	40	1	(365)
Suburban	12	55	32	1	(595)
Rural	12	42	45	1	(296)

Source: *The Prevention Index, 1996 Summary Report*, Rodale Press, Inc., Emmaus, PA, 1996

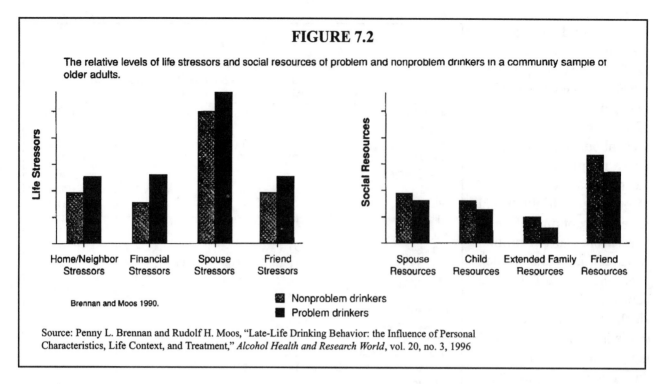

FIGURE 7.2

The relative levels of life stressors and social resources of problem and nonproblem drinkers in a community sample of older adults.

Brennan and Moos 1990.

Nonproblem drinkers
Problem drinkers

Source: Penny L. Brennan and Rudolf H. Moos, "Late-Life Drinking Behavior: the Influence of Personal Characteristics, Life Context, and Treatment," *Alcohol Health and Research World*, vol. 20, no. 3, 1996

central nervous system degeneration, often do not tolerate alcohol well.

Complications in Diagnosis and Treatment

Diagnosis of problem drinking among the aging population is complicated by the fact that many psychological, behavioral, and physical symptoms of problem drinking also occur in people who do not have drinking problems. For example, brain damage, heart disease, and gastrointestinal disorders often develop in older adults but may also occur with drinking. In addition, mood disorders, depression, and changes in employment, economics, or marital status often accompany aging as well as alcoholism. The resulting failure to identify the signs of drinking in an older person may aggravate health, relationships, and legal problems associated with alcohol abuse.

Older problem drinkers make up a relatively small proportion of the total number of clients seen by most agencies for treatment of alcohol abuse. Chances for recovery among older drinkers is considered good because older clients tend to complete their therapy more often than younger clients. Problem drinkers with a severe physical disorder or persistent organic brain syndrome (OBS) are often placed in nursing homes, although the staff members generally have limited experience and training in treating alcoholics.

The elderly may have conceptions of alcoholism that prevent them from realizing their abuse. Current theories suggest that alcoholism is a mental or physiological disease. However, only a small segment of the elderly consider it a disease, and a proportionately higher number of elderly claim alcoholism is a lack of willpower or a moral weakness. It is, therefore, more likely that an older person may attach a stigma or moral judgment to alcoholism and not seek treatment out of shame.

CHAPTER VIII

CARING FOR THE ELDERLY — CAREGIVERS

Societies generally recognize a moral obligation to care for their elderly and needy. In earlier, smaller communities, the care of an elderly person was usually provided by his or her family. The family often included several generations living in close contact with each other and with other members of the community who could share the responsibility and burden. In fact, family members were the mainstay of the nation's elder care system.

In America today, family units are much smaller, and family members may live great distances from each other. Communities are often made up of commuters and families with two working parents who may lack the time or desire to care for the elderly. Nonetheless, elder care still usually falls to the family and, more specifically, to the wife, daughter, or daughter-in-law.

Women generally live longer than men. The larger numbers of elderly women in American society result in the situation that most elderly men live in family settings (not necessarily with spouses) where they may be more easily assisted, while many elderly women live alone.

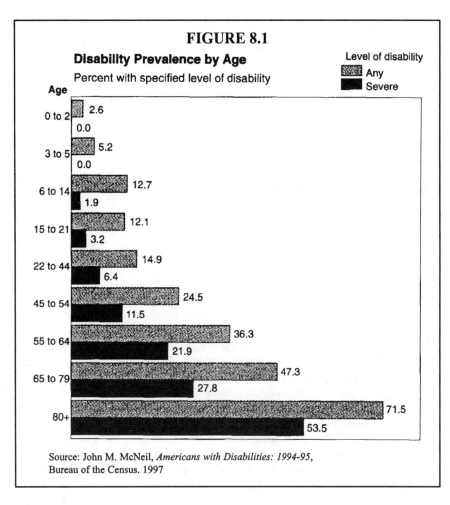

FIGURE 8.1

Disability Prevalence by Age

Percent with specified level of disability

Level of disability
Any
Severe

Source: John M. McNeil, *Americans with Disabilities: 1994-95*, Bureau of the Census. 1997

DISABILITY AND DEPENDENCY RATES

After the age of 65, the need for assistance increases sharply as the elderly grow older. The Bureau of the Census reported that, in 1994, from age 55 to 64, 36.3 percent of Americans had some disability, and 21.9 percent had a severe disability. From 65 to 79, 47.3 percent had some disability, and 27.8 were severely disabled. Among those 80 and above, 71.5 percent were disabled, while 53.5

percent suffered from severe disability (Figure 8.1). Blacks were more likely to need assistance than Whites or Hispanics, and females were more likely to require assistance than males. (For more information on disability, see Chapter VI — Health.)

Experts estimate that almost half of the elderly need help with at least one activity, such as getting dressed, going for a walk, or going to the bathroom. Another third need help with two to three activities, and approximately one-fifth require assistance with four or more activities. (Activities of daily living — ADLs — consist of getting in or out of bed, bathing, using the toilet, eating, and other personal chores.)

TYPES OF DISABILITY

Older people vary greatly in their health and dependency needs. One measure of health status is an elder's ability to perform activities necessary for day-to-day living, such as personal hygiene and moving about.

Many people have difficulty with "instrumental" activities of daily living (IADLs). These chores also include preparing meals, doing housework and laundry, shopping, getting to medical services, using the telephone, and managing finances. Most caregivers are needed to help with household tasks (meal preparation, housecleaning and laundry), shopping, and transportation. Table 8.1 shows the various limitations among the disabled.

In addition, some people have functional disabilities such as lifting and carrying weight as heavy as 10 pounds, reading newsprint, hearing normal conversation, or climbing a flight of stairs. These disabilities may vary greatly from person to person. One person may have *difficulty* reading newsprint; another may be *unable* to read it. Other disabilities included in the Bureau of the Census list of disabilities were the necessity to use a wheelchair; use of a cane, crutches, or walker for more than 6 months; Alzheimer's disease or mental retardation; any condition that limits the amount of work an individual is able to perform; and any condition that makes it difficult to do housework.

A GROWING ELDERLY POPULATION — A GROWING NEED FOR CAREGIVERS

The supply of caregivers is not keeping pace with the growth in the older population. The number of elderly persons for every 100 adults of working age (aged 18 to 64) is called the old-age dependency ratio. In 1990,

---

TABLE 8.1

Definition of Disability Including Functional Limitations, ADLs, and IADLs

People 15 years old and over were identified as having a disability if they met any of the following criteria:

- Used a wheechair or were a long-term user of a cane, crutches, or a walker
- Had difficulty performing one or more functional activities (seeing, hearing, speaking, lifting/carrying, using stairs, or walking)
- Had difficulty with one or more activities of daily living (the ADLs included getting around inside the home, getting in or out of bed or a chair, bathing, dressing, eating, and toileting)
- Had difficulty with one or more instrumental activities of daily living (the IADLs included going outside the home, keeping track of money and bills, preparing meals, doing light housework, taking prescription medicines in the right amount at the right time, and using the telephone)
- Had one or more specified conditions (a learning disability, mental retardation or another developmental disability, Alzheimer's disease, or some other type of mental or emotional condition)
- Were limited in their ability to do housework
- Were 16 to 67 years old and limited in their ability to work at a job or business
- Were receiving federal benefits based on an inability to work

People age 15 and over were identified as having a severe disability if they were unable to perform one or more functional activities; needed personal assistance with an ADL or IADL; used a wheelchair; were a long-term user of a cane, crutches, or a walker; had a developmental disability or Alzheimer's disease; were unable to do housework; were receiving federal disability benefits; or were 16 to 67 years old and unable to work at a job or business.

Source: John M. McNeil, *Americans with Disabilities: 1994-95*, Bureau of the Census, Washington, DC, 1997

there were 20 elderly persons for every 100 working-aged adults. When the youngest baby boomers approach retirement age in 2025, there will be 32 elderly persons for every 100 people of working age.

The National Long-Term Care Survey

As life expectancy has increased and the number of elderly has grown, some observers have predicted a nation burdened with people living longer who are crippled with disabilities and riddled with pain. Certainly, in some cases, that does occur. However, the predicted pandemic of pain and disability has not materialized to the extent some have feared. Instead, recent research shows that not only are Americans living longer, but they are developing fewer chronic diseases and disabilities. America's elderly are defying stereotypes that aging is synonymous with increasing disability and dependence.

Researchers at Duke University, in the *National Long Term Care Survey*, a federal study that surveyed nearly 20,000 people age 65 and older in 1982, 1984, 1989, and 1994, found that every year there has been a smaller and smaller percentage of older people unable to take care of themselves. Although the annual declines have been only 1 to 2 percent per year, they have been steady since 1982, when the survey began. In addition, the percentage of old people with chronic diseases, such as high blood pressure, arthritis, and emphysema, has steadily declined.

Dr. Kenneth Manton, Larry Corder, and Eric Stallard, demographers at Duke University who analyzed the survey data, calculated that declining disability rates from 1982 until 1994 saved Medicare $200 million. They explained that if the disability rates of 1982 had held constant into 1994, there would have been nearly 300,000 more disabled people age 65 to 74 in the population. The researchers found 1.2 million fewer people, a 65-percent reduction, disabled in 1994 than would have been expected had the disability rate remained the same as in 1982.

An important traditional measurement of the extent and severity of disability is the number of people at advanced age in nursing homes or other institutions. In 1994, there were an estimated 1.7 million elderly people in institutions. If the 1982 rates had prevailed (adjusted for population), 2.1 million persons would have been institutionalized. The net difference of 400,000 persons represents actual improvement in rates of chronic disability. At an annual per capita nursing home cost in 1994 of $43,300, the difference suggests savings of up to $17.3 billion in nursing home expenses. (Some costs may be transferred to other sectors, such as assisted living arrangements or even life sustaining medical technology. Experts believe this cost still represents substantial progress.)

These findings have led researchers on aging to ask why it is that older Americans are less frail and feeble than before. One answer is that people either are not developing the diseases that cripple or disable them, or they are developing them later in life. Why? There are a number of explanations, all of which probably contributed to the improved health of the nation's elderly. One possible explanation attributes the decline to increased education — greater availability of medical knowledge to the public, in general, as well as increasing educational levels among the elderly. Education level has been associated with better health. In addition, higher levels of education are also associated with greater wealth, which enables a person to live a more healthful life and to get adequate health care. Many elderly people practice better health habits today, such as exercising more and eating a more healthful diet, which likely improve not only the quality of their lives but also, perhaps, their longevity.

Another possible explanation for the improved health of the elderly is that old people are reaping the benefits of improvements in public health (nutrition, water quality, hygiene) that occurred when they were young. In addition, medical advances, like hip replacements, lens replacements for cataract sufferers, and better pain relievers, can delay or prevent the burdens of chronic diseases that afflicted previous generations.

109

PROFILE OF AMERICA'S CAREGIVERS

The Majority Are Women

The 1997 *National Survey of Caregivers*, conducted by the National Alliance for Caregiving and the American Association of Retired Persons (AARP), found that 22.4 million U.S. households — nearly 1 in 4 — were involved in family caregiving of elderly relatives or friends. Since 1987, the number of households caring for an older adult has tripled.

The survey found that the typical caregiver is a married woman in her mid-forties who works full time, is a high school graduate, and has an annual household income of $35,000. The average age is 46. Seventy-three percent are female. Among Asians, however, almost equal percentages of men and women are caregivers. Asian caregivers were more highly educated than other racial/ethnic groups. (See Table 8.2.)

Caregivers provided anywhere from less than one hour of care per week to "constant care." The average caregiver provided care for 18 hours per week. Table 8.3 shows the hours per week that caregivers estimated they gave. (Level refers to demand and intensity of care, from Level 1 to Level 5, with 5 being the highest and most demanding. Level 5 caregivers provided more than 40 hours per week or "constant care.") Forty-one percent of caregivers were caring for children under 18 at the same time as elderly relatives or friends. Eleven percent of caregivers provided long-distance care (one hour or more from the caregiver's residence).

Women spend more time than men in caregiving activities — 18.8 hours per week for women and 15.5 hours for men. While women constituted 73 percent of all caregivers, they were 79 percent of the constant/40-hour-per-week caregivers. Asians spent significantly less time than other minority groups in providing care — 15.1 hours for Asians, 20.6 hours for Blacks, 19.8 hours for Hispanics, and 17.5 hours for Whites.

The average caregiver today spends less time giving care than her counterpart a decade ago. She

TABLE 8.2

CAREGIVER PROFILE
(Base = Total Caregivers)

	TOTAL	WHITE	BLACK	HISPANIC	ASIAN
Number interviewed (unweighted)	n=1,509	n= 623	n=306	n=307	n=264
Number in U.S. population (weighted)*	n=2,241	n=1,829	n=238	n=105	n= 40
GENDER					
Female	72.5%	73.5%	76.8%	67.4%	52.3%
Male	27.5	26.5	23.2	32.6	47.7
AGE OF CAREGIVER					
Under 35	22.3%	20.5%	23.5%	37.1%	38.6%
35-49	39.4	39.0	44.4	37.5	43.6
50-64	26.0	26.8	22.5	21.2	14.4
65 or Older	12.4	13.6	9.5	4.2	3.4
Mean (years)	46.15	46.93	44.75	40.01	39.01
MARITAL STATUS					
Married or living with partner	65.7%	67.8%	50.9%	63.8%	64.4%
Single, never married	12.6	11.1	19.3	18.2	26.1
Separated or divorced	13.0	12.1	19.0	15.7	6.0
Widowed	8.0	8.3	9.8	2.0	3.0
CHILDREN UNDER AGE 18 IN HOUSEHOLD					
Yes	41.3%	38.8%	51.0%	58.3%	51.1%
No	57.8	60.2	48.4	41.7	48.1
EDUCATIONAL ATTAINMENT					
Less than high school	9.0%	8.2%	16.3%	11.1%	2.3%
High school graduate	35.3	36.0	32.0	35.2	18.2
Some college	22.5	22.2	26.8	26.7	17.0
College graduate	20.1	20.4	15.4	18.2	39.0
Graduate School +	8.8	8.8	5.6	6.5	20.8
Technical school	3.5	3.5	3.3	2.3	1.9
EVER ON ACTIVE DUTY/ U.S. ARMED FORCES	11.5%	11.1%	11.1%	11.4%	7.2%

Continued on following page.

is also more likely to use paid services (75 percent), such as personal and nursing care, wheelchairs, home modification, etc. (Table 8.4). The financial burden on caregivers has eased. Those who provide financial help to their dependents spend a median of 3 percent of monthly income, compared with 7 percent in 1987. Caregivers are spending out-of-pocket about $2 billion per month for groceries, medicine, and cash supports for their relatives.

Recipients of Care

Eighty-five percent of caregivers took care of a relative, and 15 percent, a friend or neighbor. Care recipients were usually female: 31 percent of caregivers took care of their own mothers, 9 percent, their mothers-in-law, and 12 percent took care of grandmothers. Only 5 percent reported taking care of spouses. The average age of care recipients was 77 years. Figure 8.2 shows the main illnesses of care recipients. One-fifth of care recipients live in the same household as their caregiver.

Slightly more than half of all care recipients lived alone. Asian care recipients were more likely than Whites to live with their caregivers.

Competing Demands

Sixty-four percent of caregivers were working full- or part-time. Half of them reported making adjustments to their work schedule (rearranging their work schedules, taking time off without pay, working part-time, or quitting their jobs) for caregiving responsibilities. Six percent said they gave up work entirely, and 6 percent took early retirement. (See Table 8.5.) Although working men also reported these conflicts, fewer of them rearranged their work lives to accommodate caregiving.

Caregivers Need Care, Too

Caregivers have become the casualties of our ability to live longer. — Jack Nottingham, executive director, Rosalyn Carter Institute for Human Development, Georgia Southwestern College

For many people, caring for an ill or disabled elderly person may, over time, become an enormous burden. Elder caretakers may neglect their own health and needs because no one else is available to care for their elderly spouse or parent.

The *National Survey* reported that slightly less than half of caregivers said their caregiving duties caused them to give up time with other family members; 43 percent gave up vaca-

---

TABLE 8.2 (Continued)

CAREGIVER PROFILE

	TOTAL	WHITE	BLACK	HISPANIC	ASIAN
Number interviewed (unweighted)	n=1,509	n= 623	n=306	n=307	n=264
Number in U.S. population (weighted)*	n=2,241	n=1,829	n=238	n=105	n= 40
CURRENT EMPLOYMENT					
Employed full-time	51.8%	51.0%	55.6%	51.8%	63.3%
Employed part-time	12.3	12.7	10.5	13.4	14.0
Retired	15.9	17.0	13.7	6.8	4.2
Not employed	19.7	18.9	20.3	28.0	18.2
HOUSEHOLD INCOME					
Under $15,000	14.0%	11.7%	29.1%	21.1%	8.3%
$15K-24.9K	18.0	17.3	24.8	22.5	11.0
$25K-29.9K	9.3	9.5	9.8	7.8	8.0
$30K-39.9K	14.0	14.0	12.4	16.3	13.3
$40K-49.9K	10.3	10.4	7.8	11.1	14.0
$50K-74.9K	14.0	14.4	9.5	10.4	15.5
$75K or higher	10.9	12.1	3.0	6.2	19.7
Median	$35K	$35K	$22.5K	$27.5K	$45K

Note: Column percentages may not total 100% because of refusals.
*Weighted numbers refer to numbers of caregiving households in the U.S. population. Each number must be multiplied by 10,000 to determine the U.S. population prevalence for that cell. For example, 2,241 means 22,410,000 (i.e., there are an estimated 22,410,000 caregiving households in the U.S.). All percentages are based on weighted data.

Source: *Family Caregiving in the U.S. — Findings from a National Survey*, National Alliance for Caregiving and American Association of Retired Persons, Bethesda, MD and Washington, DC, 1997

TABLE 8.3

MEAN HOURS OF CARE PROVIDED PER WEEK BY CAREGIVER LEVEL

	Number in Sample	Hours Per Week
All Caregivers	1,509	17.9
Level 1	389	3.6
Level 2	208	8.2
Level 3	287	9.1
Level 4	355	27.3
Level 5	185	56.5

• *All Level 5 caregivers, by definition, provide "constant care" or 40 or more hours of care per week (an estimated 2,910,000 caregiver households nation-*

Source: *Family Caregiving in the U.S. — Findings from a National Survey*, National Alliance for Caregiving and American Association of Retired Persons, Bethesda, MD and Washington, DC, 1997

cent said it was the recipient's attitude (uncooperative, demanding); and 4 percent mentioned problems with location, inconvenience, or distance.

When asked what were the greatest rewards of caregiving, 16 percent each said knowing their recipient was well cared for, satisfaction of doing a good deed, and the recipient's appreciation. Also mentioned was watching the recipient's health improve, family loyalty, "giving back," fulfilling family obligations (11 percent each), and spending time together (10 percent).

When asked to describe their caregiving experience in one word, 57 percent chose positive words, such as "rewarding," "thankful," "loving," and "OK." Just over one-third used negative words — "stressful," "burdened," "exhausting" — to describe their caregiving. Eight percent said they did not know how they felt about caregiving.

tions, hobbies, or other activities. Fifteen percent reported experiencing physical or mental health problems due to caregiving. The number one mechanism mentioned to cope with stress was prayer (74 percent); 88 percent of Black caregivers used prayer. Talking with friends (66 percent), exercise (38 percent), and hobbies (36 percent) were also indicated. Relatively few mentioned help from professionals or other counselors (16 percent), use of medications (7 percent), or resorting to alcohol (3 percent). Asian caregivers (6 percent) were far less likely than Whites (17 percent) or Blacks (14 percent) to seek professional help.

Biggest Difficulty and Greatest Rewards of Caregiving

One in 5 caregivers said the biggest difficulties they faced in providing care were the demands on their time and not being able to do what they wanted; 15 percent said it was watching or worrying about their recipient's deterioration; 10 per-

TABLE 8.4

UTILIZATION OF SERVICES (Base = Total Caregivers) (percentages)

Acquiring a wheel chair, walker, or other device	46.7
Personal or nursing care services	37.8
Home modification	28.1
Home-delivered meal services	15.6
Assistance with housework	15.6
Financial information service	15.5
Transportation service	14.9
Respite care	14.1
Adult day care/senior center	9.5
Support group	6.6

Source: *Family Caregiving in the U.S. — Findings from a National Survey*, National Alliance for Caregiving and American Association of Retired Persons, Bethesda, MD and Washington, DC, 1997

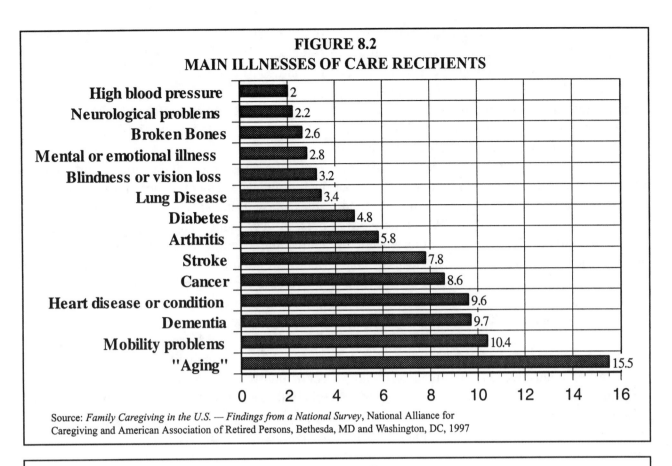

FIGURE 8.2
MAIN ILLNESSES OF CARE RECIPIENTS

Illness	Value
High blood pressure	2
Neurological problems	2.2
Broken Bones	2.6
Mental or emotional illness	2.8
Blindness or vision loss	3.2
Lung Disease	3.4
Diabetes	4.8
Arthritis	5.8
Stroke	7.8
Cancer	8.6
Heart disease or condition	9.6
Dementia	9.7
Mobility problems	10.4
"Aging"	15.5

Source: *Family Caregiving in the U.S. — Findings from a National Survey*, National Alliance for Caregiving and American Association of Retired Persons, Bethesda, MD and Washington, DC, 1997

TABLE 8.5

WORK-RELATED ADJUSTMENTS BY LEVEL OF CARE
(Base = Caregivers Ever Employed while Providing Care to This Care Recipient)
(percentages)

	Total	Level 1	Level 2	Level 3	Level 4	Level 5
Total unweighted+	(N=1,193)	(n=330)	(n=174)	(n=240)	(n=277)	(n=113)
Total weighted+	(N=1,716)	(n=530)	(n=245)	(n=331)	(n=363)	(n=166)
Made any changes listed below	54.2	40.8	45.1	58.2*	66.5*	75.0*
Changed daily schedule: go in late, leave early, take time off during work	49.4	36.3	44.0	54.0*	61.5*	64.0*
Took leave of absence	10.9	5.5	5.9	9.1	17.8*	26.0*
Worked fewer hours, took less demanding job	7.3	2.0	3.8	6.5	11.7*	25.0*
Lost any job benefits	4.2	2.4	3.4	1.7	7.5	11.0*
Turned down a promotion	3.1	1.2	2.1	0.7	6.0	10.4*
Chose early retirement	3.6	1.2	0.3	3.0	5.1	14.8*
Gave up work entirely	6.4	1.3	0.2	4.4	10.2*	30.3*

+Unweighted numbers refer to numbers of caregivers in the sample, while weighted numbers refer to numbers of caregiving households in the U.S. population nationwide.

*Differences in percentages are significant at the .05 level.

Source: *Family Caregiving in the U.S. — Findings from a National Survey*, National Alliance for Caregiving and American Association of Retired Persons, Bethesda, MD and Washington, DC, 1997

Experts agree that even a small break from the responsibilities of elder care can be of enormous benefit to a caregiver, and many believe that it can prevent older people from being placed in nursing homes prematurely. In fact, studies have found that more elderly people are placed in institutions because of the caregiver's burnout than because of a decline in their own condition. Recent attention to the special needs of caretakers has resulted in a variety of formal and informal programs designed to provide some relief for them. While these programs generally provide services to the dependent elderly, their purpose is primarily to assist the caregiver.

RESPITE CARE

Families caring for elderly relatives often do not think of themselves as caregivers. Although they may know they need a break, they may not be aware of the concept of respite care, nor do they know how to arrange for it. The dictionary definition of respite is "an interval of temporary relief or rest, as from pain, work, duty, etc." The Foundation of Long-Term Care (FLTC) has formulated a working definition of geriatric respite care as, "the temporary supportive care of an elder who normally lives in the community with a caregiver, by a substitute caregiver, in order to strengthen and maintain the regular caregiver's well-being and ability to maintain care at home."

Respite care takes many forms. In some cases, the respite worker comes to the home to take care of the elderly person so that the caregiver can take a few hours for personal needs, relaxation, or rest. Respite care is also available for longer periods so that caregivers can recuperate from their own illnesses or even take a vacation.

Adult day care programs around the country provide structured daytime programs through which functionally impaired adults can receive the social, health, and supportive services needed to restore or maintain optimal functioning. While not designed specifically to aid caregivers, adult day care programs serve in a similar purpose as formal respite programs by temporarily giving the caregiver physical and psychological relief from the burden of elder care.

FROM INFORMAL TO FORMAL SERVICES

At the same time that the elderly population is increasing, the segment of the general public available to provide unpaid care, generally family members, is decreasing. The once familiar extended family has become less common in the United States. In addition, several other trends continue to decrease the availability of caregivers, including more women employed outside the home, greater geographical separation of families, high divorce rates, and smaller families. Fewer caregivers will be available for the increasing number of elderly needing support. As a result, the elderly will likely have to pay for a higher proportion of professional services. (See Chapter IX for information on health care.)

Foster Care

Although many elderly do not need intensive nursing home care, some of those who need limited assistance are increasingly being cared for in foster homes. It is an alternative that gives an older person safe and comfortable care at a cost much less than nursing home care — monthly costs averaging about $1,000 — one-third that of nursing homes.

Foster care for adults is like foster care for children; a person or a family is paid to take in other people and provide them a home — meals, laundry, a place to sleep, and someone to talk to and watch over them. In some programs, the residents pay for the care with their own money, although often a government agency or non-profit agency brings the family and the participant together. Some elderly pay for their care with their Social Security or pension income, some from Supplemental Security income (SSI). In some cases, states have received Medicaid waivers that allow them to spend federal long-term nursing funds for community-based care programs like adult foster homes. Licensing regulations vary from state to state.

There are no overall figures on how many older people are living in foster homes since no single agency monitors the dozens of programs nationwide. Experts estimate that tens of thousands of older people are in foster care, and they see those numbers increasing.

The benefits of foster care, in addition to cost, are considerable: residents report enjoying family life and personal relationships with their foster care families, they tend to focus less on their infirmities and be more independent, and their families are happier not to have to admit them to nursing homes.

"Cluster" Care

Begun as an experiment in New York State in the mid-1980s, *cluster care* is another alternative form of personal care for those elderly who do not need full-time, trained nursing care. In cluster care, a team of workers employed by one home attendant agency is responsible for the care of a group of clients who live in close proximity. With the supervision of a nurse and a case manager, the clients schedules are set by evaluating which activities of daily living they need help with and how long it takes to perform those tasks. One worker (a "shared aide") can coordinate visits to several clients in a day. Said one family member, "Cluster care approximates the kind of care we are used to giving those we love in extended families."

Experts predict the program will become increasingly popular across the country as states strapped for money face a population growing older and in need of care. However, some elderly and disabled cannot be served by such a program — those so frail they need constant monitoring during their waking, and often sleeping, hours, and those living far from other personal-care clients.

The On Lok Program

One comprehensive-care program for frail elderly people that is winning support across the country is based on a San Francisco model. The On Lok center in San Francisco's Chinatown weaves medical care, home care, social services, and case management into a single web of care. Founded 20 years ago, the On Lok center was named from the Chinese words for "peaceful" and "happy."

"It's not for everyone," said Don Sherwood, who tracks the On Lok program for the Office of Research and Demonstration at the Health Care Financing Administration, the federal agency that manages Medicare and Medicaid. "Only 5 percent of those over 65 are frail enough to be eligible, and many don't want to change doctors and go to a day health center. But for those who want comprehensive care, it's very good."

Clients sign over their Medicaid and Medicare policies. In return, they receive housing and total care free of charge, as long as they use the program's doctors and nurses. Central to the On Lok model is the day health center, a vastly expanded version of the social day programs that proliferated in the 1970s. In addition to recreational activities, the centers have added health services with on-site geriatricians, rehabilitation therapists, nurse-practitioners, and other health professionals. When needed, clients are hospitalized. They may also receive, if necessary, intravenous antibiotic or hydration therapy at the center.

Most participants like the program because they are guaranteed health care, including hospitalization or nursing home care, until they die or leave the program. Despite the support services, which are more extensive than would be generally supplied under Medicaid, the program is less expensive than nursing home care. Because the health of participants is constantly monitored, their use of hospitals is so sharply reduced that On Lok facilities cost less than regular care under Medicaid or Medicare, despite all the extra services that the model provides.

CORPORATE INVOLVEMENT

Corporations are not welfare agencies. Their focus is on a profitable balance sheet. Nevertheless, many companies are exploring elder care issues because, for many reasons, it may be in their best interest.

Labor Costs

Companies with a high average age among employees, or with more female workers, are more likely to have a higher number of caregivers and, hence, more work time lost to elder care tasks. Tardiness and increased use of the telephone frequently occur among some caregivers; work disruptions that can affect the morale of other employees, who may feel they must work harder to compensate for co-workers who assume the duties of caregivers. Employees distracted on the job were more likely to make mistakes and have higher accident rates, as well as increased conflict with fellow employees.

Caregiving problems can also remain hidden from the employer because employees may "cover up" their activities when late or absent. Caregivers may work fewer hours, change schedules, and take time off without pay, which leads to increased hiring and training by the employer. However, until recently, the additional labor losses attributable to caregiving had not been quantified.

The MetLife Study of Employer Costs for Working Caregivers

Employers, as well as employees, bear a financial burden from personal caregiving. In response to the growing evidence that caregiving for older family members is exacting a cost on U.S. business, the National Alliance for Caregiving and Metropolitan Life Insurance Company conducted a 1997 study, *Family Caregiving in the United States: Findings from a National Survey*, to collect new data on the cost of caregiving. The study included only full-time employees and only those identified as Levels III, IV, and V caregivers. These caregivers provided assistance with at least two Activities of Daily Living (ADLs; bathing, toileting, feeding, transferring, or walking) and at least four Instrumental Activities of Daily Living (IADLs; financial management, transportation, help with medications, shopping, preparing meals, etc.). They provided between 9 (Level III) and 56 hours (Level V) of care each week.

TABLE 8.6

Replacement Costs for Employees Who Quit			
Full-Time Employed Caregivers by Gender (Levels III, IV, and V)	Number who quit in a given year (4.2%)	Median Weekly Wage	Cost to Employers (75% of annual wage)
Men	59,642	$ 701	$ 1,630,553,866
Women	180,981	$ 468	$ 3,303,262,439
Total	240,623		$ 4,933,816,305

TABLE 8.7

Costs Due to Absenteeism			
Full-Time Employed Caregivers by Gender (Levels III, IV, and V)	Number absent average 6 days per year (10.5%)	Median Weekly Wage	Cost to Employers
Men	156,205	$ 701	$ 131,399,945
Women	473,997	$ 468	$ 266,196,973
Total	630,203		$ 397,596,918

Source of both tables: *The MetLife Study of Employer Costs for Working Caregivers*, Metropolitan Life Insurance Company, Westport, CT, 1997

According to the study, 23.2 percent of all households, or 22.4 million households, were involved in caregiving. The majority (64.2 percent) of caregivers were employed, most (52 percent) full-time. Based on these findings, 14.4 million employed caregivers were balancing work with their caregiving roles.

Replacing Employees Who Quit

Over 17 percent of caregivers said they had to quit their jobs or take early retirement because of caregiving tasks. These people provided care an average of four years. Table 8.6 shows the replacement costs — a total of almost $5 billion — for employees who quit.

Absenteeism

The study found that 10.5 percent of employed caregivers were absent a minimum of three or more days in the previous six months due to caregiving chores. The total cost to employers was almost $400 million annually (Table 8.7). Most (59 percent) employed caregivers arrived late for work, left early, took extended lunch breaks, or in some other way altered their work schedule. These caregivers lost an estimated 1 hour per week that could not be made up, for a total cost to employers of $488 million annually (Table 8.8).

Interruptions at Work

Many caregivers were interrupted during their workdays by phone calls to the care recipient or service providers or by other caregiving chores. These breaks in work were estimated at 1 hour per week, a total cost to employers of $3.8 billion (Table 8.9). Sixty percent of caregivers reported experiencing an elder care crisis in the previous months that caused additional phone calls, loss of concentration, and partial absenteeism that caused a loss of 3 days per year and a total cost of more than $1 billion (Table 8.10).

Supervising Caregivers

Eighty-one percent of employed caregivers said their supervisors were sympathetic regarding their caregiving burdens. However, the cost to employers in providing emotional support, arranging coverage for caregivers to be absent, counseling about benefits, and dealing with work disruptions was estimated to be one hour per month and $805 million (Table 8.11).

Total Cost to Business

The total costs of caregiving in lost productivity to U.S. business is $11.5 billion per year (Table

TABLE 8.8

Costs Due to Partial Absenteeism				
Full-Time Employed Caregivers by Gender (Levels III, IV, and V)	Number experiencing partial absenteeism (59%)	Number unable to make up 50 hours/year (22%)	Median Weekly Wage	Cost to Employers
Men	837,082	184,166	$ 701	$ 161,375,558
Women	2,540,085	558,843	$ 468	$ 326,923,158
Total	**3,377,168**	**743,009**		**$ 488,298,715**

TABLE 8.9

Costs Due to Workday Interruption				
Full-Time Employed Caregivers by Gender (Levels III, IV, and V)	Number experiencing workday interruptions	Hours lost due to interruptions (avg. 50 hr/yr)	Median Weekly Wage	Cost to Employers
Men	1,420,049	71,002,434	$ 701	$ 1,244,317,663
Women	4,309,068	215,453,391	$ 468	$ 2,520,804,670
Total	**5,729,117**	**286,455,825**		**$ 3,765,122,333**

Source of both tables: *The MetLife Study of Employer Costs for Working Caregivers*, Metropolitan Life Insurance Company, Westport, CT, 1997

8.12), a conservative figure because it is based on median wages and do not include those giving Level I and Level II care or those working part-time. If those caregivers were also included in the calculations, the study concluded that the total costs to U.S. business would exceed $29 billion per year.

TABLE 8.10

Costs Due to Eldercare Crises				
Full-Time Employed Caregivers by Gender (Levels III, IV, and V)	Number affected by crises (60%)	Days lost to crises (3 per year)	Median Weekly Wage	Cost to Employers
Men	852,029	2,556,088	$ 701	$ 358,363,487
Women	2,585,441	7,756,322	$ 468	$ 725,991,745
Total	3,437,470	10,312,410		$ 1,084,355,232

Source: *The MetLife Study of Employer Costs for Working Caregivers*, Metropolitan Life Insurance Company, Westport, CT, 1997

Physical and Mental Costs to Caregiver

Working caregivers are subject to more frequent headaches, weight loss or gain, anxiety or depression, and are slightly more likely to be under a physician's care. Twenty percent of caregivers reported being under a doctor's care, compared to 16 percent of employees who were not caregivers. Twenty-two percent of caregivers compared to 8 percent of non-caregivers reported anxiety and depression. (It should be noted that caregivers to the elderly may be older than many other workers and perhaps under care for reasons not associated with their caregiving status.)

Unless the workplace offers some kind of support for the caregiver through assistance programs or other benefits, the employee may not seek help until physical symptoms occur. Thus, health care benefits may end up becoming the major source of corporate support available to most caregivers — a very expensive program for such a purpose.

Caregivers often use their "sick days" or vacation days for caregiving responsibilities. This places the employee in need of such time for his or her own recuperation or recreation, but having it already used up for caregiving. Caregivers are one-third more likely to report their health as "poor."

"Trailing Parents"

Just when corporations were getting used to the "trailing spouse" — the wife or husband whose career puts obstacles in the way of business moves — a new problem has appeared. The graying of America is creating "trailing parents," who pose even greater relocation problems for employees and corporations. This is a problem in an economy that has always depended on a high degree of mobility.

Nobody knows the exact extent of the problem, but already an estimated 20 percent of the work force is responsible for an aging relative, and that figure will rise. Companies are beginning to

TABLE 8.11

Costs Associated with Supervising Personal Caregivers				
Full-Time Employed Caregivers by Gender (Levels III, IV, and V)	Number with supportive supervisors (81%)	Supervisor's time (12 hours per year)	Median Weekly Wage	Cost to Employers
Men	1,150,239	13,802,873	$ 771	$ 266,084,889
Women	3,490,345	41,884,139	$ 515	$ 539,048,871
Total	4,640,584	55,687,012		$ 805,133,760

Source: *Family Caregiving in the U.S. — Findings from a National Survey*, National Alliance for Caregiving and American Association of Retired Persons, Bethesda MD and Washington, DC, 1997

118

TABLE 8.12

All Costs to Employers		
	Cost per Employee	Total US Employer Costs
Replacing Employees		$ 4,933,816,305
Absenteeism	$ 69	$ 397,596,918
Partial Absenteeism	$ 85	$ 488,298,715
Workday Interruptions	$ 657	$ 3,765,122,333
Eldercare Crises	$ 189	$ 1,084,355,232
Supervisor's Time	$ 141	$ 805,133,760
Total	**$ 1,142**	**$ 11,474,323,263**

Source: *The MetLife Study of Employer Costs for Working Caregivers*, Metropolitan Life Insurance Company, Westport, CT, 1997

deal with the implications of trailing parents. A few, like Apple Computer, have sometimes agreed to foot the bill for moving elderly relatives rather than settle for a second choice in important personnel appointments.

Meanwhile, corporations are eager for a mobile work force. In 1995, an Atlas Van Lines survey of 147 companies found they expected to transfer more employees in 1995 than in 1994. Sixty-two percent of companies said they expected to move more people in 1999 than in 1994. And those numbers do not include the outside talent that companies seek to fill crucial slots. With larger numbers of people looking after elderly relatives, corporations are likely to see some of their choices turn down an offer — even at top levels.

Recruiters report that applicants who are caregivers usually drop out of the job-changing market, at least temporarily, or restrict how far they will move, or both. Relocation specialists claim that people often do not volunteer the information that they are caregivers, lest they be left out of the running for promotions.

Even so, in a 1995 Rodgers and Associates, a Boston research firm, survey of employees at eight large companies, 37 percent of those who identified themselves as caregivers said they were not interested in relocating. Among all employees, only 26 percent said they would not be interested in such jobs. In an Atlas Van Lines questionnaire, "family ties," cited by 64 percent of respondents, edged out "spousal employment" for two consecutive years as the primary reason employees turned down a relocation.

Many companies have not decided how to respond to the elder care problem. IBM, for example, has no formal policy on moving elderly parents unless they live with an employee. Then they move with the household. In the Atlas questionnaire, only 3 percent of the companies said they would pay to move an elderly relative of a newly hired employee.

However, sometimes companies disregard the rules and make decisions on an individual basis. When a manager wants a particular employee, the company often makes an exception and pays for a relocation of any family members. They may also arrange for referrals to nursing homes and research doctors, hospital, and home health aides. This is especially true at the upper management level of companies. And that fact alone may explain growing corporate interest in elder care — it affects an increasing number of older, upper-level employees.

Looking for Answers

Employers are beginning to understand they are incurring elder care-related costs in terms of lost work time, impaired productivity, higher use of health benefits, turnover rates, and size of applicant pools (some job seekers do not even apply for some jobs because they know in advance their caregiving responsibilities will interfere). Just as employers now recognize the value of addressing child care issues in the workplace, many of them are now looking for ways to deal with the care of elders.

In 1986, Dana Friedman, of the Conference Board and co-president of the Families and Work Institute, suggested ("Eldercare: The Employee Benefit of the 1990s") that "company support for eldercare is likely to become the new pioneering benefit of the 1990s." She explained that corporate decision-makers were more likely to be caring for older relatives than for young children. However, in 1992, Ms. Friedman followed up ("The Corporate Commitment to Elder Care"):

It is now five years since the first flurry of activity in employer-supported eldercare services. To my surprise, not much has happened. There are many more companies offering information and referral services — perhaps an estimated 300-400. A few hundred more offer seminars on caring for the elderly. Several others allow support groups or arrange for caregiver fairs.... There are about 110 companies offering long-term care insurance to help offset the expenses of a lengthy illness among elderly relatives. Given the staggering numbers of employees expecting to have elder care responsibilities in the next five to ten years, I would have expected a lot more experimentation among employers in finding ways to meet the varied needs of employed caregivers.... What explains the slower-than-expected movement of employer support for elder care?

Ms. Friedman suggested three primary reasons:

- Financial cost-cutting — when companies are forced to trim expenses, these benefits are viewed as unnecessary expenses;

- The numbers of caregivers currently employed remain *relatively* small and diffuse;

- Companies just do not know what to do.

The Families and Work Institute thinks that will change as greater numbers of employees become caregivers in the next few years.

CHAPTER IX

PROVIDING HEALTH CARE FOR THE ELDERLY

While providing health care for the elderly is an important issue today, it will become a concern of gigantic proportion as the elderly population of the United States increases. The elderly are the biggest group of users of health services, accounting for more than one-third of the nation's total personal health expenditures. Rising costs, demands for additional services, the further development of life-sustaining technologies, and the role of government are, and will continue to be, subjects of intense debate.

In this chapter, health care facilities, costs, and private and government health programs are discussed separately, although there is considerable overlap between the three areas.

WHERE DO THE ELDERLY GET HEALTH CARE?

Getting proper health care is difficult for many elderly people. Even if they can afford to pay for the best care, and many cannot, they may not be able to find a facility or the skilled health care professionals to provide the services they need. As with living arrangements, there is no single answer as to the best way to deliver health care to the elderly; there are advantages and disadvantages to all the programs.

Home Care

In Their Own Homes

Most Americans prefer to live independently as long as possible. Many elderly people with moderate and even severe health problems manage to remain in their own homes for many years by adjusting their lifestyles, modifying their environments, taking the proper medication, and using outside resources such as relatives, friends, or paid nurses or caregivers to assist them.

At some point, most elderly people with health problems need outside assistance. If family members do not have the time or knowledge to provide the needed care, they must find someone who can. Unfortunately, there is a severe shortage of workers who are trained (and willing) to provide at-home medical care. Finding a dependable, skilled caregiver is often very difficult.

Home health care is a rapidly growing industry in today's U.S. health care system. In 1994, 1.4 million elderly persons were served by home health care agencies. Elderly patients were predominantly female (71 percent), in the age group 75 to 84 (42 percent), White (68 percent), widowed (47 percent), living in private residences (93 percent), and living with family members (51 percent). (See Table 9.1.)

The most frequent services rendered were bathing or showering, transferring to or from a bed or chair, using the toilet, and eating. The most common instrumental services provided were light housework, preparing meals, administering medications, shopping, placing telephone calls, and managing money. Of those discharged from home health care, most (31 percent of men and 37 percent of women) had met their goals (recovered or stabilized to the point that they or another person could resume the activities). About 18 percent had recovered or stabilized; 21 percent of men were hospitalized, as were 13 percent of women; and 2.9 percent of men and 4.4 percent of women transferred to nursing homes. About 8 percent died. (See Figure 9.1.)

Three factors account for the growth in home health care:

- Advancements in medical technology that allow for care at home at a lower cost than in an institution;

- The enactment of Medicare in 1965, which allowed for payment for certain home services; and

- The increase in the number of elderly.

In the Homes of Others

When chronic health problems prevent elderly people from living alone or with spouses, they may move in with their children or other relatives. Families take ill relatives into their homes because they want to care for them as long as possible or because they cannot find suitable or affordable long-term care facilities. Having an elderly, ill parent or relative in the home can place an emotional and/or financial strain on any family, depending on the type and degree of the health problem. In Alzheimer's cases, for example, the burden can be severe and prolonged. (See Chapter VI.)

Hospitals

While most elderly people receive medical treatment in doctors' offices or health clinics, the incidence of hospitalization rises with age. In 1995, those 65 to 74 were hospitalized at a rate of 257.6 per 1,000 people; those 75 and older were hospitalized at the rate of 455.2 per 1,000. These rates compared to 89.8 per 1,000 for those 15 to 44 years of age and 118.2 per 1,000 for those 45 to 64. The average length of stay in 1995 was 6.5 days for those 65 to 74 years old and 7.1 days for those older than 75 years. As with the general population, the average stay of those over 65 has been shortening over time—from 10.7 days in 1980 to 6.8 days in 1995. (See Table 9.2.)

Part of the cost of hospitalization for most elderly patients is covered under Medicare. Since the enactment of the Diagnosis Related Groups (DRG) system (see *How Medicare Pays*, below), Medicare payments to hospitals have fallen below many of the hospitals' own expenses. This led hospitals to make the patient's stay as short as possible. It also forced some community hospitals to close. Over 50 percent of the closures were in rural communities.

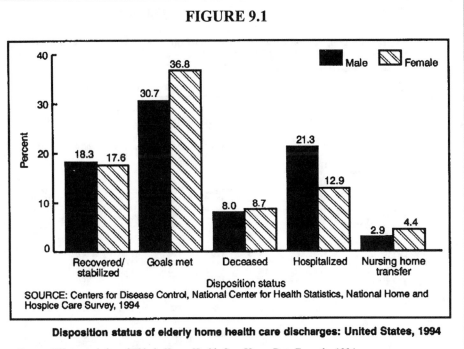

FIGURE 9.1

SOURCE: Centers for Disease Control, National Center for Health Statistics, National Home and Hospice Care Survey, 1994

Disposition status of elderly home health care discharges: United States, 1994

Source: "Characteristics of Elderly Home Health Care Users: Data From the 1994 National Home and Hospice Care Survey," *Advance Data,* National Center for Health Statistics, September 26, 1996

Hospices

Hospice care is a program of care involving physical, psychological, social, and spiritual care for dying persons, their families, and other loved ones. Hospice services are available in both the home and inpatient setting. Those persons in hospice care are generally there for relatively short periods of time. Hospices provide skilled nursing care and pain relief for those who are terminally ill (less than six months to live).

The Health Care Financing Administration reported that, in 1995, 1,959 hospices operated in the United States with a large concentration (36 percent) in the South. These facilities served an estimated 305,530 people. The number of hospices participating in the Medicare program has increased from 355 in 1985 to 1,959 in 1995. The average number of covered days of care per person in 1995 was 59, and the average payment per person was $6,078. In 1986, the hospice program cost an estimated $77 million; by 1995,

TABLE 9.2

Discharges, days of care, and average length of stay in non-Federal short-stay hospitals, according to selected characteristics: United States, selected years 1980–95

[Data are based on a sample of hospital records]

Characteristic	1980[1]	1985[1]	1988	1989	1990	1992	1993[2]	1994	1995
				Discharges per 1,000 population					
Total[3]	158.5	137.7	117.6	115.4	113.0	110.5	107.6	106.5	104.7
Sex[3]									
Male	140.3	124.4	106.9	105.1	100.9	98.6	95.2	94.2	92.3
Female	177.0	151.8	129.3	126.6	126.0	123.2	120.5	119.1	117.4
Age									
Under 15 years	71.6	57.7	49.8	48.8	44.6	45.2	37.7	39.2	41.7
15–44 years	150.1	125.0	103.9	102.7	101.6	96.0	95.4	93.2	89.8
45–64 years	194.8	170.8	142.1	136.8	135.0	131.0	126.8	124.1	118.2
65 years and over	383.7	369.8	336.8	333.4	330.9	336.5	341.6	341.6	344.6
65–74 years	315.8	297.2	266.8	261.9	259.1	264.5	262.2	261.6	257.6
75 years and over	489.3	475.6	435.5	433.1	429.9	432.7	446.3	445.3	455.2
Geographic region[3]									
Northeast	147.6	129.1	126.1	124.6	121.0	123.9	118.3	121.3	120.0
Midwest	175.4	143.4	120.3	117.2	115.1	105.3	102.2	102.6	99.5
South	165.1	143.5	118.9	119.0	119.2	116.3	116.9	111.8	110.9
West	136.9	130.3	103.0	97.7	92.1	93.7	87.6	87.6	86.0
				Days of care per 1,000 population					
Total[3]	1,129.0	872.1	750.8	727.5	705.0	659.3	626.9	594.0	544.3
Sex[3]									
Male	1,076.0	848.2	748.2	729.8	690.4	656.3	616.3	580.8	533.1
Female	1,187.1	902.0	760.6	734.0	725.3	667.5	640.5	609.5	556.7
Age									
Under 15 years	315.7	263.0	248.4	237.4	215.4	219.6	195.5	189.2	185.6
15–44 years	786.8	603.3	492.6	480.3	465.3	416.1	399.3	390.4	346.0
45–64 years	1,596.9	1,201.6	966.5	915.9	911.5	827.1	785.0	727.5	655.6
65 years and over	4,098.4	3,228.0	2,994.1	2,959.2	2,867.7	2,771.7	2,676.2	2,516.3	2,352.4
65–74 years	3,147.0	2,437.3	2,248.8	2,153.2	2,067.7	2,040.8	1,927.1	1,798.8	1,669.0
75 years and over	5,578.7	4,381.4	4,045.2	4,082.6	3,970.7	3,747.8	3,664.6	3,445.7	3,220.1
Geographic region[3]									
Northeast	1,204.7	953.5	922.4	909.1	878.0	838.6	787.2	774.9	722.1
Midwest	1,296.2	952.0	747.0	726.0	713.4	626.2	600.5	553.9	502.9
South	1,105.5	848.9	725.6	727.8	704.1	676.2	655.1	618.0	564.9
West	836.2	713.2	602.7	532.5	509.9	483.1	445.2	420.3	385.2
				Average length of stay in days					
Total[3]	7.1	6.3	6.4	6.3	6.2	6.0	5.8	5.6	5.2
Sex[3]									
Male	7.7	6.8	7.0	6.8	6.8	6.7	6.5	6.2	5.8
Female	6.7	5.9	5.9	5.9	5.8	5.4	5.3	5.1	4.7
Age									
Under 15 years	4.4	4.6	5.0	4.9	4.8	4.9	5.2	4.8	4.5
15–44 years	5.2	4.8	4.7	4.7	4.6	4.3	4.2	4.2	3.9
45–64 years	8.2	7.0	6.8	6.7	6.8	6.3	6.2	5.9	5.5
65 years and over	10.7	8.7	8.9	8.9	8.7	8.2	7.8	7.4	6.8
65–74 years	10.0	8.2	8.4	8.2	8.0	7.7	7.3	6.9	6.5
75 years and over	11.4	9.2	9.3	9.4	9.2	8.7	8.2	7.7	7.1
Geographic region[3]									
Northeast	8.2	7.4	7.3	7.3	7.3	6.8	6.7	6.4	6.0
Midwest	7.4	6.6	6.2	6.2	6.2	5.9	5.9	5.4	5.1
South	6.7	5.9	6.1	6.1	5.9	5.8	5.6	5.5	5.1
West	6.1	5.5	5.9	5.5	5.5	5.2	5.1	4.8	4.5

[1]Comparisons of data from 1980–85 with data from later years should be made with caution as estimates of change may reflect improvements in the design (see Appendix I) rather than true changes in hospital use.
[2]In 1993 children's hospitals had a high rate of nonresponse that may have resulted in underestimates of hospital utilization by children.
[3]Age adjusted.

NOTES: Rates are based on the civilian population as of July 1. Some numbers in this table have been revised and differ from previous editions of *Health, United States*. Estimates of hospital utilization from the National Health Interview Survey (NHIS) and the National Hospital Discharge Survey (NHDS) may differ because NHIS data are based on household interviews of the civilian noninstitutionalized population and exclude deliveries, whereas NHDS data are based on hospital discharge records of all persons. NHDS includes records for persons discharged alive or deceased and institutionalized persons, and excludes newborn infants. Differences in hospital utilization estimated by the two surveys are particularly evident for the elderly and for women. See Appendix I.

SOURCE: Centers for Disease Control and Prevention, National Center for Health Statistics, Division of Health Care Statistics. Data from the National Hospital Discharge Survey.

benefit payments for hospice care had increased to $1.8 billion. (See Table 9.3.)

Many more persons received a combination of hospice and home health care. Most of the hospices (88 percent) were nonprofit; only 5 percent were proprietary (for-profit), and 6.7 percent were owned by the government agencies. Most (66 percent) of the hospices were certified by Medicare; Medicaid had certified 57 percent.

TABLE 9.3

Number of Hospices, Number of Persons, Covered Days of Care, Total Charges, and Program Payments for Hospice Services Used by Medicare Beneficiaries, by Area of Residence: Calendar Year 1995

Area of Residence	Number of Hospices	Persons	Covered Days of Care		Total Charges in Thousands	Program Payments in Thousands	Program Payments per Person[1]
			Number	Per Person			
All Areas[2]	1,992	309,336	18,196,624	59	$1,882,499	$1,872,698	$6,058
United States	1,959	305,530	17,990,578	59	1,865,538	1,855,739	6,078
Northeast	315	51,337	2,674,467	52	291,427	286,713	5,591
Midwest	554	76,895	4,591,255	60	463,781	463,103	6,025
South	713	114,561	7,264,116	63	729,525	725,494	6,336
West	377	62,737	3,460,740	55	380,803	380,427	6,068

Source: *1997 Statistical Supplement*, *Health Care Financing Review*, Health Care Financing Administration, Washington, DC, 1997

(Medicaid/ Medicare had approved the hospices for payment by their programs.)

NURSING HOMES — A REVOLUTION IN PROGRESS

Nursing homes provide long-term care for those whose health problems are so severe that they require specialized, intensive, or prolonged medical treatment.

The Declining Nursing Home Population

Approximately 5 percent of the population 65 years and older reside in nursing homes at any one time, but more will likely live in nursing homes at some period during their lifetimes. In 1995, nursing homes provided care for nearly 1.4 million residents. The majority of elderly nursing home residents are female, over the age of 75, White, and widowed. About 60 percent were 65 to 84 years of age, and 40 percent were over the age of 85. (See Table 9.4.) In the 1980s, many investors assumed that growing numbers of elderly would lead to rapid increases in nursing home populations. As a result, they added 147,000 nursing home beds between 1985 and 1995 to accommodate an expected 2.1 million elderly. The occupancy rate, however, fell from 92 percent to 87 percent over that time because many of the elderly suffered less disability and were able to live elsewhere.

Length of Stay

Contrary to popular belief, many people do not go to nursing homes to die. In fact, in 1995,

residents were discharged after an average stay of 838 days (Table 9.5), compared to 1,026 days in 1985. This decline in nursing home use may be due to the increases in availability of home care services. The majority of nursing home residents are there because they suffer from serious health problems, but there are some whose problems would not normally require institutionalization. Their needs may not be primarily medical, but they have nowhere else to go. They are usually poor and/or have no one in the community who is able or willing to care for them. Many of these people are also now able to be cared for by home health care providers.

The Cost of Nursing Home Care

Nursing home care is expensive. An average one-year stay in a nursing home costs more than $43,300. In 1995, at the time of admission, most (38 percent) nursing home residents relied on Medicaid. The second most common source of payment at admission was insurance, own income, or family support (32 percent), followed by Medicare (25 percent) and other sources (4 percent). The primary source of payment changed as a stay proceeded. Among those on Medicare, 40 percent shifted to Medicaid, until approximately 58 percent were Medicaid-funded, with 29 percent funded by private insurance, 13 percent by Medicare, and 3 percent other.

Conditions Have Improved

For some people, the prospect of living in a nursing home is terrifying. The unsavory

125

TABLE 9.4

Number and percent distribution of elderly nursing home residents 65 years and over by selected demographic characteristics, according to sex: United States, 1995

Selected demographic characteristics	Both sexes		Male		Female	
	Number	Percent distribution	Number	Percent distribution	Number	Percent distribution
Total.	1,385,400	100.0	342,700	100.0	1,042,700	100.0
Age at admission						
65–74 years.	242,000	17.5	93,500	27.3	148,600	14.2
75–84 years.	586,300	42.3	143,400	41.8	442,900	42.5
85 years and over	557,100	40.2	105,900	30.9	451,200	43.3
Race						
White.	1,240,000	89.5	294,500	85.9	945,500	90.7
Black.	117,900	8.5	37,000	10.8	80,900	7.8
Black and other	137,600	9.9	44,500	13.0	93,200	8.9
Other and unknown.	27,500	2.0	11,100	3.2	16,400	1.6
Hispanic origin						
Hispanic.	32,300	2.3	13,000	3.8	19,300	1.8
Non-Hispanic.	1,276,000	92.1	312,600	91.2	963,400	92.4
Unknown.	77,100	5.6	17,100	5.0	60,100	5.8
Marital status						
Married.	229,300	16.5	126,800	37.0	102,500	9.8
Widowed.	914,800	66.0	127,900	37.3	786,900	75.5
Divorced and/or separated.	75,800	5.5	31,600	9.2	44,200	4.2
Never married and/or single.	154,300	11.1	53,000	15.5	101,300	9.7
Unknown.	11,300	0.8	*	*	*7,900	*0.8
Living quarters						
Private residence.	509,700	36.8	124,500	36.2	385,200	36.9
Retirement home.	31,100	2.2	*6,600	*1.9	24,400	2.3
Board and care and/or residential facility	68,600	4.9	15,200	4.4	53,400	5.1
Nursing home.	160,400	11.6	43,600	12.7	116,800	11.2
Hospital.	562,300	40.6	138,500	40.4	423,800	40.6
Mental health facility.	14,900	1.1	*	*	*9,700	*0.9
Other or unknown.	38,500	2.8	*9,100	*2.7	29,400	2.8
Living arrangement						
Family members.	280,500	20.2	84,400	24.6	196,100	18.8
Nonfamily members.	28,400	2.0	*6,300	*1.8	22,100	2.1
Alone.	215,900	15.6	39,000	11.4	177,000	17.0
Other or unknown.	860,600	62.1	213,100	62.2	647,600	62.1

* Figure does not meet standard of reliability or precision.

NOTES: Numbers may not add to totals because of rounding. Percents are based on the unrounded figures.

Source: "Characteristics of Elderly Nursing Home Residents: Data from the 1995 National Nursing Home Survey," *Advance Data*, National Center for Health Statistics, Washington, DC, July 2, 1997

reputation of some nursing homes is not entirely undeserved. However, living conditions in these facilities have become better over the past few years. Both physical conditions and workers' attitudes towards residents have improved as a result of media attention, government regulation, demands by families, and the concern of the nursing home industry itself.

The industry recognizes the potential market of an aging population and is anxious to convey a positive image. Nonetheless, reports of abuse and inadequate health care continue. A major problem is retaining good employees. Next to child-care facilities, nursing homes have the highest employee turnover rate of any occupation, especially among unskilled and semi-skilled workers. Nursing home aides, the people who provide most of the direct patient care, are very poorly paid. In many areas of the country, a person can earn a higher hourly wage at a fast-food restaurant than in a nursing home.

Competition in the Industry

As with virtually all segments of the health care industry, change is sweeping the nursing home industry. With the growing numbers of elderly, nursing homes are prospering. For nursing homes, the critical group is people 85 and older, which is the fastest growing part of the elderly population. By the year 2000, their number is expected to swell by 40 percent, and to double by 2010. Experts estimate that more than half of those over 85 need long-term care.

In order to stay competitive with the growing home care industry and the increasing array of services available for the elderly, nursing homes have begun to reinvent themselves, offering additional programs and services along with traditional institutional care. Among those services are adult day care, visiting nurses, respite care (short-term stays when primary caregivers are not available, as on a vacation), transportation, and minimal care apartment units. Craig Duncan, executive director of the Eddy Nursing Home in Troy, New York, explained,

> We are moving away from an institutional base except for the frailest population, and that's because we have better-educated older consumers telling us what they want, and that is to stay out of a nursing home. If we want to maintain and gain a share of that market—and let's face it, all of us are revenue-driven—we had better respond.

Sub-Acute Care

In order to make nursing homes more profitable, nursing home operators have begun to compete with hospitals for sub-acute care patients. Patients recovering from cancer, heart bypass operations, joint replacement surgery, or serious

TABLE 9.5

Average length of stay of elderly nursing home residents 65 years and over by age, marital status, sex, and standard error: United States, 1995

Selected demographic characteristics	Both sexes (S.E.)	Male (S.E.)	Female (S.E.)
	Number in days		
Total.	1,385,400	342,700	1,042,700
Average length of stay in days	838(13.6)	689(23.5)	887(15.8)
Age			
65–74 years.	1,064(38.9)	893(58.7)	1,172(50.8)
75–84 years.	864(19.0)	677(30.8)	925(22.3)
85 years and over	713(15.6)	526(28.7)	756(17.4)
Marital status			
Married.	562(25.2)	518(36.1)	616(31.3)
Widowed.	877(16.4)	736(34.6)	900(17.8)
Divorced and/or separated	802(49.9)	839(90.3)	775(55.5)
Never married and/or single	1,050(44.3)	916(71.0)	1,121(54.7)

NOTE: S.E. is standard error.

Source: "Characteristics of Elderly Nursing Home Residents: Data From the 1995 National Nursing Home Survey," *Advance Data*, National Center for Health Statistics, Washington, DC, July 2, 1997

accidents are increasingly receiving post-operative therapy in nursing homes rather than in hospitals because nursing home care is much less expensive. The average daily charges for sub-acute care in nursing homes range from $300 to $550; the same treatment in hospitals costs between $700 and $1,000. Health care analysts estimate that 10 to 20 percent of general acute care hospital patients could be cared for in sub-acute units of nursing homes. Thousands of nursing home beds are being shifted from caring for lower-profit traditional patients to providing for people who no longer need the services of acute-care hospitals but who are still too sick to go home.

The Crisis in Nursing Home Care

For much of the past decade, advocates for the elderly and disabled have fought to expand the nation's long-term care system to meet the demands of an aging population. Most industry analysts believe progress has been made. Nonetheless, governmental budget cuts to Medicare, Medicaid, and Social Security, along with attempts in Congress to lessen regulation may threaten the quality of long-term care. The American Association of Retired Persons (AARP), the nation's largest organization of older people, predicted that more than two million people could lose coverage for long-term care — including nursing home coverage and assistance at home — by 2002 if proposed budget cuts become law. The supporters of less regulation counter that strict regulation is no longer necessary and that free-market conditions will both improve the quality of care and decrease the cost of nursing home care.

THE HIGH COST OF HEALTH CARE

The elderly make up 12 percent of the U.S. population, but account for one-third of total personal health care expenditures (money spent for the direct consumption of health care goods and services). In 1995, health care spending was approximately 13.5 percent of gross domestic product (GDP), and has remained relatively stable since 1993 (Figure 9.2).

An Especially Severe Burden on the Elderly

The cost of health care in the United States is a serious problem for the elderly. Health care is the only budget expense for the elderly which is both a higher percentage of their income and a greater dollar amount than for the nonelderly. Many elderly Americans are forced into poverty paying for health care for themselves or for loved ones. Before a family can qualify for some forms of assistance such as Medicaid, it must often "spend down," that is, spend its assets to the poverty level. This leaves the surviving spouse and families in financial ruin. Robert M. Ball, chairman of the National Academy of Social Insurance, a non-profit research organization in Washington, DC, stated in 1995 that,

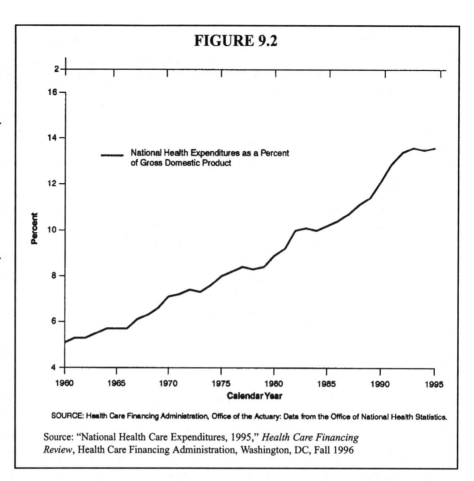

FIGURE 9.2

National Health Expenditures as a Percent of Gross Domestic Product

SOURCE: Health Care Financing Administration, Office of the Actuary: Data from the Office of National Health Statistics.

Source: "National Health Care Expenditures, 1995," *Health Care Financing Review*, Health Care Financing Administration, Washington, DC, Fall 1996

Sometime in the not-too-distant future, we will get a major national program protecting families against the cost of long term care.... I expect it to come, not primarily because of the potential power of the elderly ... but because of pressure from those middle-aged, the sons and daughters of the elderly. They are the ones most at risk.

Where Does the Money Go?

The typical person 65 to 74 years of age spends 10 percent of his/her expenditures on health care, while the average person 75 years of age and over spends 14 percent. Of this expenditure, health insurance accounts for 47 percent; medical services, 31.4 percent; physicians' services, 10.8 percent; and prescription drugs, 18.7 percent. Costs increase with age in all categories of service. People over 85 spend, by far, the greatest amount per capita on health care.

128

TABLE 9.6

Health care coverage for persons 65 years of age and over, according to type of coverage and selected characteristics: United States, 1989, 1993, 1994, and 1995

[Data are based on household interviews of a sample of the civilian noninstitutionalized population]

Characteristic	Medicare and private insurance				Medicare and Medicaid				Medicare only[1]			
	1989	1993[2]	1994	1995[3]	1989	1993[2]	1994	1995[3]	1989	1993[2]	1994	1995[3]
	Number in millions											
Total[4]	21.5	23.7	23.3	22.6	1.7	1.7	1.7	2.2	4.9	4.8	4.6	5.1
	Percent of population											
Total, age adjusted[4]	73.5	75.5	75.1	72.0	5.7	5.2	5.3	7.0	16.8	15.3	14.8	16.2
Total, crude[4]	73.5	75.4	75.1	72.1	5.7	5.3	5.4	7.1	16.9	15.4	14.8	16.2
Age												
65–74 years	74.2	76.0	74.9	71.6	5.0	4.6	4.5	6.1	15.5	14.2	14.4	16.3
75 years and over	72.3	74.5	75.3	72.8	6.8	6.4	6.9	8.6	19.0	17.2	15.4	16.0
75–84 years	74.1	76.5	77.3	74.1	6.4	5.8	5.8	8.1	17.4	15.6	14.4	15.0
85 years and over	64.8	66.7	67.4	68.2	8.5	8.5	11.0	10.3	26.1	23.7	19.5	19.2
Sex[5]												
Male	73.9	76.5	75.8	72.5	4.0	3.0	3.0	4.6	17.2	15.7	15.8	17.3
Female	73.4	74.7	74.7	71.8	6.8	6.9	7.0	8.8	16.4	15.0	13.9	15.3
Race[5]												
White	77.3	79.1	78.8	75.6	4.5	4.2	4.4	5.5	14.7	13.2	12.9	14.8
Black	39.3	43.6	42.4	40.1	16.5	13.3	14.9	22.2	37.9	36.2	34.5	31.3
Hispanic origin and race[5]												
All Hispanic	38.8	38.1	49.2	33.8	20.4	23.6	19.5	27.9	24.1	31.7	23.2	28.4
Mexican American	33.5	30.2	41.8	24.1	23.5	15.7	22.0	25.1	26.7	45.8	29.5	37.3
Puerto Rican	*18.5	*6.3	48.4	41.3	*30.6	*21.9	17.5	26.6	*27.6	59.0	28.3	28.5
Cuban	45.7	59.0	55.9	41.7	*20.6	39.7	*24.8	44.1	*23.7	*3.2	12.9	*14.1
Other Hispanic	49.5	42.6	56.3	40.3	13.0	*19.1	12.9	19.8	19.2	27.9	17.9	25.1
White, non-Hispanic	78.5	80.9	80.3	77.8	3.9	3.4	3.7	4.4	14.4	12.4	12.3	14.0
Black, non-Hispanic	39.3	43.8	42.9	39.9	16.3	13.2	14.4	22.3	38.0	36.1	34.6	31.4
Family income[5]												
Less than $14,000	64.8	58.3	59.0	54.9	11.4	14.1	15.0	19.6	21.5	24.3	22.8	23.1
$14,000–$24,999	81.2	82.8	82.5	79.5	2.6	1.6	2.0	3.4	13.4	13.1	12.3	13.7
$25,000–$34,999	80.0	85.7	83.5	80.6	2.4	1.5	1.4	2.1	12.5	9.4	9.5	12.1
$35,000–$49,999	80.3	83.6	83.9	80.9	*1.9	*2.1	*2.0	*1.4	10.2	9.4	9.3	11.4
$50,000 or more	76.5	81.3	79.1	78.4	*1.1	*2.4	*1.4	*2.0	12.6	8.5	8.4	10.4
Geographic region[5]												
Northeast	73.1	79.0	75.5	72.8	4.0	3.5	4.3	5.1	18.0	12.1	15.6	16.9
Midwest	79.6	81.7	82.4	81.4	2.9	3.5	2.5	3.9	14.1	12.3	11.3	11.4
South	70.6	70.8	69.8	69.1	7.7	7.4	7.7	9.8	18.3	19.0	18.1	17.1
West	71.4	71.7	74.0	63.5	7.6	5.7	6.1	8.2	16.0	16.3	12.7	20.2
Location of residence[5]												
Within MSA[6]	73.6	75.2	75.3	71.9	5.1	5.1	5.0	6.6	16.8	15.1	14.4	15.9
Outside MSA[6]	73.4	76.3	74.5	72.6	7.2	5.8	6.3	8.5	16.8	15.9	15.9	17.0

* Relative standard error greater than 30 percent.

[1] Includes persons not covered by private insurance or Medicaid and a small proportion of persons with other types of coverage, such as CHAMPUS or public assistance.

[2] July 1 to Dec. 31, 1993. The questionnaire changed in 1993 compared with previous years.

[3] January 1 to June 30, 1995, preliminary data.

[4] Includes all other races not shown separately and unknown family income.

[5] Age adjusted.

[6] Metropolitan statistical area.

NOTES: Percents do not add to 100 because the percent without Medicare is not shown, and because persons with Medicare, private insurance, and Medicaid appear in both columns. In 1995, 5.5 percent of all persons 65 years of age and over had no Medicare, but only 0.8 percent were without health insurance.

SOURCE: Centers for Disease Control and Prevention, National Center for Health Statistics, Division of Health Interview Statistics and Division of Health and Utilization Analysis: Data from the National Health Interview Survey.

Where Does the Money Come From?

Almost all Americans 65 years and older receive some help with medical expenses from government programs such as Medicare and Medicaid (see below) and/or are covered by private medical insurance. Many elderly people mistakenly believe that Medicare will pay for all their health costs.

No single government or private program covers all health costs. It is possible, however, to obtain total, or almost total, financial coverage for medical costs with a combination of government programs, private health insurance, and out-of-pocket payments by the patient. The cost of such a package, though, is prohibitive for many elderly people, and qualifications for enrollment in some programs may be difficult or impossible to meet. Table 9.6 shows the sources of health care coverage for the elderly from 1989 to 1995. In 1995, about 16 percent had Medicare only, around 72 percent had Medicare and private insurance, and approximately 7 percent had Medicare and Medicaid. It is often the family of an elderly person who pays for nursing home care.

GOVERNMENT HEALTH CARE PROGRAMS

The United States is one of the few industrialized nations that does not have a national health care program. In most other developed countries, government programs cover almost all health-related costs, from maternity care to long-term care.

In the United States, the two major government health care programs are Medicare and Medicaid. They provide financial assistance for the elderly, the poor, and the disabled. Before the existence of these programs, a large number of older Americans could not afford adequate medical care.

Medicare

The Medicare program, enacted under Title XVIII ("Health Insurance for the Aged") of the Social Security Act, was signed into law by President Lyndon Johnson and went into effect on July 1, 1966. Table 9.7 shows the enrollment from 1967 through 1995. In 1995, 37.5 million elderly were enrolled in Medicare, with a total expenditure of $184 billion. The program is composed of two parts:

• Part A provides hospital insurance. Coverage includes doctors' fees, nursing services, meals, a semiprivate room, special care units, operating room costs, laboratory tests, and some drugs

and supplies. Part A also covers rehabilitation services, limited post-hospital skilled nursing facility care, home health care, and hospice care for the terminally ill.

• Part B (Supplemental Medical Insurance or SMI) is elective medical insurance; enrollees must pay premiums to get coverage. It covers private physicians' services, diagnostic tests, outpatient hospital services, outpatient physical therapy, speech pathology services, home health services, and medical equipment and supplies.

In 1994, the average enrollee received $3,934 in benefits, although, in a typical year, approximately 17 percent of the elderly covered by Medicare do not file a single claim. The fastest growing segment of Medicare enrollees is the over-85 age group. The impact of an aging Medicare population on health care expenditures is significant since, on the average, the aged tend to be sicker and incur much greater expense per capita.

How Medicare Pays

Doctors are reimbursed on a fee-for-service basis. This system presents a number of problems. Because of paperwork, inadequate compensation, and delays in reimbursements, some doctors will not provide service under the Medicare program; the system includes incentives that may encourage doctors to treat patients in a hospital rather than in a less-expensive outpatient setting; and patients may receive treatment that provides only marginal health benefits.

The (George) Bush Administration initiated a fee schedule that went into effect in 1992 that substantially cut payments to doctors. Critics claim such reductions make it harder for elderly people to gain access to health care because fewer doctors will participate in the program. However, effective January 1998, the law allows doctors to contract privately with Medicare enrollees for services that are covered by Medicare (they agree to pay the doctor out of their own pocket).

Since 1983, hospitals have received reimbursement under the prospective payment system (PPS), in which a Medicare patient is classified into one of 477 diagnosis-related groups (DRGs) for which there is a fixed, pre-determined payment. Hospitals which can provide care for less than the payment keep the difference, those whose costs run over the payment must absorb the loss. There is, however, a mounting effort within the Medicare program to compensate for different market conditions, for example, between rural and urban hospitals.

Many health care and elderly advocacy organizations and members of Congress are concerned that PPS may be affecting the care Medicare patients receive. Since hospitals are paid a fixed reimbursement for a DRG regardless of their expenses, they may find it expedient to provide less service than necessary, to discharge a patient sooner than usual, or not to admit certain patients. Several studies have found that cost control measures enacted in 1983 did not result in reduced quality of care while an elderly patient was hospitalized, but did increase the likelihood that the elderly patient would be discharged in a medically unstable condition.

The Home Health Agency Program — A Booming Business

Some people can receive in-home health services from Medicare's Home Health Agency program. Available services include periodic, part-time skilled nursing care; physical, occupational, or speech therapy; part-time home health aide services; medical social services; and durable medical equipment. To be eligible for services, a person must be homebound and have a plan of treatment developed by an attending physician.

Home health care is one of the fastest growing segments of the health care industry. Since 1985, the number receiving care in their homes from Medicare, the main payer, has more than doubled.

One cause of this surge is the vastly improved technology that makes a wider range of care possible at home and has put increasing numbers of older, sicker patients on life-support services like oxygen, drugs, and nutrition for months at a time. It also offers the opportunity for people to receive skilled care in the comfort of their own homes, where most prefer to be.

Providing Only Limited Protection

Medicare has been an extremely successful program. In 1965, when President Johnson signed the bill creating it into law, only half of America's elderly had any health insurance. Today, Medicare pays hospital and doctor bills for more than 37.5 million Americans over 65, making this age group the only one in America with virtually universal coverage. Medicare, along with increased Social Security benefits, has helped transform a group that has suffered from high rates of poverty into a more economically secure group.

However, Medicare does not provide complete health care coverage. It does not pay for basic medical expenses such as routine physical examinations, prescription drugs, eyeglasses, prostheses (artificial body parts), and, perhaps most importantly, long-term at-home or nursing-home care. Older Americans are, in fact, spending a higher proportion of their incomes on health care now than they were in 1965 before Medicare and Medicaid were enacted. The House Select Committee on Aging reported that Medicare pays less than half (48 percent) of older persons' health care cost. Contributing to high health costs are the skyrocketing price of health care in general and the rapid escalation of Medicare premiums, deductibles, and co-insurance.

Older people sometimes find it difficult to locate doctors who accept Medicare patients. For the reasons mentioned above, many doctors choose not to participate in the Medicare program, and there is no requirement that they participate in the program.

TABLE 9.7

Medicare enrollees and expenditures and percent distribution, according to type of service: United States and other areas, selected years 1967–95

[Data are compiled by the Health Care Financing Administration]

Type of service	1967	1970	1975	1980	1985	1990	1993	1994	1995[1]
Enrollees					Number in millions				
Total[2]	19.5	20.5	25.0	28.5	31.1	34.2	36.3	36.9	37.5
Hospital insurance	19.5	20.4	24.6	28.1	30.6	33.7	35.9	36.5	37.1
Supplementary medical insurance	17.9	19.6	23.9	27.4	30.0	32.6	34.6	35.2	35.7
Expenditures					Amount in millions				
Total	$4,737	$7,493	$16,316	$36,822	$72,294	$110,984	$150,370	$164,862	$184,204
Total hospital insurance[3]	3,430	5,281	11,581	25,577	48,414	66,997	94,391	104,545	117,604
Inpatient hospital	3,034	4,827	10,877	24,116	44,940	59,451	76,402	81,517	89,130
Skilled nursing facility	282	246	278	395	548	2,575	5,780	7,596	9,541
Home health agency	29	51	160	540	1,913	3,666	10,049	12,559	15,503
Hospice	...	...	...	...	43	358	1,059	1,421	2,002
Administrative expenses[4]	77	157	266	526	970	947	1,101	1,452	1,236
Total supplementary medical insurance	1,307	2,212	4,735	11,245	23,880	43,987	55,979	60,317	66,600
Physician	1,128	1,790	3,416	8,187	17,312	29,609	34,688	36,900	40,457
Outpatient hospital	33	114	643	1,897	4,319	8,482	12,418	14,034	15,405
Home health agency	10	34	95	234	38	74	118	154	182
Group practice prepayment	19	26	80	203	720	2,827	4,743	5,480	6,883
Independent laboratory	7	11	39	114	558	1,476	2,012	2,050	2,046
Administrative expenses[4]	110	237	462	610	933	1,519	2,000	1,699	1,627
Percent distribution of expenditures									
Total hospital insurance[3]	100.0	100.0	100.0	100.0	100.0	100.0	100.0	100.0	100.0
Inpatient hospital	88.5	91.4	93.9	94.3	92.8	88.7	80.7	78.0	75.8
Skilled nursing facility	8.2	4.7	2.4	1.5	1.1	3.8	6.1	7.3	8.1
Home health agency	0.8	1.0	1.4	2.1	4.0	5.5	10.9	12.0	13.2
Hospice	...	...	...	...	0.1	0.5	1.1	1.4	1.7
Administrative expenses[4]	2.2	3.0	2.3	2.1	2.0	1.4	1.2	1.4	1.1
Total supplementary medical insurance	100.0	100.0	100.0	100.0	100.0	100.0	100.0	100.0	100.0
Physician	86.3	80.9	72.1	72.8	72.5	67.3	63.0	61.2	60.7
Outpatient hospital	2.5	5.2	13.6	16.9	18.1	19.3	20.6	23.3	23.1
Home health agency	0.8	1.5	2.0	2.1	0.2	0.2	0.2	0.3	0.3
Group practice prepayment	1.5	1.2	1.7	1.8	3.0	6.4	8.9	9.1	10.3
Independent laboratory	0.5	0.5	0.8	1.0	2.3	3.4	3.7	3.4	3.1
Administrative expenses[4]	8.4	10.7	9.8	5.4	3.9	3.5	3.6	2.8	2.4

... Category not applicable.
[1] Preliminary figures.
[2] Number enrolled in the hospital insurance and/or supplementary medical insurance programs on July 1.
[3] In 1967 includes coverage for outpatient hospital diagnostic services.
[4] Includes research, costs of experiments and demonstration projects, and peer review activity.

NOTE: Table includes data for Medicare enrollees residing in Puerto Rico, Virgin Islands, Guam, other outlying areas, foreign countries, and unknown residence.

SOURCE: Health Care Financing Administration. Office of Medicare Cost Estimates, Office of the Actuary and Bureau of Data Management and Strategy. Washington.

A Program in Crisis

The spirit in which this law is written draws deeply upon the ancient dreams of all mankind. In Leviticus, it is written, 'Thou shall rise up before the hoary head, and honor the face of an old man'. — Russell B. Long, Democratic Senator, Louisiana, at the Medicare vote in 1965

Policy makers generally agree that Medicare cannot be sustained in its current form. Its costs are rising and must be controlled before the wave of baby boomers begin receiving benefits around 2010. The cost for medical procedures often used by the elderly, such as angioplasty and coronary bypass surgery, have increased. In addition, people are living longer. In 1995, for the first time since 1972, Medicare's trust fund lost money, a sign that the financial condition of Medicare was worse than assumed. The Health Care Financing Administration (HCFA), which runs Medicare, had not expected a deficit until 1997. Income to the trust fund, primarily from payroll taxes, was slightly less than expected, and spending was somewhat higher.

The deficit is significant because once the trust fund has started to lose money, the losses are expected to grow from year to year. No tax increases are scheduled under current law, and federal officials do not expect a reduction in the rate of spending unless a budget deal is made or is reached between President Clinton and the Congress. No such deals seem likely. There are enough assets to cover the shortfall over the next few years, but once the assets of the trust fund are depleted, there is no way to pay all the benefits that are due.

Politicians and policy-makers are bitterly divided over how Medicare should be changed, and how quickly. The Medicare payroll tax has not been increased since 1986. Medicare remains essentially unchanged since its beginning, a promise by the government to give the

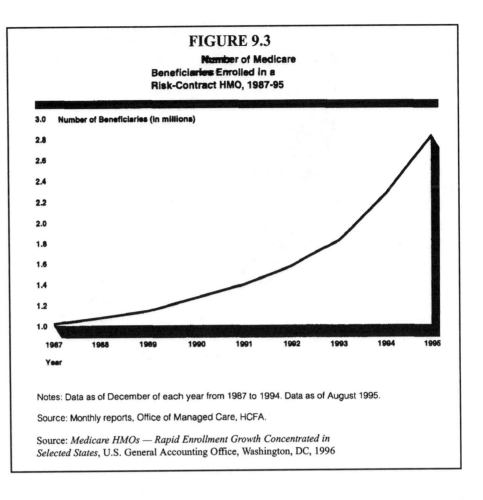

FIGURE 9.3

Number of Medicare Beneficiaries Enrolled in a Risk-Contract HMO, 1987-95

Notes: Data as of December of each year from 1987 to 1994. Data as of August 1995.

Source: Monthly reports, Office of Managed Care, HCFA.

Source: *Medicare HMOs — Rapid Enrollment Growth Concentrated in Selected States*, U.S. General Accounting Office, Washington, DC, 1996

elderly free choice of doctors and specialists and to reimburse those doctors on the basis of each service they perform. Beneficiaries are responsible for deductibles, copayments, and many other costs not covered by Medicare. Most (70 percent) elderly people buy "Medigap" insurance with private agencies to help cover these costs.

Some Democrats have argued that only a true social insurance program, financed by payroll taxes and covering everyone, would spread the risk sufficiently and insure that all the elderly, rich and poor, could receive complete medical coverage. Republicans, by and large, have argued for a voluntary system. Both Democrats and Republicans, in general, believe that recipients should have more choices and more financial responsibility for what they choose.

While almost no one advocates an abrupt withdrawal of benefits from today's retirees, most observers believe that those benefits cannot last

forever in their current form. Richer recipients will likely have to contribute more, benefits will have to decline, or Medicare payments to doctors and hospitals, already very low, will have to be cut even more. None of these options are politically appealing to a congressman or congresswoman running for re-election.

Medicare Health Maintenance Organizations

Medicare's fee-for-service system was the norm for medicine in 1965, but it is no longer. In the past two decades, the elderly have had the option of receiving managed care through health maintenance organizations (HMOs). HMOs provide health care services for a fixed prepayment. For monthly pre-paid premiums, HMO enrollees receive benefits not available under Medicare alone, such as free prescription drugs, dental care, eyeglasses, hearing aids, and hospitalization. The HMOs, in turn, receive fixed payments from the HCFA. This managed care

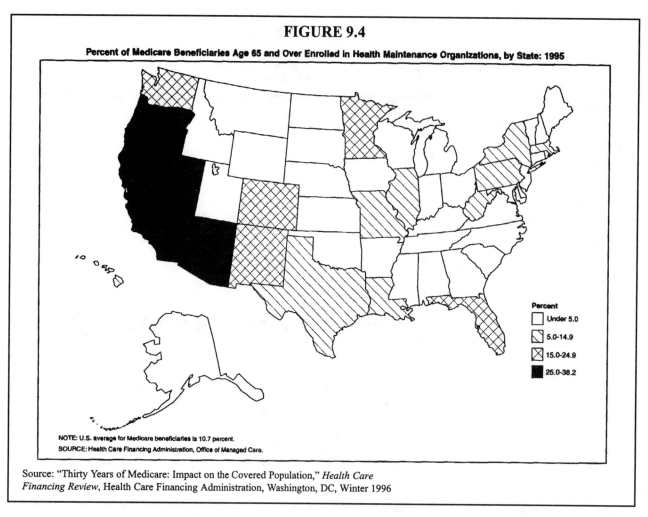

FIGURE 9.4

Percent of Medicare Beneficiaries Age 65 and Over Enrolled in Health Maintenance Organizations, by State: 1995

Percent
- [ ] Under 5.0
- [/] 5.0-14.9
- [⊠] 15.0-24.9
- [■] 25.0-38.2

NOTE: U.S. average for Medicare beneficiaries is 10.7 percent.
SOURCE: Health Care Financing Administration, Office of Managed Care.

Source: "Thirty Years of Medicare: Impact on the Covered Population," *Health Care Financing Review*, Health Care Financing Administration, Washington, DC, Winter 1996

system is supposedly intended to control costs while maintaining quality medical care.

To date, Medicare beneficiaries have enrolled in HMOs at a much lower rate than persons with private-sector insurance. Nonetheless, many observers see HMOs as the way to control rising Medicare costs and want to encourage greater use of HMOs. In 1995, fewer than 10 percent of the 37 million (2.8 million) Medicare recipients had enrolled in an HMO, although this was almost triple the number enrolled in 1987 (Figure 9.3). Medicare HMO coverage is not evenly spread among the states and, in fact, there is a strong concentration in a handful of states (Figure 9.4). In fact, 19 states had no enrollees.

Public Opinion

A December 1995 *New York Times*/CBS News nationwide poll found that, generally, Medicare recipients were concerned about proposals to reorganize the plan, while younger generations were less fearful. Sixty-four percent of the elderly, 53 percent of those 30 to 64 years, and 41 percent of those 18 to 29 years said the proposals to cut back Medicare will be "bad." When asked if it would be acceptable for Medicare recipients to be required to enter HMOs, 38 percent of the elderly said it would be acceptable; 56 percent of those 45 to 64 years, and 69 percent of those 18 to 44 thought so. To the question, "Do you think the Medicare program will have the money available to provide you with the benefits you expect in your retirement?" 79 percent of those 18 to 44, 54 percent of those 45 to 64, and only 14 percent of those over 65 said "no."

A 1997 nationwide poll of 1,258 Americans by the *Los Angeles Times* found 59 percent of those over 65 willing to pay more for health care, including higher premiums. Thirty-two percent

TABLE 9.8

Medicaid recipients and medical vendor payments, according to basis of eligibility: United States, selected fiscal years 1972–95

[Data are compiled by the Health Care Financing Administration]

Basis of eligibility	1972	1975	1980	1985	1990	1992	1993	1994	1995
Recipients					Number in millions				
All recipients	17.6	22.0	21.6	21.8	25.3	31.2	33.4	35.1	36.3
					Percent of recipients[1]				
Aged (65 years and over)	18.8	16.4	15.9	14.0	12.7	12.0	11.6	11.5	11.4
Blind and disabled	9.8	11.2	13.5	13.8	14.7	14.4	15.0	15.6	16.1
Adults in families with dependent children[2]	17.8	20.6	22.6	25.3	23.8	22.6	22.4	21.6	21.0
Children under age 21[3]	44.5	43.6	43.2	44.7	44.4	48.8	48.7	49.0	47.3
Other Title XIX[4]	9.0	8.2	6.9	5.6	3.9	1.9	1.9	1.7	1.7
Vendor payments[5]					Amount in billions				
All payments	$ 6.3	$ 12.2	$ 23.3	$ 37.5	$ 64.9	$ 91.5	$101.8	$107.9	$120.1
					Percent distribution				
Total	100.0	100.0	100.0	100.0	100.0	100.0	100.0	100.0	100.0
Aged (65 years and over)	30.6	35.6	37.5	37.6	33.2	31.8	31.0	30.9	30.4
Blind and disabled	22.2	25.7	32.7	35.9	37.6	37.2	38.0	39.1	41.1
Adults in families with dependent children[2]	15.3	16.8	13.9	12.7	13.2	13.6	13.4	12.6	11.2
Children under age 21[3]	18.1	17.9	13.4	11.8	14.0	16.1	16.2	16.0	15.0
Other Title XIX[4]	13.9	4.0	2.6	2.1	1.6	1.2	1.2	1.2	1.2
Vendor payments per recipient[5]					Amount				
All recipients	$ 358	$ 556	$1,079	$1,719	$2,568	$2,937	$3,042	$3,080	$3,311
Aged (65 years and over)	580	1,206	2,540	4,605	6,717	7,759	8,168	8,264	8,868
Blind and disabled	807	1,276	2,618	4,459	6,564	7,578	7,706	7,735	8,435
Adults in families with dependent children[2]	307	455	662	860	1,429	1,762	1,813	1,791	1,777
Children under age 21[3]	145	228	335	452	811	971	1,013	1,007	1,047
Other Title XIX[4]	555	273	398	657	1,062	1,814	1,856	2,165	2,380

[1]Recipients included in more than one category for 1980 and 1985. From 1990 to 1995 between 0.2 and 2.5 percent of recipients have unknown basis of eligibility.
[2]Includes adults in the Aid to Families with Dependent Children (AFDC) program.
[3]Includes children in the AFDC program.
[4]Includes some participants in Supplemental Security Income program and other people deemed medically needy in participating States.
[5]Payments exclude disproportionate share hospital payments ($19 billion in 1995) and payments to health maintenance organizations and Medicare ($11 billion in 1995).

NOTES: 1972 and 1975 data are for fiscal year ending June 30. All other years are for fiscal year ending September 30.

SOURCE: Health Care Financing Administration. Bureau of Data Management and Strategy. Unpublished data.

opposed such proposals, predominantly those 18 to 44. Sixty-eight percent of all ages opposed increasing the age of eligibility for benefits from 65 to 67.

Some people have predicted a "generational war" over benefit programs for the elderly, with baby boomers at odds with their children, who may be increasingly resentful over the heavy financial burden they are expected to bear for the programs. Many policy analysts see the young and the old locked in an ugly struggle, epitomized in a *Newsweek* cover showing a weary young man with an old woman in a wheelchair on his back.

This does not seem to be the case. Younger voters seem to be just as concerned about protecting Medicare and Social Security as their parents. Scholars believe the reason for this is that, despite the talk about the breakdown of the extended family, the bonds between generations remain surprisingly strong. Senator Bob Kerrey (D-NE), a leader in the effort to overhaul benefit programs, believes the young want [the elderly] to be secure. "They want them to have quality health care. And they don't want them to be dependent on them [the young]." This is a matter of self-interest—curtailing benefits for the elderly will likely translate into additional burdens and/or worries for their families.

Medicaid

Medicaid ("Grants to States for Medical Assistance Programs," Title XIX of the Social Security Act) is a program established in 1966 to provide medical assistance to certain categories of low-income Americans: the aged, blind, disabled, or members of families with dependent children. The costs of the Medicaid program are financed

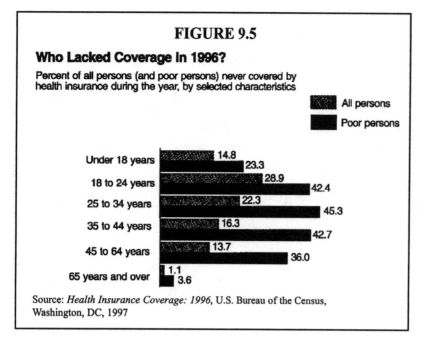

FIGURE 9.5

Who Lacked Coverage in 1996?

Percent of all persons (and poor persons) never covered by health insurance during the year, by selected characteristics

■ All persons
■ Poor persons

Age	All persons	Poor persons
Under 18 years	14.8	23.3
18 to 24 years	28.9	42.4
25 to 34 years	22.3	45.3
35 to 44 years	16.3	42.7
45 to 64 years	13.7	36.0
65 years and over	1.1	3.6

Source: *Health Insurance Coverage: 1996*, U.S. Bureau of the Census, Washington, DC, 1997

jointly by the federal government and the states. Medicaid covers hospitalization, doctors' fees, laboratory fees, X-rays, and long-term nursing home care. It is the largest source of funds for medical and health-related services to America's poorest people.

In 1995, while the elderly represented 11.4 percent of the 36.3 million Americans receiving Medicaid (down from 17.6 percent in 1972), the elderly received 30.4 percent of Medicaid benefits, an average of $8,868 per person. (See Table 9.8.)

Medicaid is the principal source (52 percent) of public financing for nursing home care. Two-thirds of the people in nursing homes get assistance from Medicaid. With the average cost of a year's nursing home service at $43,000, it generally does not take long for most Americans to deplete their savings and qualify for Medicaid coverage; half of them do so within six months. "The fact is," said Jeff Eagan, executive director of the Long Term Care Campaign, a coalition representing the disabled, "right now, Medicaid is the long-term care safety net." In addition, it is the primary source of prescription drug coverage for a large number of the poor elderly. Although home health services presently account for a small share

of Medicaid expenditures for the aged, it is the fastest growing sector.

PRIVATE HEALTH CARE PROGRAMS

Recognizing that Medicare (or Medicaid) will not cover all of their health care costs, many people seek other types of coverage to cover the gap between Medicare benefits and actual expenses. Additional coverage, however, can be costly, and beyond the reach of some elderly persons.

Employer Health Insurance

Persons over 65 who are actively employed may be covered under a company health care policy. Coverage may not be denied or reduced just because of age or because a person is eligible for benefits under a federal program. Even after retirement, a person may be able to receive continued coverage under a company policy.

Private Health Insurance

Medigap

An increasing number of private insurance companies are offering policies (often called co-insurance or "Medigap" insurance) that pay for services not included in Medicare. These policies can be expensive and, in some cases, do not provide complete coverage. Abuses in the Medigap insurance field have included overlapping coverage, selling clients more coverage than they need, and deceptive advertising. Because federal and state laws set a minimum level of benefits for a supplemental policy, one such policy is enough in virtually every case. Nonetheless, in 1995, the Health Insurance Association of America found that 25 percent of such policyholders had more than one policy.

TABLE 9.9

Percent and standard error of persons 65 years of age and over with a regular source of medical care by age and selected demographic characteristics: United States, 1993

Selected demographic characteristics	All persons 65 years of age and over	65–74 years of age	75 years of age and over
	Percent and standard error		
Total[1]	93.9(0.3)	93.6(0.5)	94.2(0.6)
Sex			
Male	93.3(0.5)	92.7(0.6)	94.4(0.7)
Female	94.3(0.4)	94.3(0.5)	94.2(0.7)
Race[2]			
White	93.9(0.4)	93.8(0.5)	94.1(0.6)
Black	93.4(1.0)	92.2(1.3)	95.3(1.3)
Region			
Northeast	94.3(0.6)	94.2(1.1)	94.4(1.3)
Midwest	93.9(0.6)	93.9(0.8)	94.0(1.0)
South	93.9(0.6)	93.4(0.7)	94.7(0.9)
West	93.3(1.0)	93.0(1.1)	93.7(1.5)
Place of residence			
MSA[3]	93.7(0.4)	93.7(0.5)	93.8(0.7)
Central city	93.0(0.8)	92.9(0.9)	93.1(0.9)
Noncentral city	94.2(0.5)	94.2(0.6)	94.2(0.9)
Not MSA[3]	94.2(0.6)	93.3(0.9)	95.6(0.8)
Family income			
Less than $10,000	92.1(0.9)	88.4(1.5)	95.2(0.9)
$10,000–$19,999	93.0(0.7)	92.6(1.0)	93.6(0.9)
$20,000–$34,999	95.4(0.6)	95.5(0.8)	95.3(1.0)
$35,000–$49,999	94.2(1.3)	95.1(1.1)	91.7(3.0)
$50,000 or more	95.7(0.9)	95.3(1.3)	96.8(1.3)
Race and family income			
White:			
Less than $20,000	92.7(0.5)	91.7(0.8)	93.7(0.7)
$20,000–$34,999	95.3(0.6)	95.4(0.8)	95.1(1.0)
$35,000 or more	95.2(0.8)	95.4(0.8)	94.6(1.9)
Black:			
Less than $20,000	92.5(1.1)	90.7(1.7)	95.4(1.3)
$20,000–$34,999	97.1(2.0)	97.2(2.6)	97.1(2.9)
$35,000 or more	93.6(3.5)	94.0(4.0)	*92.4(7.7)
Poverty index			
At or above poverty threshold	94.4(0.4)	94.1(0.5)	94.8(0.6)
Below poverty threshold	91.8(1.0)	89.8(1.7)	93.8(1.4)
Insurance coverage			
Medicare and private	95.4(0.4)	95.3(0.4)	95.5(0.5)
Medicare and public	94.1(1.1)	94.4(1.7)	93.7(1.7)
Medicare only	88.0(1.0)	86.1(1.5)	90.3(1.4)
Other	91.5(2.3)	91.0(2.7)	92.5(4.1)
No insurance	63.1(6.2)	59.2(7.4)	70.8(10.1)
Health status			
Excellent, very good, good	93.2(0.5)	93.1(0.6)	93.4(0.7)
Fair or poor	95.6(0.5)	95.3(0.6)	95.9(0.8)

*Figure does not meet standard of reliability or precision.

[1]Persons of races other than white or black, persons with unknown income, unknown poverty status, unknown health insurance coverage, and unknown health status are included in the total but not shown separately.

[2]Other races are not shown separately. Persons of Hispanic origin are not separated from the white and black race categories.

[3]MSA is metropolitan statistical area.

NOTE: Persons with unknown regular source of care were excluded from the analysis.

Source: "Access to Health Care, Part 3: Older Adults," *Vital and Health Statistics*, Series 10, No. 198, National Center for Health Statistics, Washington, DC, 1997

Nearly 68 percent of the elderly have some form of private insurance in addition to Medicare. Blacks were only half as likely to have supplemental coverage as their White counterparts.

Public Law 101-508, the Omnibus Budget Reconciliation Act of 1990, allowed people reaching the age of 65 to buy Medigap policies regardless of the condition of their health, provided they do so within six months after enrolling in Medicare. These protections apply to new beneficiaries, approximately 2 million people a year.

Having No Health Insurance

The Bureau of the Census reported, in 1996, that only 1.1 percent of all Americans over 65, or 3.6 percent of poor people over 65, have no health insurance. The remainder are covered by Medicare (Figure 9.5).

LONG-TERM HEALTH CARE

FIGURE 9.6

Unavailable or inconvenient 22.8%

Does not trust doctor 7.4%

Cannot afford 6.9%

Other 10.2%

Unknown 5.6%

Does not need doctor 47.1%

SOURCE: National Center for Health Statistics, National Health Interview Survey, 1993.

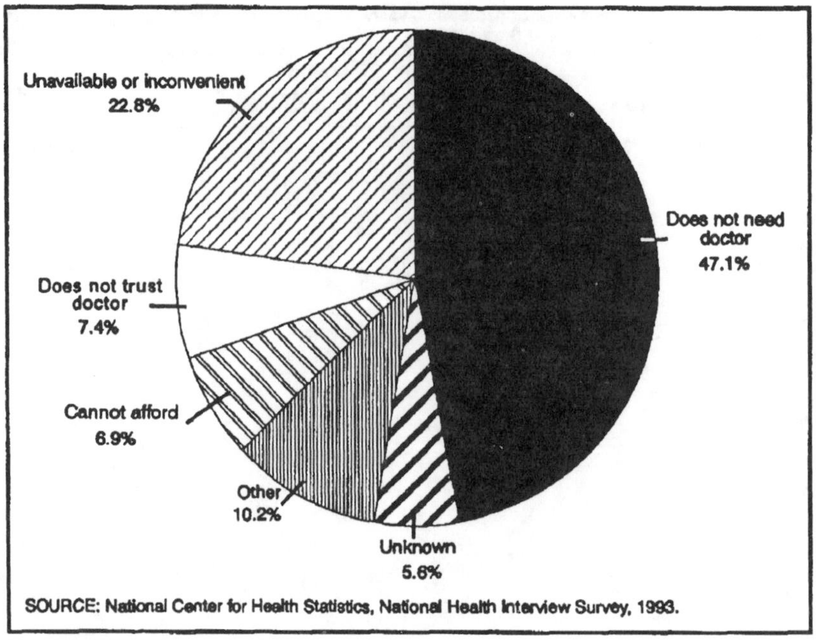

Reason for no regular source of care for persons 65 years of age and over: United States, 1993

Source: "Access to Health Care, Part 3: Older Adults," *Vital and Health Statistics*, Series 10, No. 198, National Center for Health Statistics, Washington, DC, 1997

Perhaps the most pressing and most difficult health care problem facing America today is long-term care. Long-term care refers to services needed by individuals with chronic illnesses or mental or physical conditions so severe that they cannot care for themselves over long periods of time. Longer life spans and improved life-sustaining technologies are increasing the possibility that an individual may eventually require long-term care.

In 1996, the John Hancock Mutual Life Insurance Company, in conjunction with the National Council on Aging, surveyed Americans about their plans for future long-term medical need. The study found that less than half of all adults have planned for the possibility of debilitating illness. Among the reasons given for lack of planning were "the issue is difficult to face," having more immediate needs, procrastination, lack of affordability, and unwillingness to take financial risks.

Predominating reasons varied depending upon age group. Baby boomers most often (75 percent) cited being too busy, although the youngest boomers claimed to have more pressing needs associated with child rearing; those 51 to 75 said the issue is better dealt with when it arises, and two-thirds said the issue is too hard to face; and the oldest Americans, born before 1925 believed it was too late to save meaningfully toward the possibility of need. Three-fourths of respondents of working age claimed they would take advantage of long-term insurance if it were offered by their employers.

Options Are Limited and Expensive

The options for good, affordable long-term care in the United States are few. One year's stay in a nursing home currently costs, on average, between $40,000 and $50,000 depending on the amount of care required. Even hiring an unskilled caregiver who makes home visits can cost more

TABLE 9.10

Estimated Prevalences of Failure to Receive Selected Preventive Care Services
Among Behavioral Risk Factor Surveillance System Respondents with Health Insurance
Who Were 65 Years of Age or Over, by Region[1], Sex, and Race/Ethnicity: United States, 1995

Region and Characteristic	Percent Not Receiving an Influenza Immunization in Past 12 Months	95-Percent Confidence Interval	Percent Never Receiving a Pneumonia Vaccination	95-Percent Confidence Interval	Percent Not Receiving a Mammogram in Past 2 Years[2]	95-Percent Confidence Interval	Percent Not Receiving a Digital Rectal Examination in Past Year	95-Percent Confidence Interval
United States Total	40.9	39.9, 41.9	62.7	61.7, 63.7	--	--	49.6	48.4, 50.8
Male	40.4	38.6, 42.2	63.6	61.8, 65.4	--	--	41.2	39.4, 43.0
Female	41.2	39.8, 42.6	62.1	60.7, 63.5	32.1	30.9, 33.3	55.5	54.1, 56.9
White, not Hispanic	39.1	37.9, 40.3	61.0	59.8, 62.2	32.0	30.6, 33.4	48.9	47.7, 50.1
Black, not Hispanic	59.4	55.5, 63.3	78.9	75.6, 82.2	36.4	31.7, 41.1	53.1	49.0, 57.2
Hispanic	47.2	40.7, 53.7	72.8	66.9, 78.7	25.9	19.4, 32.4	56.5	50.0, 63.0
Other	41.6	31.4, 51.8	63.6	53.0, 74.2	23.0	14.6, 31.4	59.7	49.1, 70.3

Source: "Behavioral Risk Factor Surveillance of Aged Medicare Beneficiaries, 1995," *Health Care Financing Review*, Health Care Financing Administration, Washington, DC, Summer 1997

than $25,000 a year; skilled care costs much more. Most elderly people and young families cannot afford this expense. Lifetime savings can be consumed before the need for care ends.

A Dilemma for the Entire Family

The inability to care for oneself not only affects the patient, but the entire family. Most people prefer to care for disabled parents or relatives at home as long as they can, but the emotional and financial strain on all family members can be great. As a loved one's condition deteriorates, there may come a time when home care is impossible, and the family has no alternative but to find an outside source of help.

Families who provide long-term care often sacrifice their own needs and wishes to meet the physical and financial obligations inherent in long-term care. They may delay sending a child to college, quit jobs or reduce hours, or they may exhaust their savings or go deeply into debt to pay for nursing home or specialized care.

Little Relief from Government Programs

Most government or "social" programs are funded with taxpayer dollars. Yet the elderly, most of whom have paid taxes over long, productive lifetimes, are often on their own at a time when it comes to long-term care.

The only government program that provides any substantial assistance for long-term health care is Medicaid, the federal-state health program designed to aid the poor. In order for elderly persons to qualify for nursing home care under Medicaid, they usually must reduce their personal financial status to the poverty level. Often they reach the poverty level by spending most of their hard-earned assets and income on their nursing home care. If the person is married, his or her spouse is now not only alone, but also poor.

... or Private Insurance Policies

A few insurance companies offer policies that claim to cover long-term care. However, they may contain loopholes and exclusions that limit actual coverage. A joint study by the United Seniors Health Cooperative and the University of North Carolina investigated 77 policies offered by 21 companies in Washington, DC, in 1991, and found that 61 percent of people in nursing homes would not have received any benefits from any of the policies.

Although advocates for the elderly have long campaigned for a more comprehensive system — particularly a broad-based insurance system like Social Security or Medicare — the political climate of the past 15 years has not been conducive to any expansion of the social welfare system.

National Health Expenditures Aggregate and per Capita Amounts, Percent Distribution, and Average Annual Percent Growth, by Source of Funds: Selected Years 1960-95

Item	1960	1970	1980	1985	1990	1991	1992	1993	1994	1995
					Amount in Billions					
National Health Expenditures	$26.9	$73.2	$247.2	$428.2	$697.5	$761.7	$834.2	$892.1	$937.1	$988.5
Private	20.2	45.5	142.5	253.9	413.1	441.4	478.8	505.5	517.2	532.1
Public	6.6	27.7	104.8	174.3	284.3	320.3	355.4	386.5	419.9	456.4
Federal	2.9	17.8	72.0	123.3	195.8	224.4	253.9	277.6	301.9	328.4
State and Local	3.7	9.9	32.8	51.0	88.5	95.9	101.6	108.9	118.0	128.0
					Number in Millions					
U.S. Population[1]	190.1	214.8	235.1	247.1	260.0	262.6	265.2	267.9	270.4	273.0
					Amount in Billions					
Gross Domestic Product	$527	$1,036	$2,784	$4,181	$5,744	$5,917	$6,244	$6,553	$6,936	$7,254
					Per Capita Amount					
National Health Expenditures	$141	$341	$1,052	$1,733	$2,683	$2,901	$3,145	$3,330	$3,465	$3,621
Private	106	212	606	1,027	1,589	1,681	1,805	1,887	1,913	1,949
Public	35	129	446	705	1,094	1,220	1,340	1,443	1,553	1,672
Federal	15	83	306	499	753	855	957	1,036	1,116	1,203
State and Local	20	46	140	206	341	365	383	407	436	469
					Percent Distribution					
National Health Expenditures	100.0	100.0	100.0	100.0	100.0	100.0	100.0	100.0	100.0	100.0
Private	75.2	62.2	57.6	59.3	59.2	58.0	57.4	56.7	55.2	53.8
Public	24.8	37.8	42.4	40.7	40.8	42.0	42.6	43.3	44.8	46.2
Federal	10.9	24.3	29.1	28.8	28.1	29.5	30.4	31.1	32.2	33.2
State and Local	13.9	13.5	13.3	11.9	12.7	12.6	12.2	12.2	12.6	12.9
					Percent of Gross Domestic Product					
National Health Expenditures	5.1	7.1	8.9	10.2	12.1	12.9	13.4	13.6	13.5	13.6
					Average Annual Percent Growth from Previous Year Shown					
National Health Expenditures	—	10.6	12.9	11.6	10.2	9.2	9.5	6.9	5.1	5.5
Private	—	8.5	12.1	12.3	10.2	6.8	8.5	5.6	2.3	2.9
Public	—	15.3	14.2	10.7	10.3	12.7	11.0	8.7	8.6	8.7
Federal	—	19.8	15.0	11.4	9.7	14.6	13.1	9.4	8.7	8.8
State and Local	—	10.2	12.7	9.2	11.6	8.3	6.0	7.2	8.4	8.4
U.S. Population	—	1.2	0.9	1.0	1.0	1.0	1.0	1.0	1.0	0.9
Gross Domestic Product	—	7.0	10.4	8.5	6.6	3.0	5.5	4.9	5.8	4.6

[1] July 1 Social Security area population estimates for each year, 1960-95.

NOTE: Numbers and percents may not add to totals because of rounding.

SOURCE: Health Care Financing Administration, Office of the Actuary: Data from the Office of National Health Statistics.

Source: "National Health Care Expenditures, 1995," *Health Care Financing Review*, Health Care Financing Administration, Washington, DC, Fall 1996

NOT ALWAYS TAKING THE BEST CARE OF THEMSELVES

A 1997 Public Health Service study found that, in 1993, 6 percent — 3.3 million — of the elderly reported that they did not have a regular source of medical care (Table 9.9). Older persons with Medicare and private health insurance or Medicare and public insurance coverage were more likely to have a regular source of care than those who had Medicare only or who were uninsured. Among the reasons cited for their lack of care were "does not need a doctor" (47 percent), inconvenience (23 percent), "does not trust doctor" (7 percent), cannot afford (7 percent), and other (10 percent). (See Figure 9.6.)

Unmet needs were most likely to include dental care (1.4 million elderly), glasses (1 million), medical care (500,000), and prescription medications (600,000). Although the majority of elderly people had a regular source of care, many did not get routine preventive services such as immunizations, Pap smears, or mammograms. Forty-one percent did not get influenza immunization, 63 percent did not get pneumonia immunizations, 32 percent of women did not get mammograms, and 50 percent did not receive digital rectal examinations (for colon or prostate cancer (Table 9.10). For whatever reasons, many elderly are not taking the time to get preventive care services.

PROVIDING HEALTH CARE — A NATIONAL CONCERN

Health care costs continue to rise mainly because of increased prices for services, higher technology, rising demand for services, and inflation. In 1960, national health care cost $23.9 billion; in 1995, Americans spent $988.5 billion for health care. Of that, federal health programs, including Medicare, Medicaid, public health programs, and health research accounted for approximately 46 percent of the cost. In 1995, health expenditures were 13.6 percent of the total gross domestic product (the total value of a nation's annual output of goods and services). (See Table 9.11.) By most estimates, health care will account for 15 percent of the gross domestic product by the year 2000.

How much and what kind of health care protection should be available are on-going questions with no easy answers. The problems have not gone unnoticed by Congress. A wide array of bills have been introduced with proposals ranging from almost total protection under federal programs to almost complete dependence on the private sectors. There is little consensus on a solution. Faced with an aging population and ever-rising medical costs, the government's and the nation's health care predicament will likely worsen.

CHAPTER X

ELDERLY VICTIMS

CRIMES AGAINST THE ELDERLY

The U.S. Department of Justice, Bureau of Justice Statistics, in *Changes in Criminal Victimization 1994-95* (Washington, DC, April 1997), reported that, in 1995, Americans 65 years and older were considerably less likely to be crime victims than younger people (Table 10.1). Similarly, the Federal Bureau of Investigation, in *Crime in the United States — 1996* (1997) reported that persons over the age of 65 made up only 4.5 percent of the total 1996 murder victims (Table 10.2). Crime victimization rates among the elderly have generally declined since 1973 (Figure 10.1). Over 20 years, the lowest rate of violent crime against the elderly was recorded in 1990 — 3.5 per 1,000 persons age 65 or older.

The Emotional Impact of Crime

The consequences of victimization, however, can be much more severe for the elderly. Speaking before the House Select Committee on Aging, Irwin I. Kimmelman, Attorney General for the New Jersey Department of Law and Safety, noted that it is not the number of crimes, but the "terrible and tragic impact that crime has on [the elderly] that is significant. Crime simply causes much more fear among the elderly and has a far more deleterious impact on the quality of their lives."

Crimes against the elderly are particularly devastating because older people are often less resilient than younger people. They may not be able to cope with the trauma and "get on with their lives," especially if their lives are static, with few new pleasant experiences to replace the memory of painful ones. Even so-called non-violent crimes, such as purse snatching, vandalism, and burglary, can be devastating. Stolen or damaged articles and property are often irreplaceable, either because of the sentimental or monetary value. Even non-violent crimes leave victims with a sense of violation and vulnerability.

Once victimized, older people may become obsessed with the idea that they will be victimized again (a not uncommon reaction in younger victims, as well). They may develop a negative outlook on life and even alter their lifestyle, as they resort to extreme precautionary measures. Sixty-four percent of violent crimes against the elderly in 1992 (the latest data available) were committed by a person who was a total stranger to them (Table 10.3). Fear of strangers can make an elderly person reluctant to leave his or her home.

CHARACTERISTICS OF ELDERLY CRIME VICTIMS

Among the elderly, certain groups are generally more likely to experience a crime than others. More than 60 percent of the elderly live in metropolitan areas, and many live in inner cities where crime rates are the highest. Overall, in 1992, half of violent crimes against older people occurred in or near their homes (compared to 25 percent for younger victims) (Table 10.4). For the elderly, the homes and neighborhoods where they generally spend most of their time do not necessarily offer escape from victimization, but, in fact, may make them especially vulnerable. As a

TABLE 10.1

Personal crime victimization, by sex, age, race, Hispanic origin, household income, region, and location of residence of victims, 1995

Characteristic of victims	Population	Rates of personal crime in 1995 (per 1,000 persons)							
			Violent crimes						Personal theft
		Total	Total	Rape/Sexual assault	Robbery	Assault			
						Total	Aggravated	Simple	
Sex									
Male	104,268,820	54.4	53.2	.3	7.5	45.3	11.9	33.5	1.3
Female	111,440,640	38.5	36.4	2.8	3.2	30.4	5.9	24.6	2.1
Age									
12-15	15,575,940	110.9	107.1	2.2	9.5	95.4	15.4	80.1	3.8
16-19	14,539,170	110.3	107.7	5.7	9.0	93.0	24.4	68.6	2.7
20-24	17,813,630	79.8	78.8	3.0	10.8	65.0	15.4	49.6	1.1
25-34	41,138,060	55.9	54.7	2.0	6.9	45.8	11.7	34.1	1.2
35-49	60,635,010	35.6	33.8	1.4	4.7	27.7	6.8	20.9	1.8
50-64	34,451,280	15.6	14.0	.1	1.8	12.1	2.6	9.5	1.6
65 or older	31,556,350	6.9	5.9	0.0	1.3	4.6	1.3	3.3	1.0
Race									
White	181,880,850	44.6	43.1	1.6	4.2	37.3	8.2	29.1	1.4
Black	25,998,040	58.4	55.4	1.6	12.5	41.3	12.6	28.7	3.1
Other	7,830,570	43.8	40.9	1.2	6.3	33.4	9.2	24.2	2.9
Hispanic origin									
Hispanic	19,674,030	56.1	53.4	1.3	10.6	41.5	13.6	27.9	2.6
Non-Hispanic	193,918,300	45.0	43.4	1.6	4.8	37.0	8.2	28.8	1.6
Household Income									
Less than $7,500	15,917,890	74.6	71.0	3.5	11.8	55.7	16.5	39.2	3.6
$7,500 - 14,999	25,169,790	49.7	48.4	1.6	9.1	37.7	10.0	27.7	1.3
$15,000 - 24,999	32,095,240	49.2	47.7	1.6	6.5	39.5	9.1	30.4	1.5
$25,000 - 34,999	29,608,960	48.1	46.4	1.5	5.1	39.8	8.9	30.8	1.7
$35,000 - 49,999	34,914,380	45.8	44.2	1.8	3.6	38.9	8.8	30.1	1.5
$50,000 - 74,999	29,657,010	44.1	42.7	1.2	3.1	38.4	8.5	29.9	1.5
$75,000 or more	22,091,400	37.9	36.2	.8	2.4	33.0	5.5	27.6	1.7
Region									
Northeast	42,930,170	41.1	38.5	1.3	6.2	31.0	5.5	25.5	2.6
Midwest	51,592,700	46.7	45.2	2.3	4.3	38.6	7.9	30.7	1.5
South	75,910,170	39.6	38.4	.9	4.3	33.1	8.4	24.8	1.3
West	45,276,420	61.5	59.7	2.1	7.2	50.4	13.5	36.9	1.8
Residence									
Urban	62,255,840	59.9	56.8	2.0	9.7	45.1	11.7	33.4	3.1
Suburban	98,073,550	43.5	42.1	1.6	4.0	36.6	8.1	28.4	1.4
Rural	55,380,060	35.5	34.9	1.2	2.6	31.1	6.6	24.5	0.6

Source: *Changes in Criminal Victimization, 1994-95,* Bureau of Justice Statistics, Washington, DC, 1997

group, the elderly are more dependent on walking and public transportation, which increases their exposure to possible criminal attack.

Crimes of violence were highest for those who lived in the city, rented their homes, were divorced or separated, were Black, and had incomes below $7,500. Crimes of theft were greatest for those elderly with incomes over $25,000, those who lived in cities, and those who were divorced or separated. Household crime rates were highest for males, Blacks, homeowners, and those with

incomes above $25,000. (See Table 10.5.) Elderly Whites had the lowest violent crime rates; elderly Blacks had the lowest personal theft rates (Figure 10.2).

Approximately one-third of the older violent crime victims, compared to a fourth of those younger than 65, received medical attention at a hospital as a result of being victims of crime. Older victims also received more serious injuries. (See Table 10.6.) Among younger victims, 5 percent suffered serious injuries, such as broken bones and

TABLE 10.2

Age, Sex, and Race of Murder Victims, 1996

Age	Total	Sex			Race			
		Male	Female	Unknown	White	Black	Other	Unknown
Total	15,848	12,195	3,631	22	7,647	7,638	425	138
Percent distribution[1]	100.0	76.9	22.9	.1	48.3	48.2	2.7	.9
Under 18[2]	1,960	1,385	572	3	973	907	57	23
Under 22[2]	4,366	3,511	852	3	1,923	2,295	113	35
18 and over[2]	13,669	10,661	3,003	5	6,564	6,659	364	82
Infant (under 1)	247	124	120	3	153	80	7	7
1 to 4	375	204	171	—	198	159	15	3
5 to 8	101	57	44	—	63	36	2	—
9 to 12	81	42	39	—	46	34	1	—
13 to 16	692	557	135	—	320	344	21	7
17 to 19	1,669	1,447	222	—	667	954	36	12
20 to 24	2,739	2,379	360	—	1,050	1,601	72	16
25 to 29	2,219	1,807	411	1	908	1,234	63	14
30 to 34	1,838	1,389	447	2	867	904	53	14
35 to 39	1,685	1,235	450	—	878	756	39	12
40 to 44	1,212	897	315	—	660	511	32	9
45 to 49	877	628	248	1	493	358	24	2
50 to 54	539	398	141	—	320	190	25	4
55 to 59	362	277	85	—	232	116	12	2
60 to 64	276	205	71	—	179	91	5	1
65 to 69	223	152	71	—	156	62	5	—
70 to 74	174	106	68	—	125	44	5	—
75 and over	320	142	177	1	222	92	4	2
Unknown	219	149	56	14	110	72	4	33

[1] Because of rounding, percentages may not add to total.
[2] Does not include unknown ages.

Source: *Uniform Crime Reports — Crime in the United States, 1996,*
Federal Bureau of Investigation, Washington, DC, 1997

---

loss of consciousness; 9 percent of the elderly suffered serious injuries.

Older People Are Considered Easy Prey

Because of their physical limitations, criminals often consider older people easy prey. The elderly usually do not resist a criminal attack. They are aware that they may lack the strength to repel a younger aggressor and that they are particularly susceptible to broken bones and fractured hips, which could permanently cripple them.

The Bureau of Justice reports that victims age 65 and older take protective measures in 58 percent of their victimizations, compared to 73 percent of younger victims. Those over 65 who try to protect themselves most often use nonphysical actions, such as arguing, reasoning, screaming, or running away. Younger victims are more likely to use physical actions, such as attacking, resisting, or chasing the offender. Most criminals are likely less concerned about nonphysical defenses than they are about physical resistance.

Older people are also a favorite target of fraud and confidence schemes. They often live on fixed incomes and limited savings. "Get rich" schemes can appear very attractive to the elderly because they offer the promise of economic security.

TREATMENT BY THE COURTS

Elderly victims are sometimes poorly treated by the criminal justice system. Because of physical impairments, such as poor hearing and vision and slowness of movement and speech, older persons can encounter impatience and insensitivity when they attempt to report a crime committed against themselves. This kind of treatment adds to their frustration and sense of helplessness.

Victim compensation for crimes against the elderly is currently provided on the state level, and amounts vary from state to state. Most states compensate for medical, counseling, and physical therapy expenses associated with the crime and reimburse for lost wages, loss of support to dependents, and for funeral expenses.

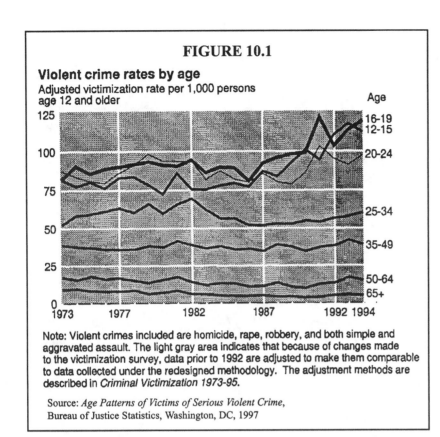

FIGURE 10.1

Violent crime rates by age

Adjusted victimization rate per 1,000 persons age 12 and older

Note: Violent crimes included are homicide, rape, robbery, and both simple and aggravated assault. The light gray area indicates that because of changes made to the victimization survey, data prior to 1992 are adjusted to make them comparable to data collected under the redesigned methodology. The adjustment methods are described in *Criminal Victimization 1973-95.*

Source: *Age Patterns of Victims of Serious Violent Crime,* Bureau of Justice Statistics, Washington, DC, 1997

DOMESTIC VIOLENCE AGAINST THE ELDERLY*

Domestic violence against the elderly is a phenomenon that has only recently gained public attention. It is impossible to determine exactly how many elderly people are the victims of domestic violence. As with child abuse, the number of actual cases is larger than the number of reported cases. However, experts agree that elder abuse is far less likely to be reported than child or spousal abuse. Definitions of abuse and reporting methods vary greatly both between states and among different government agencies.

Research done in 1981 concluded that 10 percent of the elderly population were victims of elder abuse. A much-publicized report, *Elder Abuse: A Decade of Shame and Inaction* (1990), released by the now-defunct Subcommittee on Aging of the U.S. House of Representatives, estimated that "about 1 out of every 20 older Americans, or more than 1.5 million persons," may be victims of elder abuse each year. The National Center on Elder Abuse (NCEA), in *Elder Abuse: Questions and Answers — An Information Guide for Professionals and Concerned Citizens*, June 1996, estimated there were 820,000 to 1.8 million abused elders in the country in 1996.

Nationwide, reports of domestic elder abuse have increased steadily in the past several years. The National Aging Resource Center on Elder Abuse, predecessor of the NCEA, reported 117,000 incidents in 1986, 128,000 in 1987, 140,000 in 1988, 211,000 in 1990, and 213,000 incidents in 1991. The NCEA reported 227,000 incidents in 1993 and 241,000 in 1994, nationwide. (See Figure 10.3.) With enhanced public awareness and improved reporting systems, experts anticipate reports of elder domestic abuse will continue to increase.

Types of Mistreatment

Research on domestic elder abuse is still in its infancy, but studies conducted over the past 10 years have revealed several recurring forms of abuse. Federal definitions of elder abuse, neglect, and exploitation appeared for the first time in the 1987 Amendments to the Old Americans Act. Broadly defined, there are three basic categories of abuse: (1) domestic elder abuse, (2) institutional elder abuse (see below), and (3) self-neglect, or self-abuse.

Domestic elder abuse generally refers to any form of maltreatment of an older person by someone who has a special relationship with the

---

*For a complete discussion of domestic violence against the elderly, see *Violent Relationships — Battering and Abuse Among Adults*, Information Plus, Wylie, Texas, 1997.

TABLE 10.3

Percent of violent crime victims whose offenders are:

	Relatives	Acquaint-ances	Strangers	Relationship unknown
Crimes of violence				
Under 65	8%	33%	56%	3%
65 or older	8	20	64	8
Robbery				
Under 65	5	17	74	4
65 or older	3	5	83	9
Assault				
Under 65	9	36	52	3
65 or older	13	32	47	8

Source: *Elderly Crime Victims*, Bureau of Justice Statistics, Washington, DC, 1994

TABLE 10.4

Place of occurrence

	Total	At home	Near home	On the street	In public or business facility	Else-where
Crimes of violence						
Under 65	100%	14%	11%	39%	21%	15%
65 or older	100	25	25	31	9	10
Robbery						
Under 65	100	13	9	52	16	10
65 or older	100	20	21	37	13	10
Assault						
Under 65	100	14	12	36	21	15
65 or older	100	27	29	27	7	10

Source: *Elderly Crime Victims*, Bureau of Justice Statistics, Washington, DC, 1994

elder (a spouse, sibling, child, friend, or caregiver). Most sources have identified the following categories of domestic elder mistreatment. :

- **Physical abuse** — inflicting physical pain or injury.

- **Sexual abuse** — non-consensual sexual contact of any kind with an older person.

- **Emotional or psychological abuse** — inflicting mental anguish by, for example, name calling, humiliation, making threats, or isolation.

- **Neglect** — willful or unintentional failure to provide basic necessities, such as food and medical care due to caregiver indifference, inability, or ignorance.

- **Material or financial abuse** — exploiting or misusing an older person's money or assets.

The NCEA reported that the majority of the confirmed cases, or about one-third of all reports of elder abuse, usually turn out to be self-neglect or self-abuse cases. For example, 32 percent of the confirmed cases in 41 states during 1994 were self-neglect or self-abuse. The NCEA estimates the incidence of specific types of elder maltreatment for 1994 were physical abuse, 15.7 percent; sexual abuse, 0.5 percent; emotional abuse, 7.3 percent;

neglect, 58.5 percent; financial exploitation, 12.3 percent; all other types, 5.1 percent; and unknown 0.6 percent (Figure 10.4).

A Canadian study of service providers ("Learning from Service Providers Working with

TABLE 10.5

Number of victimizations per 1,000

Victim characteristics	Persons 65 or older — Violence	Persons 65 or older — Theft	Households headed by a person 65 or older — Household crime
Sex			
Male	4.9	19.8	82.2
Female	3.4	19.4	74.3
Age			
65 to 74	4.7	22.9	82.2
75 and over	3.0	14.2	74.3
Race			
White	3.6	19.5	70.9
Black	7.6	19.6	154.1
Family income			
Less than $7,500	12.0	29.1	76.3
$7,500-$14,999	8.4	30.4	70.2
$15,000-$24,999	6.5	40.3	81.3
$25,000 or more	6.1	60.8	96.0
Marital status			
Never married	3.0	18.2	77.6
Widowed	4.2	4.2	75.1
Married	7.6	26.3	71.1
Divorced/separated	11.3	35.4	110.4
Place of residence			
Urban	7.1	26.4	112.6
Suburban	2.9	19.6	61.2
Rural	2.2	11.4	64.5
Form of tenure			
Own	3.1	17.8	82.0
Rent	7.7	26.7	66.8

Source: *Elderly Crime Victims*, Bureau of Justice Statistics, Washington, DC, 1994

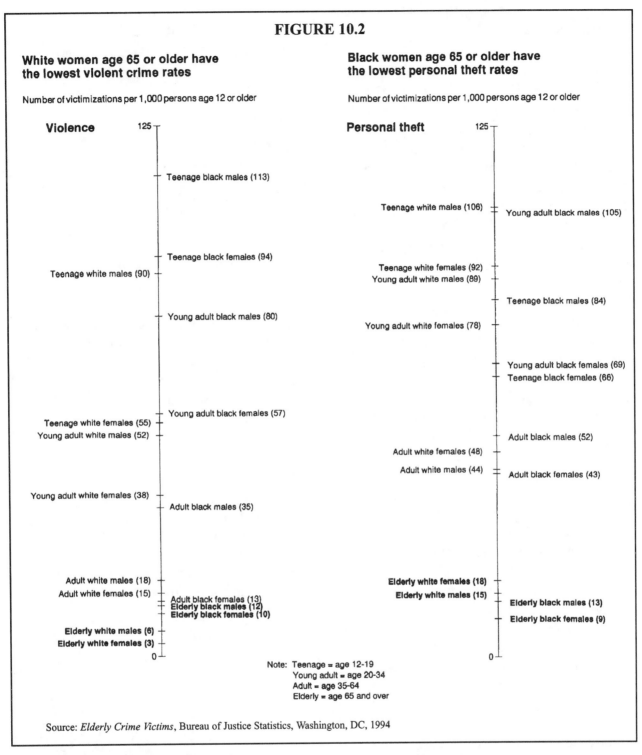

FIGURE 10.2

White women age 65 or older have the lowest violent crime rates

Number of victimizations per 1,000 persons age 12 or older

Violence

125

Teenage black males (113)

Teenage black females (94)

Teenage white males (90)

Young adult black males (80)

Young adult black females (57)
Teenage white females (55)
Young adult white males (52)

Young adult white females (38)

Adult black males (35)

Adult white males (18)
Adult white females (15)
Adult black females (13)
Elderly black males (12)
Elderly black females (10)

Elderly white males (6)
Elderly white females (3)

0

Black women age 65 or older have the lowest personal theft rates

Number of victimizations per 1,000 persons age 12 or older

Personal theft

125

Teenage white males (106)   Young adult black males (105)

Teenage white females (92)
Young adult white males (89)

Teenage black males (84)

Young adult white females (78)

Young adult black females (69)
Teenage black females (66)

Adult black males (52)
Adult white females (48)

Adult white males (44)   Adult black females (43)

Elderly white females (18)
Elderly white males (15)

Elderly black males (13)

Elderly black females (9)

0

Note: Teenage = age 12–19
Young adult = age 20–34
Adult = age 35–64
Elderly = age 65 and over

Source: *Elderly Crime Victims*, Bureau of Justice Statistics, Washington, DC, 1994

Abused Seniors," Connie Chapman, 1994) found that of 176 abused elderly, 38 percent were emotionally abused, 31 percent suffered financial or material abuse, and 23 percent were physically abused. Of the 73 cases of suspected abuse, about one-third of the victims were thought to be emotionally or financially abused; another 16 percent were neglected. (See Table 10.7.)

Theft by Kin and Friends (Financial Abuse)

As reflected in the NCEA and Chapman studies (see above), criminal justice professionals are finding that money and property are being stolen from today's elderly at alarming rates and that a large portion of the crimes are being committed not by professional criminals but by relatives, friends, health aides, household workers, and neighbors.

Like child and sexual abuse crimes, many crimes against the elderly are not reported because the victims are physically or mentally unable to summon help or because they are reticent or afraid to publicly accuse relatives or those they are dependent upon. In-home care for elderly persons often allows persons access to the financial and property assets of those cared for. Officials suspect that fully 80 percent of such cases go unreported and that conditions for the material exploitation of older Americans will likely grow.

Medical advances are lengthening lives and resulting in greater numbers of older and, in many cases, infirm persons. Increasing numbers of these elderly people have substantial bank and investment accounts. Also vulnerable are those too sick to manage even their Social Security or pension checks. Financial exploitation is likely to grow as the number of older Americans who are most vulnerable to it, the lonely and those in poor health, rises.

Women are frequent victims of such crimes, primarily because there are so many more elderly women. Loneliness causes many victims not to report the crimes, even when they are aware of them, simply because they are afraid to lose the companionship of the perpetrator. When a case of financial abuse is reported, the source of the information is likely to be someone other than the victim — a police officer, ambulance attendant, bank teller, neighbor, or other family member.

Most states require doctors and other social service professionals to report evidence of abuse. The most common outcome of intervention is that the victim is moved to an institution. Many elderly, however, refuse to be removed from an abusive situation in order to be put in an alternative setting, and without the victim's cooperation, little can be done.

TABLE 10.6

Outcome	Percent of violent crime victims	
	Under 65	65 or older
Injured	31%	33%
Serious	5	9
Minor	26	24
Received medical care	15	19
Hospital care	8	14

Source: *Elderly Crime Victims*, Bureau of Justice Statistics, Washington, DC, 1994

Who Are the Abusers of the Elderly?

The NCEA reports that among the abusers of the elderly, 35 percent were adult children; 5.9 percent, grandchildren; 13.4 percent, spouses; 2.9 percent, siblings; 13.6 percent, other relatives; 6.2 percent, service providers; 5.2 percent, friends/ neighbors; 10.3 percent, all other; and 7.4 percent, unknown (Figure 10.5).

Chapman's 1994 Canadian study found, however, that one-third of abuse was perpetrated by a husband, compared to only 3 percent of wives who were accused. Fifty-one percent of abusers were children or spouses of the children. (See Table 10.8.) The majority (70 percent of active cases, 87 percent of suspected) of seniors were

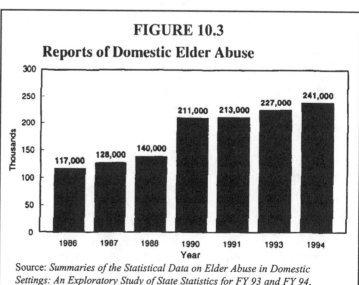

FIGURE 10.3
Reports of Domestic Elder Abuse

Source: *Summaries of the Statistical Data on Elder Abuse in Domestic Settings: An Exploratory Study of State Statistics for FY 93 and FY 94,* National Center on Elder Abuse, Washington, DC, 1996

abused by only one person, although 23 percent of victims were abused by two people, and 7 percent were abused by three people. There may be a significant number of elderly who are abused by several people.

Who Are the Abuse Victims?

The NCEA reported that almost two-thirds of elder abuse victims in domestic settings are female. Data from 36 states showed that 62 percent of the elderly who were abused in 1994 were females. In addition, older elders are more likely to be victims. Elderly over the age of 80 made up more than one-third of victims in 1994. The median age of these victims was 76.5 years.

What Are the Characteristics of Self-Neglecting Elders?

The NCEA reported that, in 1994, 62.4 percent of self-abusers were women. The median age of self-neglecting elders was 77.2 years.

Causes of Elder Abuse

The National Aging Resource Center on Elder Abuse reports that no single theory can explain why older people are abused. The causes of elder abuse are diverse and complicated. Some relate to the personality of the abuser, some are a reflection of the relationship between the abuser and the abused, and some are reactions to stressful situations. While some children truly dislike their parents and the role of caregiver, many others want to care for their parents or feel it is the right thing to do, but sometimes they may be emotionally or financially unable.

Stress

Most experts agree that stress is a contributing factor in abuse of the elderly. Meeting the daily needs of a frail and dependent elderly relative may be overwhelming for some family members. When

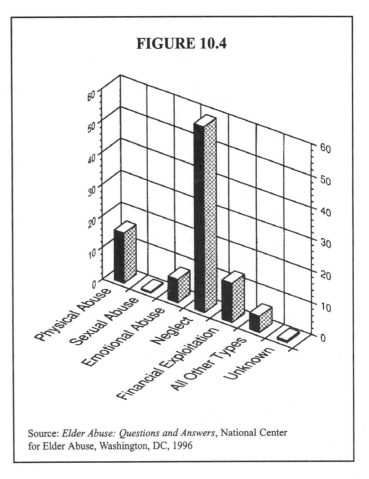

FIGURE 10.4

Source: *Elder Abuse: Questions and Answers*, National Center for Elder Abuse, Washington, DC, 1996

the elderly person lives in the same household as the caregiver, crowding, differences of opinion, and constant demands often add to the strain of providing physical care. If the elderly person lives in a different house, the added pressure of having to commute between two households, doing extra housekeeping chores, and being on call at a moment's notice may be too much for the caregiver to cope with.

The Financial Burden

In many cases, caring for an elderly person places a financial strain on a family. Elderly parents may need financial assistance at the same time that their children are raising their own families. Instead of an occasional night out, a long-awaited vacation, or a badly needed new car, families may find themselves paying for ever-increasing medical care, prescription drugs, physical aids, special dietary supplements, extra food and clothing, or therapy. Saving for their

TABLE 10.7

KIND OF ABUSE	ACTIVE INVOLVEMENT		SUSPECTED	
	Number	Percentage	Number	Percentage
Emotional	67	38%	23	31%
Material/Financial	54	31%	26	37%
Physical	40	23%	0	0
Sexual	0	0	0	0
Neglect	12	7%	12	16%
Self-Neglect	3	2%	6	8%
Abuse Unknown	0	0	6	8%
TOTALS	176	101.00	73	100.00

Source: *Learning from Service Providers with Abused Seniors,* prepared for the Elder Abuse Community Development Project, North Shore Community Services by Connie Chapman, 1994

children's college education, for a daughter's wedding, or for retirement becomes difficult. Resentment can build quickly, and it can lead to emotional if not outright physical abuse of the elderly by the caregiver.

The Cycle of Abuse

Some experts believe that persons who abuse an elderly parent or relative were themselves abused as children. Dr. Suzanne K. Steinmetz, Director for Resources for Older Americans at the University of Delaware and a recognized expert on domestic violence, found such a pattern in her studies of elderly abusers. She found that only one out of 400 children treated non-violently when his or her were raised attacked their elderly parents; one out of two children who was violently mistreated as he or she grew up abused his or her elderly parents.

Chicago psychiatrist Mitchell Messer, who treats adults who care for elderly parents, notes, "We find parent beatings when the parents set the example of solving problems through brutality when the children were growing up.... The response is simply following the example his parents set." As adults, formerly abused children often have financial, marital, or drug problems, which they blame on their parents and which make them even more abusive.

Invasion of Privacy

Most Americans believe that home is a place a person should be able to call his or her own. When that home must be shared, there is an inevitable loss of a certain amount of control and privacy. Movement may be restricted, habits may need to be changed, rivalry frequently develops between generations over decision-making, and young children may play the adults against each other to get what they want. Frustration and anxiety result as both parent and supporting child try to suppress angry feelings, sometimes unsuccessfully.

Loss of Freedom

An adult child may be obligated to care for an adult parent just at the time when his or her own children are leaving home. The resentment of being once again tied to the home, this time to care for a frail, perhaps bedridden, parent pushes many caregivers to the breaking point. To make matters worse, they may feel guilty and ashamed of their negative feelings. The dependent parent, in turn, often senses this resentment and may respond by withdrawing or becoming even more demanding. The average length of home care for a severely dependent person who is over 70 is between five and six years. In many cases, it is much longer.

Additionally, an adult child (usually a daughter) with children still in the home may find herself in the position of caring also for an elderly parent. The term "sandwich generation" (those persons who have both a younger generation and an older generation to care for) has been coined to describe these caregivers who may have anticipated enjoyment of their own interests at exactly the same time they are required to assume care for an aged parent. At the same time, it should be emphasized that the overwhelming majority of caregivers who suffer these many types of stress do not abuse the elderly people they are caring for.

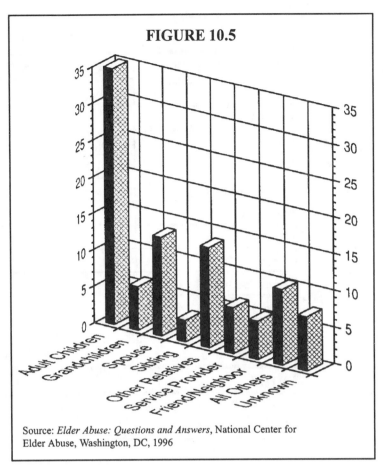

FIGURE 10.5

Source: *Elder Abuse: Questions and Answers*, National Center for Elder Abuse, Washington, DC, 1996

Reverse Dependency

Some sources believe that people who abuse an elderly person may actually be quite dependent on that person. Some experts have found that abused elderly were no more likely to have had a recent decline in health or be seriously ill or hospitalized previously than the non-abused elderly — in fact, as a group, the abused elderly were more self-sufficient in preparing meals, doing ordinary housework, and climbing stairs than were the non-abused elderly.

On the other hand, abusing caregivers often seem more dependent on their victims for housing, financial assistance, and transportation than were nonabusing caregivers. They often seem to have fewer resources and are frequently unable to meet their own basic needs. Rather than having power in

the relationship, they are relatively powerless. From these observations, some authorities have concluded that abusing caregivers may not always be driven to violence by the physical and emotional burden of caring for a seriously disabled elderly person but may have emotional problems of their own that can lead to violent behavior.

The Abusive Spouse

The high rate of spousal abuse is possibly the result of the fact that many elderly people live with spouses, so the opportunity for spousal violence is great. Violence against an elderly spouse may be the continuation of an abusive relationship that began years earlier — abuse does not end simply because a couple gets older. Sometimes, however, the abuse may not begin until later years, in which case it is often associated with alcohol abuse, unemployment, post-retirement depression, and/ or loss of self-esteem.

151

TABLE 10.8

RELATIONSHIP OF ABUSER TO VICTIM	ACTIVE INVOLVEMENT		SUSPECTED	
	Number	Percentage	Number	Percentage
Husband	41	33%	12	19%
Wife	4	3%	1	2
Son	20	16%	11	17
Daughter-in-law	19	15%	5	8
Son-in-law	11	9%	5	8
Daughter	14	11%	11	17
Grandson	2	2%	0	0
Granddaughter	6	5%	1	2
Other relative	3	3%	14	22
Neighbour	3	3%	2	3
Abuser unknown	0	0	2	3
TOTALS	123	100.00	64	101.00

Source: *Learning from Service Providers with Abused Seniors,* prepared for the Elder Abuse
Community Development Project, North Shore Community Services by Connie Chapman, 1994

Intervention and Prevention

All 50 states and the District of Columbia now have laws dealing specifically with adult abuse, but as with laws concerning child abuse and spousal abuse among younger couples, they are sometimes ineffective. The laws and the enforcing agencies vary from state to state and even from county to county within a given state. No standard definition of abuse exists among enforcement agencies.

In many cases, authorities cannot legally intervene and terminate an abusive condition unless a report is filed, the abuse is verified, and the victim files a formal complaint. An elderly person could understandably be reluctant, physically unable, or too fearful to accuse or prosecute an abuser. At the present time, 42 states and the District of Columbia operate "mandatory reporting systems," making it mandatory for certain professionals to report suspected abuse. In eight states, reporting is voluntary.

The best way to stop elder abuse is to prevent its occurrence. As noted above, researchers have identified specific situations where abuse is likely to occur and the type of person that is likely to be an abuser. Older people who know that they will eventually need outside help should carefully analyze the potential difficulties of living with a child and, if necessary and possible, make alternate arrangements. In any event, they should take care to protect their money and assets to ensure that their valuables cannot be easily taken over by someone else.

Young families or persons who must care for an older person, voluntarily or otherwise, must realize that their frustration and despair do not have to result in abuse. Social agencies can often work with families to help relieve anger and stress. Sometimes there are ways to offset the financial burden of elder care, for example, through tax deductions or subsidies for respite care. (See Chapter IX.)

INSTITUTIONAL ABUSE

Abuse of the elderly can also occur outside the private home in nursing homes charged with the care of the aged and ill patient. Institutional abuse generally refers to the same forms of abuse mentioned as domestic abuse but perpetuated by persons who have a legal or contractual obligation to provide elders with care and protection. Because data on nursing home residents' complaints are not compiled on a national level, data is scarce regarding abuse occurring in institutional settings.

Brian Payne and Richard Cikovic studied 488 cases of nursing home abuse reported to Medicaid Fraud Control Units ("An Empirical Examination of the Characteristics, Consequences, and Causes of Elder Abuse in Nursing Homes," *Journal of Elder Abuse & Neglect*, vol. 7, no. 4, 1995). Forty-two states have Medicaid Fraud Control Units, which are responsible for detecting, investigating, and prosecuting Medicaid fraud and abuse. The study found that 84.2 percent of the abuse was physical, including slapping; hitting with an object such as a hairbrush, wet towel, or spatula; kicking; and spitting. The remaining acts were sexual (8.8 percent), monetary (1.4 percent), or duty-related, in which an employee misperformed specific duties, such as removing bandages in a rough manner.

Although nurses' aides comprised the largest group of abusers (62 percent), they were also the single most numerous employees in nursing homes (Table 10.9). Of the 488 incidents, 63 percent involved a male employee. Males were also slightly more likely to be victims (57 percent), although more females are employed in nursing homes, and more residents are female. Male employees tended to abuse male residents; female employees tended to abuse female victims (Table 10.10).

TABLE 10.9
Occupations of Nursing Home Personnel Accused of Abuse

Occupation	n	%
Nurses' Aide	302	61.9
Licensed Practical Nurse	32	6.6
Direct Care Worker	15	3.1
Supervisor	15	3.1
Certified Nurse's Technician	11	2.3
Registered Nurse	9	1.8
Maintenance/Housekeeping	7	1.4
Orderly	6	1.2
Resident Counselor	6	1.2
Mental Health Caseworker	5	1.0
Licensed Caretaker	4	0.8
Human Service Worker	2	0.4
Developmental Trainer	2	0.4
Other/Missing	72	14.8
Total	**488**	**100.0**

Source: Brian K. Payne and Richard Cikovic, "An Empirical Examination of the Characteristics, Consequences, and Causes of Elder Abuse in Nursing Homes," *Journal of Elder Abuse and Neglect*, vol. 7, no. 4, 1995, pp. 61-74. Copyright 1995, Haworth Press, Inc., Binghamton, New York.

TABLE 10.10
Gender of the Accused by Gender of the Victim

Gender of Victim	Gender of Accused Male		Female	
	n	%	n	%
Male	126	(66.0)	48	(41.4)
Female	65	(34.0)	68	(58.6)
Total	191		116	

chi-square 17.66, phi = .24, p = .01

Source: Brian K. Payne and Richard Cikovic, "An Empirical Examination of the Characteristics, Consequences, and Causes of Elder Abuse in Nursing Homes," *Journal of Elder Abuse and Neglect*, vol. 7, no. 4, 1995, pp. 61-74. Copyright 1995, Haworth Press, Inc., Binghamton, New York.

In an effort to improve the quality of care and eliminate abuse in nursing homes, government regulations and laws are requiring greater supervision of nursing homes. In 1987, then-President Ronald Reagan signed into effect a landmark law, the Omnibus Budget Reconciliation Act (PL 100-203), which included sections that protected patient rights and treatment. The law went into effect October 1990. Compliance with the law varies from state to state and from one nursing facility to another. Families are increasingly filing (and winning) court suits against irresponsible nursing facilities.

CHAPTER XI

THE "AGE WAVE" — TRENDS AND PROJECTIONS

America is no longer "young." By the year 2030, one-third of the population will be over 55. By the year 2050, those over 65 will make up 20 percent of the population, up from 13 percent in 1995 (Table 11.1). Changes in age composition can have dramatic political, economic, and social effects on a nation.

INCREASING DIVERSITY

Among the elderly, racial and ethnic diversity will continue to increase. Although races other than White now constitute about 1 in 10 of the elderly, by 2050, that proportion is expected to increase to 2 in 10. The elderly Black population will likely increase from 8 to 10 percent, and elderly Hispanics from 4 percent to 15 percent. (See Figure 11.1.)

Tomorrow's elderly will be more educated and wealthier than today's elderly, just as today's older

Americans are better educated and more well-to-do than their grandparents. In addition, with the variety of living arrangements needed and the differences between individuals in health and personality, the older generation will reflect more variation than ever before.

It is increasingly likely that more and more people in their 50s and 60s will have surviving parents. The four-generation family will become common, with children knowing grandparents and even great-grandparents, especially their great-grandmothers.

Increasing age, racial, and ethnic diversity will change the everyday interactions among Americans. Having more individuals from previous generations, increasing numbers of whom are also more likely to be from diverse racial and ethnic backgrounds, will alter the social, cultural, and language interactions.

TABLE 11.1

Percent Distribution of the Population by Age: 1990 to 2050

[In percent. As of July 1. Resident population]

Year	Total	Under 5 years	5 to 13 years	14 to 17 years	18 to 24 years	25 to 34 years	35 to 44 years	45 to 64 years	65 years and over	85 years and over	100 years and over
ESTIMATE											
1990	100.0	7.6	12.8	5.3	10.8	17.3	15.1	18.6	12.5	1.2	0.0
PROJECTIONS											
Middle Series											
1995	100.0	7.5	13.1	5.6	9.5	15.5	16.2	19.9	12.8	1.4	0.0
2000	100.0	6.9	13.1	5.7	9.6	13.6	16.3	22.2	12.6	1.6	0.0
2005	100.0	6.7	12.5	5.9	9.9	12.7	14.7	24.9	12.6	1.7	0.0
2010	100.0	6.7	12.0	5.7	10.1	12.9	12.9	26.5	13.2	1.9	0.0
2020	100.0	6.8	12.0	5.3	9.3	13.3	12.3	24.6	16.5	2.0	0.1
2030	100.0	6.6	12.0	5.4	9.2	12.3	12.8	21.7	20.0	2.4	0.1
2040	100.0	6.8	11.9	5.4	9.3	12.4	11.9	22.0	20.3	3.7	0.1
2050	100.0	6.9	12.1	5.4	9.2	12.5	12.0	21.8	20.0	4.6	0.2

Source: *Population Projections of the U.S. by Age, Sex, Race, and Hispanic Origin, 1995-2050*, Bureau of the Census, Washington, DC, 1996

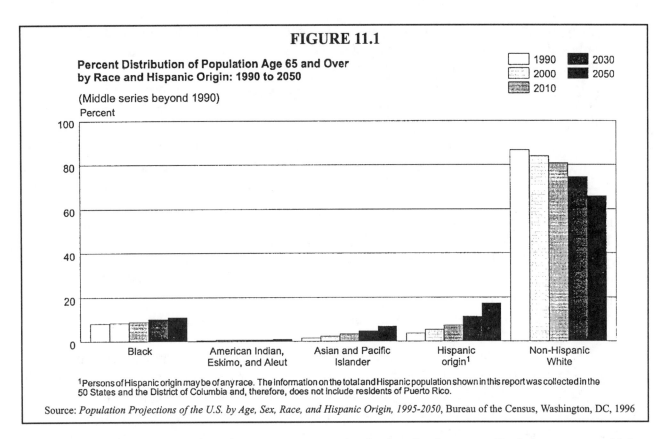

FIGURE 11.1

Percent Distribution of Population Age 65 and Over by Race and Hispanic Origin: 1990 to 2050

(Middle series beyond 1990)

Legend: 1990, 2000, 2010, 2030, 2050

Categories: Black; American Indian, Eskimo, and Aleut; Asian and Pacific Islander; Hispanic origin[1]; Non-Hispanic White

[1]Persons of Hispanic origin may be of any race. The information on the total and Hispanic population shown in this report was collected in the 50 States and the District of Columbia and, therefore, does not include residents of Puerto Rico.

Source: *Population Projections of the U.S. by Age, Sex, Race, and Hispanic Origin, 1995-2050*, Bureau of the Census, Washington, DC, 1996

THE CYCLIC LIFE

Dr. Ken Dychtwald (*Age Wave: The Challenges and Opportunities of an Aging America*, New York: Bantam, 1990) likened the increasing numbers of elderly to an awakening giant. This wave of age affects not only American institutions, but individuals as well. Added longevity often causes people to rethink the pace and plan for their lives as well as the purposes, goals, and challenges of its various stages.

Throughout human history, the average length of life was short. In a world where most people did not expect to live longer than 40 or 50 years, it was essential that certain key personal and social tasks be accomplished by specific ages. Traditionally, important activities such as getting an education, job training, parenthood, and retirement not only were designated to particular periods of life but also were expected to occur only once in a lifetime. The path from childhood to old age was linear: it moved in one direction.

This pattern of life was maintained not only by tradition, but by law. Government regulations and institutional rules prescribed the ages at which a person should go to school, begin and end work, or receive a pension. This approach to life was based on the assumptions that 1) the activities of life were to be performed on time and in sequence, and 2) most of life's periods of growth occurred in the first half of life, while the second half was, in general, characterized by decline and disinvestment.

Many people believe that as humans live longer, the traditional linear plan is evolving into a more flexible pattern, a "cyclic life plan." Having the luxury to choose how people arrange their various life tasks is becoming commonplace. For example, some people are opting to pursue careers throughout their 20s, 30s, and even 40s, followed by marriage and childrearing activities, a reversal of traditional roles. Formal learning was once the province of the young; today, middle-aged and older people are increasingly returning to school. Advances in medical technology and knowledge are making it possible to bear children later in life.

People once pursued a single career in their lifetimes; today, workers change jobs and even careers many times. The Rand Corporation, a California-based think-tank, predicted that by the year 2020, the average worker will need to be retrained up to 13 times in his or her lifetime. Except for a few specified professions (such as airline pilots), mandatory retirement has become illegal. Many older workers want to continue working (or return to work), and some must do so for financial reasons.

While the linear plan would include education, work, and recreation/retirement, in that order, a cyclic plan would be a blending, reordering, and repeating of activities, as desired. Although not everyone will choose to do things differently than in the past, they increasingly have the option to do so.

Lydia Bronte, in *The Longevity Factor* (New York: Harper Collins, 1993), followed a group of 150 people who chose to work into their 70s, 80s, 90s, and in a few cases, beyond the age of 100. Many had major achievements after age 60. Three-quarters reported that growing old was a positive experience. Bronte suggested that, while scientists in 1900 believed people could not be productive and creative over the age of 40, nearly a century later, Americans can expect a productive and creative "second middle age" between 50 and 75, and sometimes beyond, that has not existed before.

"GRAY POWER" — A POLITICAL BLOC?

People aged 55 to 74 vote more than any other age group (see Chapter V), and therefore, the increasing number of Americans in this age group will have a growing political impact. Organizations such as the American Association of Retired Persons (AARP), which claims membership of about 50 percent of persons over age 50, already exercise considerable influence in lobbying and in educating political leaders on issues pertinent to older Americans. That influence will undoubtedly grow as lawmakers, many of whom may themselves be older, respond to the increasing voting power of the elderly. Most economists predict that growing proportions of the American

budget will be dedicated to spending for the elderly.

Issues such as age discrimination, quality of care in nursing facilities, Medicare and "medigap" coverage, nontraditional living arrangements, and reform in pension plans and Social Security are vital topics for older Americans. Other areas that must be addressed are expansion of senior citizen benefits and discounts, changes in traffic and architectural design, and ethical questions raised by medical technology.

A SHIFTING ECONOMY

Older Workers

The increasing numbers of older Americans will change the work force as industry seeks both to accommodate the elderly and to profit from their attributes. With the declining number of younger workers, the work force will age, as will society in general. Many older Americans will find themselves needing to work for financial reasons, and many will want to remain active and employed. The first baby-boomer will turn 60 in 2006, so most of the changes in the work force will not begin until late in the first decade of the next century.

Marketing to the Older Consumer

People now see themselves as 10 to 15, maybe 20 years, younger than their real age.... A person turning 50 may still have half of his or her adult life ahead. There may be as many years of life after 50 as there were between 18 and 50. — Charles Allen, Modern Maturity

To appeal to this group, publications targeting those over 50, such as *Modern Maturity* and *New Choices*, have redesigned their magazines to make them cleaner, brighter, and more youthful. *Modern Maturity* announced a new design featuring two editions of its magazine — one for readers who work and one for those who are retired.

The already growing retirement-related industries are expected to increase as businesses seek to fill the needs of the older population. Health and fitness concerns will demand additional geriatricians (physicians specializing in the treatment of elderly persons), physical therapists, cataract and hearing specialists, and nutritionists. A market has emerged for pagers, remote controls, and monitoring devices for those living alone.

Comfort and security become more important as people age; they are more likely to purchase products based on comfort, value, and ease of use. Older adults are more likely to be attracted to products and appliances that they believe to be "user friendly," that is, easily understandable and useable (for example, easy-to-open medicine containers).

Most recreation centers and community programs have expanded their post-55 services. The hotel and travel industries now offer discounts and accommodations tailored to the needs of the increasingly mobile mature market and its discretionary income. Some restaurants have responded by offering smaller food portions and lowering prices on senior citizen menus. Many rural towns, indeed states, have found it profitable to attract retirees, with their pensions and savings, who make fewer demands on expensive local public services, such as schools.

ON THE ROAD

As the nation's population grows older, more older persons are on the streets both as drivers and as pedestrians. In 1998, there were 24.8 million licensed drivers over 65 in the United States, and their ranks are expected to reach 30 million by 2020. In 1998, they accounted for 14 percent of all drivers, up from 10 percent in 1980.

Drivers over 65 have a higher crash rate per mile driven than all other motorists, except those under 25. Those over 75 have the highest fatality rate per mile driven of all drivers. Reduced vision, especially night vision, reflexes, hearing, and flexibility of the head and neck are common problems of aging that can impair driving performance. However, although crash rates are high among older drivers, the actual number of crashes and deaths are relatively low because seniors usually cut down on their driving. John Eberhard, senior researcher at the National Highway Traffic Safety Administration (NHTSA), claimed, in 1998, "If you look at the number of accidents per licensed drivers, those in the 65- and-above group are the safest around."

Officials are wrestling with how to get hazardous older drivers off the roads without penalizing able ones. At what age should a person give up driving? It is a hard decision for an older person to make because the automobile is the chief means of mobility and, just as important, a sense of autonomy for most people. Studies show that the driver's state of general health and fitness is important. Only three states — Illinois, Indiana, and New Hampshire — and the District of Columbia require age-based road tests for license renewal. Seven other states offer shorter renewal periods for older drivers. In addition, some require physical examinations, others require physicians to report patients who have impairments that could affect driving safety, and many specify a wide variety of medical and mental conditions for which licenses can be suspended.

One reason states have not clamped down harder is that older drivers as a group regulate themselves quite effectively. In 1993, a study of 1,470 elderly drivers, funded by the American Automobile Association (AAA) Foundation for Traffic Safety, reported that 20.9 percent of women and 9.8 percent of men between 65 and 90 had voluntarily stopped driving because of recognized functional impairment. Nine percent of the females and 11 percent of the males reported they had been in a traffic accident in the previous five years. Women were more likely to voluntarily stop driving than men. The mean age for women deciding to stop driving was 80.9 years, while the mean for men was 82.5 years. This system of self-regulation helps explain why older drivers as a group have a better safety record than younger people. Although they make up 14 percent of all drivers, they account for less than 8 percent of all crashes.

Principal health reasons reported for stopping driving were macular degeneration of the eye and other eye conditions, stroke, hospitalization within the previous year, and Parkinson's disease. Total number of illnesses reported was the most important factor in the decision to stop driving. Age and sex were not important predictors of traffic accidents.

TABLE 11.2

Percent of U.S. Households with a Computer
By Age
By Rural, Urban, and Central City Areas

	Rural	Urban	Central City
Under 25 years	12.3	20.7	21.0
25-34 years	22.3	27.8	25.0
35-44 years	34.7	36.6	31.4
45-54 years	32.5	36.8	31.8
55 years and older	11.9	13.8	12.0

TABLE 11.3

Percent of U.S. Households with a Computer and Modem Using
On-Line Services to Search Classified Ads
By Age
By Rural, Urban, and Central City Areas

	Rural	Urban	Central City
Under 25 years	10.7	7.7	9.2
25-34 years	5.7	8.8	9.9
35-44 years	6.3	7.2	6.7
45-54 years	8.9	7.3	11.2
55 years and older	4.5	3.7	3.2

Source of both tables: *Falling Through the Net: A Survey of the "Have Nots" in Rural and Urban America*, U.S. Department of Commerce, Washington, DC, 1995

Insurance companies are now offering reduced premiums to the elderly who enroll in driver's safety classes. Highway safety engineers are studying the design of intersections and signs in an effort to keep older citizens driving safely as long as possible.

COMPUTER USE

Although computer usage is most frequently associated with the young, many older persons are increasingly using computer technology. The U.S. Department of Commerce, in its 1995 survey (*Falling Through the Net: A Survey of the Have-Nots in Rural and Urban America*), found that, among persons 55 and older, 11.9 percent of rural dwellers, 13.8 percent of urban residents, and 12 percent of those living in the central city had computers in their households (Table 11.2).

Of those households with computers and modems, among those 55 and older, 4.5 percent of

rural residents, 3.7 percent of urban residents, and 3.2 percent living in central cities used on-line services to search classified ads (Table 11.3). In addition, 11.7 percent of rural residents, 14.4 percent of urban dwellers, and 14 percent of central city residents over 55 used on-line services to take courses (Table 11.4). More than 11 percent each of rural and urban persons and 10.4 percent of central-city occupants used on-line services to gain access to government reports (Table 11.5).

In most of these categories of use, the percentages of older persons using computers were somewhat lower than other age groups. And, certainly, some of this computer use may be by the children of those over-55 persons who head the households, although by the age of 55 (and older), most parents do not have children residing in the home. Undoubtedly, in the short time since the study, even more elderly are using computers and

158

on-line systems both professionally and personally.

THE GRAYING OF THE NATION

Campuses

Universities report an increase in the age of students. This "graying" of the campus reflects the influx of older students, some of whom are elderly, who have enrolled in response to a changing job market as well as increased free time, discretionary income, and vitality among older people. The total percentage of seniors enrolled is still small; one-half of 1 percent of all college students are over 65. The percentage is greater at 2-year schools than at 4-year schools. (See Table 11.6.)

This new population has prompted changes in college life, especially at 2-year schools, including more flexible class schedules and greater accountability from faculty, since the older student is often more demanding. It is no longer unusual to read about an elderly person going to college and getting the degree he or she had always wanted or had never completed.

Lifelong Learning — A Model Program

Well-educated retirees often enjoy the chance to return to the classroom. They can concentrate on those "elective" topics of personal interest they had to forego during their work lives. Quest, affiliated with the City College of New York, the Center for Worker Education, and the Elderhostel Network, offers study groups for and by its approximately 140 well-educated members. These include men and women with careers as teachers, accountants, librarians, dentists, secretaries, business executives, lawyers, publishers, scientists, writers, public administrators, and social workers.

Annual dues entitle a member to take as many of the 42 courses offered as desired and to attend special guest lectures. Members create and lead their own courses in what is termed "peer-learning." Courses include musical theater, Plato, recreational math-

TABLE 11.4

Percent of U.S. Households with a Computer and Modem Using On-Line Services to Take Courses
By Age
By Rural, Urban, and Central City Areas

	Rural	Urban	Central City
Under 25 years	21.7	14.9	9.2
25-34 years	13.3	18.9	19.9
35-44 years	20.2	18.4	16.9
45-54 years	19.1	16.8	19.2
55 years and older	11.7	14.4	14.0

Source: *Falling Through the Net: A Survey of the "Have Nots" in Rural and Urban America*, U.S. Department of Commerce, Washngton, DC, 1995

TABLE 11.5

Percent of U.S. Households with a Computer and Modem Using On-Line Services to Access Government Reports
By Age
By Rural, Urban, and Central City Areas

	Rural	Urban	Central City
Under 25 years	12.7	16.7	21.0
25-34 years	10.7	17.9	17.5
35-44 years	12.8	15.3	19.2
45-54 years	18.2	18.3	20.5
55 years and older	11.3	11.3	10.4

Source: *Falling Through the Net: A Survey of the "Have Nots" in Rural and Urban America*, U.S. Department of Commerce, Washngton, DC, 1995

TABLE 11.6

Total fall enrollment in institutions of higher education, by type and control of institution, and age and attendance status of student: 1995

Attendance status and age of student	All institutions Total	All institutions 4-year	All institutions 2-year	Public institutions Total	Public institutions 4-year	Public institutions 2-year	Private institutions Total	Private institutions 4-year	Private institutions 2-year
1	2	3	4	5	6	7	8	9	10
All students	14,261,781	8,769,252	5,492,529	11,092,374	5,814,545	5,277,829	3,169,407	2,954,707	214,700
Under 18	285,383	120,128	165,255	232,944	71,696	161,248	52,439	48,432	4,007
18 and 19	2,796,149	1,771,315	1,024,834	2,149,691	1,171,170	978,521	646,458	600,145	46,313
20 and 21	2,617,440	1,803,281	814,159	2,006,878	1,225,544	781,334	610,562	577,737	32,825
22 to 24	2,356,678	1,619,883	736,795	1,888,417	1,183,191	705,226	468,261	436,692	31,569
25 to 29	2,113,799	1,323,542	790,257	1,629,437	872,668	756,769	484,362	450,874	33,488
30 to 34	1,295,176	710,029	585,147	1,009,461	446,471	562,990	285,715	263,558	22,157
35 to 39	980,171	500,210	479,961	769,045	306,134	462,911	211,126	194,076	17,050
40 to 49	1,234,660	650,510	584,150	967,950	401,321	566,629	266,710	249,189	17,521
50 to 64	356,036	159,542	196,494	286,672	94,425	192,247	69,364	65,117	4,247
65 and over	80,950	19,877	61,073	74,103	13,424	60,679	6,847	6,453	394
Age unknown	145,339	90,935	54,404	77,776	28,501	49,275	67,563	62,434	5,129
Full-time	8,128,802	6,151,755	1,977,047	5,925,301	4,084,711	1,840,590	2,203,501	2,067,044	136,457
Under 18	115,479	74,749	40,730	80,738	42,529	38,209	34,741	32,220	2,521
18 and 19	2,395,257	1,697,545	697,712	1,766,874	1,111,423	655,451	628,383	586,122	42,261
20 and 21	2,088,263	1,665,857	422,406	1,512,500	1,115,658	396,842	575,763	550,199	25,564
22 to 24	1,501,692	1,243,540	258,152	1,136,955	899,614	237,341	364,737	343,926	20,811
25 to 29	951,825	741,706	210,119	675,068	483,407	191,661	276,757	258,299	18,458
30 to 34	423,324	296,556	126,768	303,791	187,311	116,480	119,533	109,245	10,288
35 to 39	265,514	174,137	91,377	189,805	105,424	84,381	75,709	68,713	6,996
40 to 49	279,755	185,797	93,958	196,730	109,114	87,616	83,025	76,683	6,342
50 to 64	57,402	36,010	21,392	38,404	18,391	20,013	18,998	17,619	1,379
65 and over	6,615	3,115	3,500	4,637	1,238	3,399	1,978	1,877	101
Age unknown	43,676	32,743	10,933	19,799	10,602	9,197	23,877	22,141	1,736
Part-time	6,132,979	2,617,497	3,515,482	5,167,073	1,729,834	3,437,239	965,906	887,663	78,243
Under 18	169,904	45,379	124,525	152,206	29,167	123,039	17,698	16,212	1,486
18 and 19	400,892	73,770	327,122	382,817	59,747	323,070	18,075	14,023	4,052
20 and 21	529,177	137,424	391,753	494,378	109,886	384,492	34,799	27,538	7,261
22 to 24	854,986	376,343	478,643	751,462	283,577	467,885	103,524	92,766	10,758
25 to 29	1,161,974	581,836	580,138	954,369	389,261	565,108	207,605	192,575	15,030
30 to 34	871,852	413,473	458,379	705,670	259,160	446,510	166,182	154,313	11,869
35 to 39	714,657	326,073	388,584	579,240	200,710	378,530	135,417	125,363	10,054
40 to 49	954,905	464,713	490,192	771,220	292,207	479,013	183,685	172,506	11,179
50 to 64	298,634	123,532	175,102	248,268	76,034	172,234	50,366	47,498	2,868
65 and over	74,335	16,762	57,573	69,466	12,186	57,280	4,869	4,576	293
Age unknown	101,663	58,192	43,471	57,977	17,899	40,078	43,686	40,293	3,393
	Percentage distribution								
All students	100.0	100.0	100.0	100.0	100.0	100.0	100.0	100.0	100.0
Under 18	2.0	1.4	3.0	2.1	1.2	3.1	1.7	1.6	1.9
18 and 19	19.6	20.2	18.7	19.4	20.1	18.5	20.4	20.3	21.6
20 and 21	18.4	20.6	14.8	18.1	21.1	14.8	19.3	19.6	15.3
22 to 24	16.5	18.5	13.4	17.0	20.3	13.4	14.8	14.8	14.7
25 to 29	14.8	15.1	14.4	14.7	15.0	14.3	15.3	15.3	15.6
30 to 34	9.1	8.1	10.7	9.1	7.7	10.7	9.0	8.9	10.3
35 to 39	6.9	5.7	8.7	6.9	5.3	8.8	6.7	6.6	7.9
40 to 49	8.7	7.4	10.6	8.7	6.9	10.7	8.4	8.4	8.2
50 to 64	2.5	1.8	3.6	2.6	1.6	3.6	2.2	2.2	2.0
65 and over	0.6	0.2	1.1	0.7	0.2	1.1	0.2	0.2	0.2
Age unknown	1.0	1.0	1.0	0.7	0.5	0.9	2.1	2.1	2.4
Full-time	100.0	100.0	100.0	100.0	100.0	100.0	100.0	100.0	100.0
Under 18	1.4	1.2	2.1	1.4	1.0	2.1	1.6	1.6	1.8
18 and 19	29.5	27.6	35.3	29.8	27.2	35.6	28.5	28.4	31.0
20 and 21	25.7	27.1	21.4	25.5	27.3	21.6	26.1	26.6	18.7
22 to 24	18.5	20.2	13.1	19.2	22.0	12.9	16.6	16.6	15.3
25 to 29	11.7	12.1	10.6	11.4	11.8	10.4	12.6	12.5	13.5
30 to 34	5.2	4.8	6.4	5.1	4.6	6.3	5.4	5.3	7.5
35 to 39	3.3	2.8	4.6	3.2	2.6	4.6	3.4	3.3	5.1
40 to 49	3.4	3.0	4.8	3.3	2.7	4.8	3.8	3.7	4.6
50 to 64	0.7	0.6	1.1	0.6	0.5	1.1	0.9	0.9	1.0
65 and over	0.1	0.1	0.2	0.1	0.0	0.2	0.1	0.1	0.2
Age unknown	0.5	0.5	0.6	0.3	0.3	0.5	1.1	1.1	1.3
Part-time	100.0	100.0	100.0	100.0	100.0	100.0	100.0	100.0	100.0
Under 18	2.8	1.7	3.5	2.9	1.7	3.6	1.8	1.8	1.9
18 and 19	6.5	2.8	9.3	7.4	3.5	9.4	1.9	1.6	5.2
20 and 21	8.6	5.3	11.1	9.6	6.4	11.2	3.6	3.1	9.3
22 to 24	13.9	14.4	13.6	14.5	16.4	13.6	10.7	10.5	13.7
25 to 29	18.9	22.2	16.5	18.5	22.5	16.4	21.5	21.7	19.2
30 to 34	14.2	15.8	13.0	13.7	15.0	13.0	17.2	17.4	15.2
35 to 39	11.7	12.5	11.1	11.2	11.6	11.0	14.0	14.1	12.8
40 to 49	15.6	17.8	13.9	14.9	16.9	13.9	19.0	19.4	14.3
50 to 64	4.9	4.7	5.0	4.8	4.4	5.0	5.2	5.4	3.7
65 and over	1.2	0.6	1.6	1.3	0.7	1.7	0.5	0.5	0.4
Age unknown	1.7	2.2	1.2	1.1	1.0	1.2	4.5	4.5	4.3

NOTE.—Because of rounding, details may not add to 100.0 percent.

SOURCE: U.S. Department of Education, National Center for Education Statistics, Integrated Postsecondary Education Data System, "Fall Enrollment, 1995" survey. (This table was prepared January 1997.)

Source: *Digest of Education Statistics — 1997*, National Center for Education Statistics, Washington, DC, 1997

ematics, current ethical dilemmas, the American West, nutrition and health, crafts, languages, Shakespeare, drawing, the Islamic world, biography, God and science, Jewish authors, the Thirties, and cultural anthropology.

The members of Quest are part of a growing trend toward recreational education and educational vacations. Such learning institutions provide an alternative to stereotypical retirement activities such as playing golf or bridge. In addition, peer learning programs foster social networks and give reason to get up and go out every day, both of which are crucial to health.

Prisons

Another institution affected by the age of our society is the penal system. Eighty-one-year-old Viva LeRoy Nash, believed to be the nation's oldest death-row inmate, at Arizona State Prison, has suffered five heart attacks over the last 15 years. Like many others his age, he takes many medications each day and requires a low-fat diet. He is part of a growing number of older inmates. Some experts believe new sentencing laws mean prisons will be housing more elderly convicts and paying more money to do so. With the increasing introduction of "three strikes and you're out" programs that sentence habitual felons to life sentences, the 1987 abolition of parole for federal crimes, and the growing use of mandatory life sentences, the problems of the elderly will become a major problem for the nation's prisons. Nationwide, in 1996, about 2.5 percent of those in federal prisons were at least 60, and only 1 percent of prisoners in state prisons were over the age of 65 years of age.

As the inmate population grows older, prisoners require additional medical, dietary, and psychological services that will further stretch the already huge cost of inmate care. Surveys of the elderly population have found that among those over 65, 80 percent have one or more chronic illnesses or diseases, and 60 percent have at least three medical problems. Prisons are increasingly being asked to provide long-term medical care for an aging population.

Older inmates often suffer from more health problems than the general aged population. They are more likely to be infected with HIV and tuberculosis and have histories of drug abuse. They are often less mobile, and prisons are not designed for "easy access." Aged inmates are more affected by violence. Experts estimate that caring for aging convicts can be twice to three times as expensive. In addition, when elderly inmates have served their sentences, where do they go? Who will care for them?

Rural Areas Turning Gray — Young People Leave, Elderly Fill the Void

In rural America, as generations of young people have sought jobs and opportunity elsewhere, parents, grandparents, and great-grandparents remain. The result is a transformation across the farm belt — Nebraska, Illinois, Indiana, Kansas, and other midwestern states, as well as in rural areas of other states, especially the Sunbelt.

As the numbers of births has dropped, so has the number of students in schools. Hospitals stopped delivering babies, and in some places, hospitals, schools, and malls have closed completely. Residents have to go to nearby cities to shop or receive medical care. Some towns have died, and others are but small retirement communities of elderly, many of them in nursing homes. Many of those residents, primarily widows, help one another in what is considered the small town version of Social Security — volunteering in church, cooking for the sick, being good neighbors. As one senior explained, "There is no forced retirement here. Everyone's labor is needed." Those who are able deliver mail, drive snowplows, and serve on county boards.

Town Councils

Across the nation, particularly in small and medium-size towns, more and more older people

161

are being elected to civic positions. The National League of Cities found that the percentage of council members older than 60 rose from 14 percent in 1979 to 24 percent in 1989.

There are many reasons for this trend, including the growing demands on council members' time, something retired persons often have in abundance, the increased numbers of older people, and the growing interests older people have in protecting their resources. One advantage older people offer councils is their greater life experience and long-term perspective.

HELP IN AN INCREASINGLY COMPLEX SOCIETY

The increasing complexity of American society and the growing needs of the aged who have no one to assist them have led to the emergence of two new types of service professions — private care managers and claims companies — that provide, for a fee, what family members may once have provided. Private care (or case) managers are social workers who provide one-to-one assistance in arranging care or housing or in referral to government agencies that serve the elderly. They can oversee home-health staffing needs, monitor the quality of in-home services and equipment, and act as liaison with families living far away. Private care managers can be expensive ($50 to $150 per hour), but they may well be worth the expense. Medical claims companies assist the aged in filling out complicated insurance forms — for a charge or a percentage of the benefits received.

An estimated 500,000 U.S. elderly people need help with financial affairs. In response, new daily money management (DMM) programs have emerged, which provide help to the elderly in paying bills, filling out medical insurance forms, balancing checkbooks, making bank deposits, preparing tax returns, and budgeting. Some managers can even sign checks. There is, unfortunately, ample opportunity for abuse. Because some elderly may be confused or

forgetful, it is easy for them to be taken advantage of. The American Association of Retired Persons (AARP) offers free DMM services to low-income families through community agencies.

Elder Law

The legal profession has seen the emergence of a new specialty — elder law, which covers all the potential specialties that affect the senior population. The field of elder law includes a wide and growing range of topics. In addition to traditional work in probate, wills, and trust and estate planning, elder law specialists are now involved in such diverse areas as:

• Planning for disability or incapacity through living wills and durable power of attorney,

• Establishing eligibility for Social Security, Medicare, and Medicaid benefits,

• Long-term care, including patient rights, quality of care, and long-term care insurance,

• Elder fraud and abuse,

• Grandparents' visitation rights,

• Age discrimination at work,

• Housing problems (mortgages, housing discrimination),

• Conservatorships and guardianships, and

• Retirement and pension benefits.

Driving Services

I gave up driving this year because my eyes are going. I can't take the bus because I can't see the numbers. I won't take taxis because they smell of smoke and they cost too much. You have to reserve a week in advance for a Regional Transport van, and the seats are tough on my bad back.

I'm not frail enough to qualify for some other services. I don't want to impose on my friends or my family. Am I just supposed to sit at home? — Elderly woman, Portland, Maine

Many aging Americans face the dilemma of being unable to drive and yet, despite being otherwise healthy, find themselves prematurely lodged or housed in a nursing facility, simply because they cannot get around their communities to accomplish simple tasks, such as shopping for necessities and keeping doctors' appointments. Two-thirds of the elderly live in suburban and rural areas, and most of their homes are more than two miles from a public transportation stop. There is a large network of individual transportation services, public and private, that will pick up the elderly and disabled at their homes. But these services, known as "paratransit," do not cover the entire country. Only 11 percent of the elderly have ever used them. Most paratransit services rely on vans and paid drivers and run on fixed schedules to specific sites, such as senior centers. They are limited as to whom they can take and where and when they can go.

As the number of car-less elderly people has multiplied, federal agencies and organizations devoted to the aging have begun paying attention. AARP's Connections for Independent Living pilot project, using a mix of volunteer and paid drivers, and cars, not vans, is providing on-demand service to the elderly and disabled in Portland, Maine. Clients make a monthly payment or set up an account against which they can draw to pay for service. The network will sell the cars the elderly no longer use and start accounts with the money. Entrepreneurs in American communities might also find a market for transporting the elderly.

WAR VETERANS

The Department of Veterans Affairs reported that, in 1980, about 2 million American men over 65 were veterans. By 1995, there were close to 8.8 million veterans over 65 (Table 11.7). About 4 percent of those were women. Because of the aging of the World War II veterans, the number is expected to peak around the year 2000, when there will be about 9.3 million elderly veterans. At that point, about 60 percent of all elderly men will be veterans eligible for veteran's benefits. (Table 11.8 shows expenditures for veterans' benefits from 1980 to 1995.) The number of veterans is projected to decline after 2000 to about 8.5 million

TABLE 11.7

Veterans Living in the United States and Puerto Rico, by Age and by Service: 1995

[In thousands, except as indicated. As of July, 1. Estimated. Excludes 500,000 veterans whose only active duty military service of less than two years occurred since Sept. 30, 1980. See headnote, table 569]

AGE	Total veterans	WARTIME VETERANS						Peace-time veterans
		Total [1]	Persian Gulf	Vietnam era	Korean con-flict	World War II	World War I	
All ages	26,198	20,169	1,450	8,273	4,499	7,433	13	6,029
Under 30 years old . . .	1,133	735	735	-	-	-	-	398
30-34 years old	1,277	259	259	-	-	-	-	1,018
35-39 years old	1,587	426	146	298	-	-	-	1,161
40-44 years old	1,969	1,636	153	1,591	-	-	-	333
45-49 years old	3,535	3,422	105	3,402	-	-	-	113
50-54 years old	2,646	1,889	37	1,878	-	-	-	757
55-59 years old	2,362	844	11	526	361	-	-	1,518
60-64 years old	2,899	2,331	3	265	2,226	35	-	569
65 years old and over .	8,791	8,626	-	312	1,912	7,398	13	165

- Represents zero. [1] Veterans who served in more than one wartime period are counted only once.

Source: U.S. Dept. of Veterans Affairs, Office of Information Management and Statistics, *Veteran Population*, annual.

TABLE 11.8

Veterans Benefits—Expenditures, by Program: 1980 to 1995

[In millions of dollars. For fiscal years ending in year shown; see text, section 9. Beginning with fiscal year 1989, data are for outlays]

PROGRAM	1980	1985	1989	1990	1991	1992	1993	1994	1995
Total	23,187	29,359	30,041	28,998	31,214	33,900	35,460	37,401	37,775
Medical programs	6,042	9,227	10,745	11,582	12,472	13,815	14,603	15,430	16,255
Construction	300	557	703	661	608	639	622	695	641
General operating expenses	605	765	766	811	884	920	904	906	954
Compensation and pension	11,044	14,037	15,009	14,674	16,080	16,282	16,882	17,188	17,765
Vocational rehabilitation and education	2,350	1,164	589	452	541	695	863	1,119	1,127
All other [1]	2,846	3,609	2,228	818	629	1,549	1,586	2,062	1,034

[1] Includes insurance and indemnities, and miscellaneous funds and expenditures. (Excludes expenditures from personal funds of patients.)

Source: U.S. Dept. of Veterans Affairs, *Trend Data*, annual.

163

by 2010. With the growth in the number and proportion of older veterans, an additional strain on the Veterans Administration medical system will likely result, putting further pressure on community resources.

NONTRADITIONAL LIFESTYLES

The increasing diversity of the aging population and the shortage of caregivers to provide long-term care for them will demand different ways of living and increased use of formal community services. Figure 11.2 shows the projected increase in the use of community services by those with impairments (ADL — activities of daily living) through the year 2020. The disabled will still need nursing facilities. Hospices have established themselves as an alternative and humane solution to dying in the hospital.

Minimally physically impaired elderly may need new kinds of home care or adult day care. With more multi-generational families, a growing number of people will face the obligation and expense of caring for old or frail parents since so many people now live long enough to face multiple, chronic illnesses.

Accessory apartments, shared housing, and housing designed for the elderly will become more available. (See Chapter III.) Home equity conversion and reverse mortgages, in which an aged person "sells back" his mortgage to the lender in a gradual liquidation (as opposed to selling the house and living on the proceeds or leaving an estate for payment of debts upon one's death), may ease the housing problem for some elderly.

For the poorer elderly, the possibility of homelessness may remain all too real. American

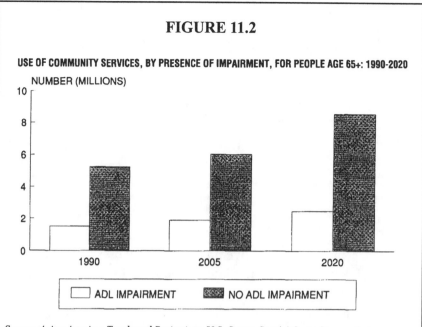

FIGURE 11.2

USE OF COMMUNITY SERVICES, BY PRESENCE OF IMPAIRMENT, FOR PEOPLE AGE 65+: 1990-2020

NUMBER (MILLIONS)

ADL IMPAIRMENT   NO ADL IMPAIRMENT

Source: *Aging America: Trends and Projections*, U.S. Senate Special Committee on Aging, American Association of Retired Persons, Federal Council on Aging, and U.S. Administration on Aging, Washington, DC, 1991

society remains challenged by an economy that forces growing numbers of aged, infirm, mentally impaired, and unemployed residents to live in its streets. (For more information on housing, see Chapter III.)

"QUITTING TIME" — RETIREMENT BECOMES AN INSTITUTION

A longer lifespan gives people the opportunity to spend more time in all the major activities of life — education, work, and retirement. In fact, retirement has become as much an institution in American life as education and work. For those who choose to retire, the retirement years can be a period to relax and do many things they have never done. On the other hand, for older persons who need or want to continue working, unemployment and age discrimination can pose serious hardships.

What do the elderly do with their time? The differences in time use between the elderly and the general population result from less time spent working. Men are likely to increase the amount of time spent on traditionally female tasks such as cooking and housework. In addition to travel, study, and socializing, the media claim the largest share of the elderly person's day, with television consuming more than half the newly available time. Loss of employment income may limit the pastime activities possible for some older Americans.

DEATH AND DYING

By far, the most frequent beneficiaries of the advances in medical technology are the elderly. Unfortunately, while technology can enhance life in certain circumstances, it may prolong life (as well as dying) at the expense of quality of life and without regard for individual wishes. The legal, ethical, religious, and economic questions raised by such technology have yet to be resolved and will certainly touch the lives of an ever-growing number of older Americans.

Among those technologies at issue are cardio-pulmonary resuscitation (CPR), respiratory ventilation, organ transplants, dialysis, nutritional support and hydration, antibiotics, and recently, euthanasia and suicide-enabling paraphernalia and procedures.

Controversy involving medical technology generally centers around terminology such as "quality versus quantity (longevity)" of life, the "high cost of dying," "living wills," and "the right to die." Court cases increasingly challenge accepted procedure. Under the Patient Self-Determination Act, part of the Omnibus Budget Reconciliation Act (PL 101-508) that went into effect in 1991, all individuals receiving medical care in hospitals, nursing homes, and certain other facilities receiving Medicare and Medicaid funds must be advised of two rights, (1) the right to make decisions about their care — including the right to refuse that care, and (2) the right to prepare binding documents stating whether they desire life-sustaining intervention in the event of their incapacitation — a "living will."

Extending a patient's life by technology is not necessarily a benefit for the person. Although today's elderly are healthier and more affluent than previous generations, the suicide rate among the elderly has risen steadily since 1981. According to the National Center for Health Statistics, in 1995, the suicide rate among persons 65 and older was 18.1 per 100,000 people, compared to an overall national rate of 11.2 per 100,000. (See Chapter VII.) Because older persons constitute the fastest-growing age group in the United States, the number of suicides will probably continue to rise. (See also *Death and Dying — Who Decides?*, Information Plus, Wylie, Texas, 1996.)

IMPORTANT NAMES AND ADDRESSES

Alzheimer's Disease and Related Disorders Association
1334 G St. NW
Washington, DC 20005
(800) 621-0379

American Association of Homes for the Aging
901 E St. NW, Suite 500
Washington, DC 20037
(202) 783-2242
FAX (202) 783-2255

American Association of Retired Persons (AARP)
601 E St. NW
Washington, DC 20049
(202) 434-2277
FAX (202) 728-4573

Children of Aging Parents (CAPS)
1609 Woodbourne Rd., Suite 302A
Levittown, PA 19057
(800) 227-7294

Eldercare Locator Directory
(800) 677-1116

Families USA
1334 G St. NW, Suite 300
Washington, DC 20005
(202) 628-3030
FAX (202) 347-2417

Gerontological Society of America
1275 K St. NW, Suite 350
Washington, DC 20005
(202) 842-1275
FAX (202) 842-1150

Gray Panthers
2025 Pennsylvania Ave. NW, Suite 821
Washington, DC 20006
(202) 466-3132
FAX (202) 466-3133

Jewish Council for the Aging
11820 Parklawn Dr., #200
Rockwell, MD 20852
(301) 881-8782
FAX (301) 231-9360

National Academy of Elder Law Attorneys
1604 N. Country Club Rd.
Tucson, AZ 86716
(520) 881-4005

National Alliance for Caregiving
4720 Montgomery Ln., Suite 642
Bethesda, MD 20814
(301) 718-8444
FAX (301) 652-7711

National Alliance for Senior Citizens
1744 Riggs NW, Third Floor
Washington, DC 20009
(202) 986-0117
FAX (202) 986-2974

National Association for Home Care
228 7th St. SE
Washington, DC 20003
(202) 547-7424
FAX (202) 547-3540

National Caucus and Center on Black Aged
1424 K St. NW, Suite 500
Washington, DC 20005
(202) 637-8400
FAX (202) 347-0895

National Center on Elder Abuse
810 First St. NE, Suite 500
Washington, DC 20002
(202) 682-2470

National Council on the Aging
409 3rd St. SW, Suite 200
Washington, DC 20024
(202) 479-6653
FAX (202) 479-0735

National Hispanic Council on Aging
2713 Ontario Rd. NW
Washington, DC 20009
(202) 265-1288
FAX (202) 745-2522

National Hospice Organization
1901 N. Moore St., Suite 901
Arlington, VA 22209
(703) 243-5900
FAX (703) 525-5762

National Institute on Aging
31 Center Dr.
Bethesda, MD 20892
(301) 496-1752
FAX (301) 496-1072

National Senior Citizens Law Center
1815 H St. NW, Suite 700
Washington, DC 20006
(202) 289-6976
FAX (202) 785-6792

National Urban League
1111 14th St. NW, #1001
Washington, DC 20005
(202) 898-1604
FAX (202) 408-1965

Older Women's League
666 11th St. NW, #700
Washington, DC 20001
(202) 783-6686
FAX (202) 638-2356

Peace Corps
1990 K St. NW
Washington, DC 20526
(202) 606-3010
FAX (202) 606-3110

Pension Rights Center
918 16th St. NW, #704
Washington, DC 20006
(202) 296-3776
FAX (202) 833-2472

Quest
City College Center for Worker Education
99 Hudson St., 6th Floor
New York, NY 10013
(212) 925-6625, Ext. 229
FAX (212) 925-0963

Salvation Army
615 Slater's Ln.
P.O. Box 269
Alexandria, VA 22313
(703) 684-5500
FAX (703) 519-5889

Service Corps of Retired Executives (SCORE)
409 3rd St. SW, 6th Floor
Washington, DC 20024
(202) 205-6762
FAX (202) 205-7636

U. S. Department of Health and Human Services
Administration on Aging
200 Independence Ave. SW, Rm. 309F
Washington, DC 20201
(202) 401-4634
FAX (202) 401-7741

Veterans Affairs Department
810 Vermont Ave. NW
Washington, DC 20420
(202) 273-5700

RESOURCES

The major source of statistics on American life is the Bureau of the Census of the U.S. Department of Commerce in Washington, DC. Many of its publications were essential for the preparation of this book, including *Marital Status and Living Arrangements: 1996* (1997), *Money Income in the United States, 1996* (1997), *Poverty in the United States: 1996* (1997), *Geographic Mobility: March 1995 to March 1996* (1997), *Asset Ownership of Households: 1993* (1995), *Americans With Disabilities 1994-95* (1997), *Household and Family Characteristics, 1996* (1997), *Voting and Registration in the Election of November 1996* (1997), *Housing of the Elderly (1995), Consumer Expenditures: 1995* (1997), *Population Projections: States, 1995-2025* (1997), *Aging in the United States — Past, Present, and Future* (1997), and *Educational Attainment in the United States: March 1995* (1996). The Department also published *Falling Through the Net: A Survey of the Have Nots in Rural and Urban America* (1995), which included information on computer use.

The Social Security Administration, an agency of the U.S. Department of Health and Human Services (HHS), is responsible for the financial security of millions of older Americans. *Fast Facts and Figures About Social Security* (Washington, DC, 1997) answers the most commonly asked questions about Social Security benefits, the Supplemental Security Income program, and Medicare.

The Health Care Financing Administration of the U.S. Department of Health and Human Services prepares the *Health Care Financing Review* and the *Medicare and Medicaid Supplement*, which were the sources of much of the material on health care coverage. The Centers for Disease Control and Prevention (CDC) of the U.S. Public Health Service supplied statistics on health issues in its *Advance Data* and *Mortality Trends for Alzheimer's Disease* (1996), *Vital and Health Statistics — Access to Health Care Part 3: Older Adults* (1997), and *Morbidity and Mortality Weekly Reports*. The Public Health Service publishes its annual *Health*, which gives information on disease issues, and *Healthy People 2000*, the service's goal for public health.

Crime in the United States — 1996 (1997), *Age Patterns of Victims of Serious Violent Crime* (1997), *Elderly Crime Victims* (1994), and *Change in Criminal Victimization 1994-95* (1997), prepared by the Federal Bureau of Investigation (FBI) and the Bureau of Justice Statistics (BJS), were helpful in providing information on elderly victims. The U.S. Department of Justice is the major source of information concerning crime and justice in America.

The National Center for Education Statistics compiles data on U.S. education. Its annual *Digest of Education Statistics 1997* (1997) was useful in understanding educational attainment among the elderly. The Bureau of Labor Statistics of the U.S. Department of Labor publishes information on the U.S. work force in its *Monthly Labor Review* and its monthly *Employment and Earnings*.

"The Older Workforce: Recruitment and Retention" (1993), a study by the American Association of Retired Persons (AARP) and the Society for Human Resource Management, includes valuable material on employment of older Americans. Information Plus thanks the Alliance for Aging Research for use of its report, *Meeting the Medical Needs of the Senior Boom* (1992), on the state of geriatric medicine. Another helpful study was "Americans Over 55 at Work Program," conducted by ICF, Inc., for the Commonwealth Fund.

Information Plus thanks the Older Women's League for permission to use material from its *1993 Mother's Day Report*, "Room for Improvement: The Lack of Affordable, Adaptable and Accessible Housing for Midlife and Older Women." *Out of Reach: Rental Housing at What Cost?* (1997), by the National Low Income Housing Coalition, provided data on rental housing. Information Plus also thanks the Gallup Poll (Princeton, NJ) for the use of its surveys. *PREVENTION INDEX* was an invaluable source of data on nutrition and exercise among the elderly. Information Plus thanks the American Heart Association for use of its data on cardiovascular disease.

Family Caregiving in the United States (1997), prepared by the National Alliance for Caregiving and the American Association of Retired Persons, was the source of much invaluable data on elder care. *The MetLife Study of Employer Costs for Working Caregivers* (1997), published by the National Alliance for Caregiving and Metropolitan Life Insurance Company, was most helpful regarding costs to business for caring for elderly relatives of employees. *Elder Abuse: Questions and Answers*, prepared by the National Center for Elder Abuse (1996), provided much helpful information on abuse of the nation's elderly. Information Plus thanks the American Association of Retired Persons (AARP) for use of its study, *The Real Golden Girls* (1997), which studied nontraditional living arrangements of the elderly.

INDEX